What Have We Learned?

What Have We Learned?

Macroeconomic Policy after the Crisis

edited by George Akerlof, Olivier Blanchard, David Romer, and Joseph Stiglitz

The MIT Press
Cambridge, Massachusetts
London, England

MIT Press books may be purchased at special quantity discounts for business or sales promotional use. For information, please email special_sales@mitpress.mit.edu.

This book was set in Sabon by Toppan Best-set Premedia Limited, Hong Kong. Printed and bound in the United States of America.

Library of Congress Cataloging-in-Publication Data

What have we learned ? : macroeconomic policy after the crisis / edited by George
Akerlof, Olivier Blanchard, David Romer, and Joseph Stiglitz.
   pages cm
Includes bibliographical references and index.
ISBN 978-0-262-02734-2 (hardcover : alk. paper)
1. Monetary policy. 2. Fiscal policy. 3. Financial crises—Government policy. 4. Economic
policy. 5. Macroeconomics. I. Akerlof, George A., 1940–
HG230.3.W49   2014
339.5—dc23
2013037345

10 9 8 7 6 5 4 3 2

Contents

Introduction: Rethinking Macro Policy II—Getting Granular

Olivier Blanchard, Giovanni Dell'Ariccia, and Paolo Mauro

The 2008–2009 global economic and financial crisis and its aftermath keep forcing policymakers to rethink macroeconomic policy. First was the Lehman crisis, which showed how much policymakers had underestimated the dangers posed by the financial system and demonstrated the limits of monetary policy. Then it was the euro area crisis, which forced them to rethink the workings of currency unions and fiscal policy. And throughout, they have had to improvise, from the use of unconventional monetary policies, to the provision of the initial fiscal stimulus, to the choice of the speed of fiscal consolidation, to the use of macroprudential instruments.

We took a first look at the issues a few years ago, both in a paper (Blanchard, Dell'Ariccia, and Mauro 2010) and at an IMF conference in 2011 (Blanchard et al. 2012). There was a clear sense among both researchers and policymakers participating in the conference that we had entered a "brave new world" and that we had more questions than answers. Two years later, the contours of monetary, fiscal, and macroprudential policies remain unclear. But policies have been tried and progress has been made, both theoretical and empirical. This introduction updates the status of the debate. It was prepared for a second conference that was hosted by the IMF on the same topic in spring 2013 and as a springboard for further discussion.

A few observations on the scope of the analysis: our comments focus on the design of macroeconomic policy after the global economy emerges from the crisis rather than on current policy choices, such as the design of exit policies from quantitative easing or the pros and cons of money-financed fiscal stimulus. The two sets of issues are obviously related, but our objective is to analyze some general principles that could be used to guide macroeconomic policy in the future rather than to suggest specific measures to be taken today. We also take a relatively narrow view of macroeconomic policy, leaving out any discussion of structural reforms and financial regulation. Although the border between financial regulation and macroprudential policies is fuzzy, we concentrate on the cyclical component of financial regulation rather than on the overall design of the financial architecture.

This introduction is organized in three main sections: monetary policy, fiscal policy, and—what may be emerging as the third leg of macroeconomic policy—macroprudential policies.

I. Monetary Policy

The monetary policy theme that emerged from the first conference on rethinking macro policy, held in March 2011, was that central banks had to move from an approach based largely on one target and one instrument (the inflation rate and the policy rate, respectively) to an approach with more targets and more instruments. Two years later the choice of both the set of targets and the set of instruments remains controversial.

A. Should Central Banks Explicitly Target Activity?

Although the focus of monetary policy discussions has been, rightly, on the role of the financial system and its implications for policy, macroeconomic developments during the crisis and after have led to new questions about an old issue, the relation between inflation and output, with direct implications for monetary policy.

One of the arguments for the focus on inflation by central banks was the "divine coincidence" aphorism: the notion that, by keeping inflation stable, monetary policy would keep economic activity as close as possible (given frictions in the economy) to its potential. So, the argument went, even if policymakers cared about keeping output at potential, they could best achieve this by focusing on inflation and keeping it stable. Although no central bank believed that divine coincidence held exactly, it looked like a sufficiently good approximation to justify a primary focus on inflation and to pursue inflation targeting.

Since the crisis began, however, the relation between inflation and output in advanced economies has been substantially different from what was observed before the crisis. With the large cumulative decline in output relative to trend and the sharp increase in unemployment, most economists would have expected a fall in inflation, perhaps even the appearance of deflation. Yet in most advanced economies (including some experiencing severe contractions in activity), inflation has remained close to the range observed before the crisis.

As a matter of logic, there are two interpretations of what is happening. Either potential output has declined nearly as much as actual output, so that the output gap (the difference between potential and actual output) is in fact small, thus putting little pressure on inflation, or the output gap is still substantial but the relation between inflation and the output gap has changed in important ways.

With regard to the first interpretation, it is possible that the crisis itself led potential output to fall, or that output before the crisis was higher than potential output—for instance, if it was supported by unsustainable sectoral (housing) bubbles—so that the actual output gap is small. This could explain why inflation has remained stable. Empirically, however, it has been difficult to explain why the natural rate of unemployment should be much higher than before the crisis, or why the crisis should have led to a large decline in underlying productivity. And although there is a fair amount of uncertainty around potential output measures (especially in the wake of large shocks such as financial crises), by nearly all estimates, most advanced economies still suffer from a substantial output gap.

This leads to the second interpretation. Indeed, convincing evidence suggests that the relation between the output gap and inflation has changed. Recent work (e.g., the IMF's 2013 *World Economic Outlook* report) attributes the change to the following two factors.

The first factor is more stable inflation expectations, reflecting in part the increasing credibility of monetary policy during the last two or three decades. By itself, this is a welcome development, and it explains why a large output gap now leads to lower (but stable) inflation rather than to steadily decreasing inflation.

The second factor is a weaker relation (both in magnitude and in statistical significance) between the output gap and inflation for a given expected rate of inflation. This is more worrisome because it implies that fairly stable inflation may be consistent with large, undesirable variations in the output gap.

Looking forward, the main question for monetary policy is whether this weaker relation is a result of the crisis itself, and thus will strengthen again when the crisis comes to an end, or whether it reflects a longer-term trend. The tentative evidence is that part of it may indeed reflect specific circumstances related to the crisis—in particular, the fact that downward nominal wage rigidities become more binding when inflation is very low. But part of the weaker relation seems to reflect as yet unidentified longer-term trends. (These actually seem to have been present before the crisis; see the IMF's 2013 *World Economic Outlook*.) Should the relation remain weak, and the divine coincidence become a really bad approximation, central banks would have to target activity more explicitly than they are doing today.

B. Should Central Banks Target Financial Stability?

The crisis has made it clear that inflation and output stability are not enough to guarantee sustained macroeconomic stability. Beneath the calm macroeconomic surface of the Great Moderation (a period of reduced macroeconomic volatility experienced in the United States beginning in the 1980s), sectoral imbalances and financial risks were growing, and ultimately led to the crisis. The severity of the ensuing crisis and the limited effectiveness of policy action has challenged the precrisis "benign neglect" approach to bubbles. And it has reignited the issue of whether monetary policy should include financial stability (proxied by, say, measures of leverage, credit aggregates, or asset prices) among its targets.

The policy rate is clearly not the ideal tool for dealing with the kind of imbalances that led to the crisis. Its reach is too broad to be cost-effective. Instead, a consensus is emerging that more-targeted macroprudential tools should be used for that task.

There are, however, important caveats. Macroprudential tools are new, and little is known about how effective they can be. They are exposed to circumvention and subject to thorny political economy constraints. (more on these tools below) Given these limitations, the issue of whether central banks should use the policy rate to lean against bubbles has made a comeback (see, e.g., Svensson 2009; Mishkin 2010; Bernanke 2011; King 2012).

Should central banks choose to lean against bubbles, an old issue—evident both in the 2008–2009 crisis and in many previous financial crises—is that bubbles are rarely identifiable with certainty in real time. This uncertainty suggests that central banks may want to react to large enough movements in some asset prices without having to decide whether such movements reflect changes in fundamentals or bubbles. In other words, given what we have learned about the costs of inaction, higher type I errors (assuming that it is a bubble and acting accordingly, when in fact the increase reflects changes in fundamentals) in exchange for lower type II errors (assuming the increase reflects fundamentals, when in fact it is a bubble) may well be justified. However, should that road be taken, setting appropriate thresholds will not be easy. One possibility would be to focus on certain types of asset-price booms, for instance those funded through bank credit, which have proven particularly dangerous.

C. Should Central Banks Care about the Exchange Rate?

The crisis has shown once again that international capital flows can be very volatile. This volatility has not generally been a major problem in advanced economies (although the flow reversals in the euro area and the drying out of dollar liquidity in the European banking system during the early stages of the crisis are a reminder that vulnerabilities exist there as well). However, shallower financial markets, greater openness and reliance on foreign-denominated assets, and less diversified real economies make emerging markets significantly vulnerable to swings in capital flows.

The volatility of capital flows can have adverse effects on macroeconomic stability, both directly (through effects on the current account and aggregate demand) and indirectly (through effects on domestic balance sheets and thus financial stability). When the exchange rate strengthens on the back of strong inflows, the traded goods sector loses competitiveness, potentially leading to an allocation of capital and labor that may be costly to undo if capital flows and the exchange rate swing back. Capital inflows can also lead to balance sheet structures that are vulnerable to reversals to the extent that the inflows promote credit booms (and hence leverage) and increase the use of foreign-denominated liabilities. (There is ample evidence, for instance, that the credit booms and widespread reliance on foreign currency borrowing in Eastern Europe in the first decade of the 2000s was associated with strong capital inflows [Dell'Ariccia et al. 2012]).

The problems with capital flow volatility have led to a reassessment of the potential role for capital controls (which the IMF calls "capital flow management tools"). But, just as in the case of macroprudential tools and financial stability, capital controls may not work well enough, raising the issue of whether monetary policy should have an additional objective (Ostry, Ghosh, and Chamon 2012).

Could central banks have two targets, the inflation rate and the exchange rate, and two instruments, the policy rate and foreign exchange intervention? (Inflation-targeting central banks have argued that they care about the exchange rate to the extent that it affects inflation, but it is worth asking whether this should be the only effect of the exchange rate they ought to consider.) Adding exchange rates to the mix raises issues of both feasibility and desirability.

The answer to the feasibility question is probably no for economies with highly integrated financial markets (and almost certainly no for small, very open, advanced economies—say, New Zealand). Under those conditions, sterilized intervention is unlikely to be effective because capital flows react immediately to interest rate differentials. But the answer is probably yes (and the evidence points in this direction) for economies with greater financial frictions and more highly segmented markets. Under those circumstances, one could thus consider an extended inflation-targeting framework, with the policy rate aimed at inflation, and foreign exchange intervention aimed at the exchange rate.

But what about desirability? The consensus that has emerged regarding the use and the limitations of capital controls is directly relevant. The issues and conclusions are very much the same. Intervention is typically not desirable when it is aimed at resisting a trend appreciation driven by steady capital flows rather than by temporary swings (that is, when the movement in the exchange rate reflects a change in underlying fundamentals rather than, for example, temporary swings between risk off and risk on). And it may raise issues from a multilateral perspective (for more, see Ostry, Ghosh, and Korinek 2012).

D. How Should Central Banks Deal with the Zero Bound?

What may be most striking about the crisis is the way in which central banks have experimented with unconventional policies, from quantitative easing, to targeted easing, to new forms of liquidity provision. Will these instruments become part of the standard toolkit, or are they specific to the crisis? To answer this question, one needs to distinguish between two characteristics of the crisis.

The first is the liquidity trap, which constrains the use of the policy rate. The second is the segmentation of some financial markets or financial institutions. Although both characteristics have played a central role in determining policy, they are conceptually separate. One can think of sufficiently adverse but nonfinancial shocks such that central banks would like to decrease the policy rate further but find themselves constrained by the zero bound. And one can think instead of financial shocks that trigger segmentation in some financial markets while the policy rate is still positive. We consider the implications of each in turn.

The crisis has shown that economies can hit the zero lower bound on nominal interest rates and lose their ability to use their primary instrument, the policy rate, with higher probability than was earlier believed. This raises two questions. The first question is what steps can be taken to minimize the probability of falling into liquidity traps in the future. We will not elaborate on the discussion given by Blanchard, Dell'Ariccia, and Mauro (2010) regarding the optimal level of inflation in this context, although the argument in that paper and the counterarguments brought up in the ensuing debate still deserve a non ideological discussion both in academia and in policy forums (see, e.g., Ball 2013).

The second question is what to do in the liquidity trap. When the crisis hit, most central banks reacted by cutting interest rates aggressively. In several cases, interest rates rapidly hit the zero lower bound. Central banks then moved to adopt unconventional policies, which have taken many forms, with an alphabet soup of acronyms. It is useful to distinguish between targeted easing (a more accurate name than credit easing) measures, that is, purchases of specific financial assets without a change in the money supply, and quantitative easing measures, which are not sterilized and thus lead to an increase in the money supply.

Available empirical evidence suggests that some targeted easing policies have had a substantial impact on the prices of the assets acquired by the central bank. Much of the impact, however, seems to have come from the unusual segmentation of financial markets associated with this crisis, as seen, for example, in the case of the mortgage-backed securities markets in the United States in 2008 and 2009 (see Gagnon et al. 2011). Although assets with different risk characteristics are always imperfect substitutes and thus relative demand always matters, the ability of the central bank to affect relative returns is likely to be much more limited in normal times than it was during the crisis.

Quantitative easing can be thought of as the combination of targeted easing (the purchase of some assets, such as long-term Treasury bonds, financed by the sale of short-term assets) and a conventional monetary expansion (the purchase of short-term assets with central bank money). The question is whether, at the zero bound, the monetary expansion component has an effect per se. The issue is particularly clear in Japan, where the central bank has announced its intention to double the monetary base. If it has an effect, it has to be through expectations of either low future nominal rates or higher future inflation. (In the Alice in Wonderland, upside-down world of the liquidity trap, higher expected inflation is welcome because it is the only way to obtain a decrease in expected real rates.) Empirical evidence is mixed. The evidence is a bit stronger for another measure with a similar intent, namely, "forward guidance." Announcements consistent with forward guidance (such as the intention or commitment to keep short-term rates low for a specific period, or for as long as some economic conditions prevail) appear to have had a significant and economically sizable impact on long-term rates both in Canada and in the United States. Similar announcements, however, appear to have been less effective for Sweden's Riksbank (Woodford 2012). With regard to future monetary policy, away from the zero bound, forward guidance may well be here to stay.

The crisis has also led to new discussions of a number of old ideas, including a shift to price-level targeting or nominal GDP targeting. Support for these rules may be partly opportunistic: a common feature of level-based approaches (i.e., rules that target the price level rather than the inflation rate, or nominal income rather than nominal income growth) is that, at this juncture, they would allow for higher inflation rates without undermining central bank credibility in the long run. A potential loss of credibility has been a major concern for central banks throughout the crisis, as evidenced by the reaffirmation by central banks of their commitment to remain vigilant against inflation with every round of unconventional policies. But these level-dependent rules have several shortcomings. An important one is that temporary price shocks are not treated as bygones and have to be absorbed through inflation, or worse, deflation.

E. To Whom Should Central Banks Provide Liquidity?

When some investors are highly specialized (have strong "preferred habitats," to use an old expression) and, for some reason, reduce their demand, outsiders may not have the specialized knowledge needed to assess whether the lack of demand comes from higher risk or from the fact that the usual buyers are unable to buy. Outsiders may then decide to stay out. When this happens, market prices may collapse, or some borrowers may lose funding. Illiquidity may then lead to insolvency. Multiple equilibria may also arise, with the expectation of insolvency leading to high interest rates and becoming self-fulfilling.

From its early stages, the crisis showed that the classical multiple-equilibrium framework, which provided a rationale for providing banks with deposit insurance and access to a lender of last resort, now also applied to wholesale funding and nonbank intermediaries. The situation in Europe later showed that the same framework could also extend to sovereigns, even in advanced economies. Indeed, sovereigns are even more exposed than financial intermediaries to liquidity problems because their assets consist mostly of future tax revenues, which are hard to collateralize. The expectation that other investors may not roll over debt in the future might lead current investors to not want to roll over, leading to a liquidity crisis.

Central banks ended up providing liquidity not only to banks but also to non-deposit-taking institutions, and (directly and indirectly) to sovereigns. From a theoretical standpoint, the logic is largely the same. Nevertheless, the extension to nonbanks raises a number of issues.

First, just as with banks, the issue of distinguishing illiquidity from insolvency arises. But for nonbanks this issue happens in the context of potentially unregulated entities about which central banks possess limited information. Second, again as for banks, is the issue of moral hazard. The promise (or expectation) of liquidity provision will induce the accumulation of even less liquid portfolios beforehand, thereby increasing the risk of a liquidity crisis (Farhi and Tirole 2012). The problem is exacerbated in the case of indirect support (through market purchases of sovereign bonds, e.g.) because, unlike with direct support to banks, it is difficult (or impossible) to administer any punishment. Haircuts (for discount window access) and conditionality (for direct purchases) can partly allay but not eliminate these concerns. And haircuts run counter to the notion of providing the "unlimited liquidity, no matter what happens" necessary to eliminate the risk of a run. During a systemic crisis, these are second-order shortcomings relative to the need to stabilize the economy. But the case for intervention appears harder to make during tranquil times.

II. Fiscal Policy

Early in the crisis, with monetary policy facing the liquidity trap and financial intermediation still in limbo, governments turned to fiscal stimulus to sustain demand and avoid what they felt could become another Great Depression. However, when the acute danger appeared to have subsided, governments found themselves with much higher levels of public debt (not so much because of the fiscal stimulus but because of the large decline in revenues caused by the recession). Since then, the focus of fiscal policy discussions has been on fiscal consolidation.

At the earlier conference, we converged on two main conclusions. First, what appeared to be safe levels of public debt before the crisis were in fact not so safe. Second, a strong case emerged for revisiting the precrisis consensus that fiscal policy had a limited cyclical role to play.

The questions are much the same today, with a few twists. In light of the high debt levels, a significant policy issue that will remain with us beyond the crisis is that of the proper speed of fiscal consolidation. The answer depends on two main factors. First, how harmful or dangerous are current debt levels? The crisis has added one more issue to the usual list of the adverse effects of high debt: multiple equilibria in which vicious cycles of high interest rates, low growth, and a rising probability of default may lead to a fiscal crisis. Second, and to the extent that fiscal consolidation is necessary, what are its effects on growth in the short run, given the state of the economy and the path and composition of the fiscal adjustment?

We take up each of these issues in turn.

A. What Are the Dangers of High Public Debt?

At the start of the crisis, the median debt-to-GDP ratio in advanced economies was about 60 percent. This ratio was in line with the level considered prudent for advanced economies, as reflected, for example, in the European Union's Stability and Growth Pact. (Somewhat ironically, the prudent level for emerging markets was considered to be lower, about 40 percent. The actual median ratio was less than 40 percent, which has given these countries more room for countercyclical fiscal policy than in previous crises.)

By the end of 2012, the median debt-to-GDP ratio in advanced economies was close to 100 percent and was still increasing. For the most part, the increase stemmed from the sharp fall in revenues caused by the crisis itself. To a lesser extent, it was attributable to the fiscal stimulus undertaken early in the crisis. And for some countries, it was due to the realization of contingent liabilities (see IMF 2012a, box 2). In Ireland and Iceland, for example, the need to rescue an oversized banking system led to unexpected increases in their debt ratios of 25 and 43 percentage points, respectively. In Portugal, to take a less well-known example, as the crisis progressed, state-owned enterprises incurred losses and, under Eurostat rules, had to be included within the general government, the deficit and debts of which increased as a result. Moreover, guarantees started being called on public-private partnerships (which were more sizable than in other countries), thereby adding to the general government's burden. Between those issues and financial sector interventions, the overall result was an increase in the Portuguese debt ratio of about 15 percentage points.

The lessons are clear. Macroeconomic shocks and the budget deficits they induce can be sizable—larger than was considered possible before the crisis. And the ratio of official debt to GDP can hide significant contingent liabilities, unknown not only to investors but sometimes also to the government itself (Irwin 2012). This suggests the need for both a more comprehensive approach to measures of public debt and lower values for what constitutes "prudent" official debt-to-GDP ratios. Unfortunately, given the extent to which actual ratios have increased, it will take a long time to attain those prudent ratios again.

The costs of high public debt, from higher equilibrium real interest rates to the distortions associated with the taxes needed to service the debt, have long been recognized. The crisis brought to light another potential cost: the risk of multiple equilibria associated with high levels of debt. If investors, worried about a higher risk of default, require higher risk premiums and thus higher interest rates, they make it more difficult for governments to service the debt, thereby increasing the risk of default and potentially making their worries self-fulfilling.

In principle, such multiple equilibria can exist even at low levels of debt. A very high interest rate can make even a low level of debt unsustainable and thus be self-fulfilling. But multiple equilibria are more likely when debt is high, for then even a small increase in the interest rate can move the government from solvency to insolvency. They are also more likely when the maturity of the debt is short and rollover needs are greater: if most of the debt has to be rolled over soon, it is more likely that current investors will worry about future rollovers, leading them to be reluctant to roll over today.

Also in principle, central banks can eliminate the bad equilibrium by providing—or simply by committing to provide—liquidity to the government if needed. However, providing this liquidity is not straightforward. The intervention may need to be very large. And in light of the usual difficulty of distinguishing between illiquidity and insolvency and the fact that the state, as distinct from banks, cannot provide collateral, the risks to the central bank may be considerable.

The experience of the crisis suggests that the issue of multiple equilibria is relevant. The evolution of Spanish and Italian sovereign bond yields can be seen in this light, with the European Central Bank's (ECB's) commitment to intervene in their sovereign bond markets having reduced the risk of a bad equilibrium. Some other euro area members, such as Belgium, have benefited from low rates despite still high levels of debt and political challenges; how much of the difference between, say, Belgium and Italy can be explained by fundamentals or by multiple equilibria is an open question. The relatively benign perception of both the United States and Japan may be seen as an example in the opposite direction. Despite high levels of debt, particularly in Japan, both countries have been perceived so far as "safe havens" and have benefited from very low rates, containing their debt-service burdens. However, the issue is the strength of their safe haven status and whether the situation might change quickly, leading to bad equilibrium outcomes in these countries too.

B. How to Deal with the Risk of Fiscal Dominance?

In light of the magnitude of the required fiscal consolidation in so many advanced economies, the issue of whether to reduce the real value of the debt through debt restructuring or inflation is unlikely to go away.

We shall limit ourselves to two brief remarks on debt restructuring. First, at least in the current international financial architecture, debt restructuring remains a costly and cumbersome process. (How to improve this situation will continue to be an important topic for research and policy analysis.) Second, in contrast to the emerging market experiences of the past, a sizable share of the debt in most advanced economies is held by domestic residents (more than 90 percent in Japan), often financial intermediaries, or by residents of neighboring or highly connected countries (including through the financial system). Thus, the scope for debt restructuring is very limited. And in any case it would call for extreme care to minimize potentially disruptive redistribution of wealth between domestic bondholders and taxpayers, and strong adverse effects on the financial system.

Against that background, governments facing the need for difficult fiscal adjustment might well put pressure on central banks to help limit borrowing costs, which raises the issue of fiscal dominance. In principle, monetary policy can help reduce the public debt burden in a number of ways. Central banks can slow down the exit from quantitative easing policies and keep sovereign bonds on their books longer. They can also delay the increase in nominal interest rates warranted by macroeconomic conditions and let inflation increase, leading, on both counts, to low real interest rates for a more prolonged period than would otherwise be optimal.

Indeed, historically, debt has often been reduced through rapid inflation; extreme examples include the well-known episodes of hyperinflation that wiped out debt in the aftermath of major wars (e.g., Germany, Japan). Less extreme cases have recently attracted renewed attention, notably the United States in the second half of the 1940s, when inflation resulted in significantly negative real interest rates and, over time, lower debt ratios (see Reinhart and Sbrancia 2011, who suggest that a return to financial repression is a potential concern).

How much difference could such monetary policies make? The answer depends largely on how long central banks can maintain low or even negative real interest rates. Under the assumption that nominal interest rates reflect one-for-one increases in inflation, so that the real interest rate remains constant (a full and immediate Fisher effect applying to all newly issued or rolled-over debt), the decrease depends on the ability to erode the value of outstanding (long-maturity) nominal debt, and is rather small. IMF staff simulations suggest that, for the G7 economies, if inflation were to increase from the current average projected pace of less than 2 percent to, say, 6 percent, the net debt ratio would decline, after five years, by about 10 percent of GDP on average (Akitoby, Komatsuzaki, and Binder, forthcoming). The effect would be larger if central banks could maintain lower real interest rates for some time. (It is sometimes argued that this would require financial repression, i.e., the ability to force banks to hold government bonds. This seems incorrect: as the current evidence shows, central banks can maintain negative real interest rates for some time if they want to. But these negative rates may lead to overheating and inflation. They may also induce investors to shift to foreign assets, leading to depreciation and further inflation. However, if central banks accept these inflation consequences, they can maintain lower real interest rates for some time, even absent financial repression.)

In short, if regular fiscal consolidation, through higher revenues or lower spending, proved infeasible, low or negative real interest rates could, in principle and within limits, help maintain debt sustainability. However, this path would have sizable costs: increases in inflation and reductions in real interest rates are, in effect, a smoother, less visible version of debt restructuring, with some of the burden of adjustment shifted from taxpayers to bondholders, and would thus face similarly significant distributional, social, and political issues.

In light of these considerations, it is essential that monetary policy decisions continue to be under the sole purview of the central bank, unencumbered by political interference. The central bank, in turn, should base its decision on the way the debt situation and fiscal adjustment (or lack thereof) would impact inflation, output, and financial stability. Indeed, central bank purchases of government bonds during the crisis have occurred against the background of large output gaps and often as part of an effort to avoid deflation or a self-fulfilling debt crisis. More generally, the central bank should be mindful of the risk that such policy could be viewed as slipping into fiscal dominance, particularly given the difficulties of assessing the effects on output of various possible strategies to keep public debt in check. The risk of fiscal dominance seems relatively limited in the euro area, where no single government can force the ECB to change its monetary policy. It is more relevant elsewhere, and may remain an issue for years to come.

C. At What Rate Should Public Debt Be Reduced?

In light of the need to decrease the ratio of public debt to GDP, the fiscal policy debate has focused on the optimal speed and the modalities of fiscal consolidation. Many of the issues consolidation raises are relevant not only for now, but more generally for fiscal policy in the future.

Identifying the dynamic effects of fiscal policy on output is difficult. It suffers from identification problems, and the effects are likely to differ depending on the state of the economy, the composition of the fiscal adjustment, the temporary or permanent nature of the measures, and the response of monetary policy.

Largely as a result of these difficulties, empirical estimates of fiscal multipliers ranged widely before the crisis (e.g., see Spilimbergo, Symansky, and Schindler 2009). Early in the crisis, some researchers and policymakers argued that positive confidence effects could dominate the adverse mechanical effects of cuts in spending or increases in revenues and lead to "expansionary fiscal consolidations." Others argued that, in a situation of impaired financial intermediation and thus tighter borrowing constraints for firms and households, together with the fact that monetary policy was facing the liquidity trap, multipliers were instead likely to be larger than in more normal times.

The wide range of fiscal policy responses to the crisis and its aftermath has stimulated new research (see, e.g., the articles in *American Economic Journal: Economic Policy* 4, no. 2, 2012). Although still a subject of some debate, the evidence shows that the multipliers have been larger than in normal times, especially at the start of the crisis (Blanchard and Leigh 2013), with little evidence of confidence effects (Perotti 2011). Beyond this conclusion, however, many questions remain unanswered—in particular, the differential effects, if any, of consolidations based on spending cuts rather than on revenue increases.

Underlying the debate about multipliers has been the question of the optimal speed of fiscal consolidation (with some in the United States actually arguing for further fiscal stimulus). In reality, for many countries severely affected by the crisis, the speed of consolidation has not been a matter of free choice; rather, it has largely been imposed on them by market pressures. Indeed, cross-country variation in the speed of adjustment has been explained in good part by differences in sovereign bond yields.

For countries that have some fiscal room, conceptually, the issue is how to trade off first moments for second moments, that is, how to trade off the adverse short-run effects on growth of faster consolidation against the decrease in risks coming from lower debt levels over time. (The argument that fiscal stimulus can more than pay for itself, and thus decrease debt levels, seems to be as weak as the earlier argument that fiscal consolidation could increase output in the short run). However, because of the relevance of multiple equilibria, and our poor understanding of the behavior of investors in this context, these risks are difficult to assess with any degree of precision. Thus, while fiscal consolidation is needed, the speed at which it should take place will continue to be the subject of strong disagreement.

Within this context, a few broad principles should still apply, as were articulated in various IMF publications (Cottarelli and Viñals 2009; Blanchard and Cottarelli 2010; IMF 2010; Mauro 2011; IMF *World Economic Outlook*, various issues; IMF *Fiscal Monitor*, various issues). In light of the distance to be covered before debt is down to prudent levels and of the need to reassure investors and the public at large about the sustainability of public finances, fiscal consolidation should be embedded in a credible medium-term plan. The plan should include the early introduction of some reforms—such as increases in the retirement age— that have the advantage of tackling the major pressures from age-related expenditures while not reducing aggregate demand in the near term.

The need to control debt has also attracted renewed interest in fiscal rules. Many countries, especially in the euro area, have introduced medium-term fiscal adjustment plans and have strengthened their commitment to fiscal rules. For example, Germany, Italy, and Spain have recently amended their constitutions to enshrine a commitment to reducing the structural deficit to zero or nearly zero by specific dates, all within a few years. More generally, many new fiscal rules have been adopted and existing ones strengthened in response to the crisis, in both advanced economies and emerging market economies (Schaechter et al. 2012). The evidence on medium-term fiscal adjustment plans shows that a wide range of shocks—especially those to economic growth—have the potential to derail implementation (Mauro 2011; Mauro and Villafuerte 2013). This potential highlights the importance of explicitly including mechanisms to deal with such shocks, thus permitting some flexibility while credibly preserving the medium-term consolidation objectives. Examples of helpful mechanisms include multiyear spending limits; the exclusion of items that are cyclical (e,g,, unemployment benefits), nondiscretionary (e.g., interest payments), or fiscally neutral (e.g., EU-funded projects); or the use of cyclically adjusted targets that let the automatic stabilizers operate in response to cyclical fluctuations.

D. Can We Do Better Than Automatic Stabilizers?

Other things equal, if the concern is output growth in the short run, weaker private demand (whether domestic or foreign) should call for slower fiscal consolidation. This argument has led several countries to shift from nominal fiscal targets to structural targets, so as to let automatic stabilizers function.

This leads to a question raised in our earlier paper. Although letting automatic stabilizers work is better than not doing so, stabilizers are unlikely to deliver the optimal cyclical fiscal policy response. First, the usual argument that the effect of automatic stabilizers on debt cancels out over time applies only to the extent that movements in output are temporary. This may not be the case. As discussed in section III, it is not clear, for example, how much of the recent decline in output (relative to trend) is temporary or permanent. Second, the overall strength of automatic stabilizers varies from country to country and depends on societal choices—on the size of the government, as well as on tax and expenditure structures—that were made on the basis of objectives other than cyclical fiscal policy. Thus, the strength of the automatic stabilizers could be insufficient, or it could be excessive.

Thus, our earlier paper asked, why not design better stabilizers (Blanchard, dell'Ariccia, and Mauro 2010)? For instance, for countries in which existing automatic stabilizers were considered too weak, proposals for automatic changes in tax or expenditure policies are appealing. Examples include cyclical investment tax credits, or prelegislated tax cuts that would become effective if, say, job creation fell below a certain threshold for a few consecutive quarters. Perhaps because the policy focus has been on consolidation rather than on the active use of fiscal policy, there has been, as far as we know, little analytical exploration (an exception is McKay and Reis 2012) and essentially no operational uptake of such mechanisms.

III. Macroprudential Instruments

One of the unambiguous lessons from the crisis is that dangerous imbalances can build beneath a seemingly tranquil macroeconomic surface. Inflation can be stable, output can appear to be at potential, but things may still not be quite right. Sectoral booms may lead to an unsustainable composition of output—for example, too much housing investment. Or financial risks may build up because of the way real activity is funded (e.g., excessively leveraged financial institutions, excess household indebtedness, excess maturity mismatches in the banking system, recourse to off-balance-sheet products entailing large tail risks). Critically, the effects of these imbalances can be highly nonlinear. Long and gradual buildups can be followed by abrupt and sharp busts, with major welfare consequences.

Beyond a desirable strengthening of prudential supervision over the financial sector, what else can be done to prevent such problems from reoccurring or to cushion their blow? Monetary and fiscal policies are not the best tools for addressing these imbalances (at least as a first line of defense). Monetary policy has too broad a reach to deal cost-effectively with sectoral booms or financial risks. Fiscal measures can be more targeted, but time lags and political economy problems limit their usefulness. These shortcomings have led to increasing interest in more targeted "macroprudential instruments" (see Borio and Shim 2007 for an early discussion). The potential use of these instruments was a major theme of our first conference, and it has been an active field of research since the start of the crisis (e.g., ECB 2012). Now that some of these tools have been adopted in practice, we better understand their effects and their limitations. But we are still a long way from knowing how to use them reliably. Empirical evidence on the effectiveness of these measures is scant, and the way they work and interact with other policies is likely to depend on a country's specific financial sector structure and institutions.

Among the conceptual issues that need to be solved are the articulations between macroprudential and microprudential regulations, and between macroprudential policies and monetary policy. We take them in turn.

A. How to Combine Macroprudential Policy and Microprudential Regulation?

Traditional microprudential regulation is partial equilibrium in nature. As a result, it does not sufficiently take into account the interactions among financial institutions and between the financial sector and the real economy. The same bank balance sheet can have very different implications for systemic risk depending on the balance sheets (and the interconnections) of other institutions and the state of the economy as a whole. Thus, prudential regulation has to add a systemic and macro dimension to its traditional institution-based focus. Regulatory ratios must reflect risk not in isolation but in the context of the interconnections in the financial sector, and must also reflect the state of the economy.

These considerations suggest that micro- and macroprudential functions should be under the same roof. However, political economy considerations may favor keeping the two functions under two different agencies. Several aspects of regulation (e.g., the degree of bank competition, policies to foster credit access, or those determining foreign bank participation) may be politically too difficult to delegate to an independent agency. On the contrary, the macroprudential function is more akin to monetary policy (with some caveats outlined below): unpopular tasks such as leaning against the wind during a credit boom are likely best performed by an independent agency. If that is the case, an alternative design could have the macroprudential authority in charge of the cyclical management of certain prudential measures, leaving the rest to the microprudential regulator. (This is the approach followed in the United Kingdom, where the Financial Policy Committee of the Bank of England will be able to vary the capital ratios to be applied by microprudential regulators.)

B. What Macroprudential Tools Do We Have, and How Do They Work?

One can think of macroprudential tools as falling roughly into three categories: (1) tools seeking to influence lenders' behavior, such as cyclical capital requirements, leverage ratios, or dynamic provisioning; (2) tools focusing on borrowers' behavior, such as ceilings on loan-to-value ratios (LTVs) or on debt-to-income ratios (DTIs); and (3) capital flow management tools.

Cyclical Capital Ratios and Dynamic Provisioning   The logic of cyclical capital ratio requirements is simple: they force banks to hold more capital in good times (especially during booms) so as to build buffers against losses in bad times. In principle, cyclical requirements can smooth a boom or limit credit growth beforehand, as well as limit the adverse effects of a bust afterward. Dynamic provisioning can do the same, by forcing banks to build an extra buffer of provisions in good times to help cope with losses if and when bad times come.

In practice, however, implementation is not so easy. First is the issue of the regulatory perimeter. Requirements imposed on banks may be circumvented through recourse to nonbank intermediaries, foreign banks, and off-balance-sheet activities. Regulators might find themselves incrementally extending the regulatory perimeter as market participants devise ever more innovative ways to circumvent it. Second is the practical question of what measures the cyclicality of requirements should be based on: the economic cycle, credit growth (as suggested under Basel III), asset-price dynamics (typically real estate)? Third, procyclicality is not effective if banks hold capital well in excess of regulatory minimums (as often happens during booms). Finally, time consistency is likely to be an issue: regulators may find it politically difficult to allow banks to reduce risk weights during a bust (when borrowers become less creditworthy and bank balance sheets are more fragile). In the past, regulators have achieved this, to some extent, through informal forbearance. A more transparent approach may be more difficult to sell to the public (recall the outcry against excessively leveraged banks in the wake of the crisis). This calls for a rules-based approach and an independent policymaker. (However, given the problems just described and the political economy issues discussed in a later paragraph, rules-based approaches present their own difficulties.)

Do these tools work? Evidence is mixed (see Saurina 2009; Crowe et al. 2011; Dell'Ariccia et al. 2012). Tighter capital requirements and dynamic provisioning have typically not stopped credit and real estate booms. But in a number of cases, they appear to have curbed the growth of particular groups of loans (such as foreign exchange–denominated loans), suggesting that these episodes would have been even more pronounced had action not been taken. In addition, in some cases, these measures provided for larger buffers against bank losses and helped to contain the fiscal costs of the crisis (Saurina 2009).

Loan-to-Value and Debt-to-Income Ratios Limits on LTV and DTI ratios are aimed at preventing the buildup of vulnerabilities on the borrower's side. After a bust, they can potentially reduce bankruptcies and foreclosures, leading to smaller macroeconomic busts.

Again, implementation is challenging. First, these measures are difficult to apply beyond the household sector. Second, attempts to circumvent them may entail significant costs. In particular, they may result in liability structures that complicate debt resolution during busts (e.g., LTV limits may lead to widespread use of second lien mortgages, which become a major obstacle to debt restructuring if a bust occurs). Circumvention may involve a shifting of risks not only across mortgage loan products but also to outside the regulatory perimeter through expansion of credit by nonbanks, less-regulated financial institutions, and foreign banks (which may result in increased currency mismatches as the proportion of foreign exchange–denominated loans rises). Undesired side effects can also occur to the extent that housing wealth is used as collateral in commercial loans (e.g., by small-business owners).

However, the limited existing empirical evidence suggests that these are promising measures. For instance, during episodes of quickly rising real estate prices, LTV and DTI limits appear to reduce the incidence of credit booms and to decrease the probability of financial distress and below par growth following the boom (see Crowe et al. 2011; Dell'Ariccia et al. 2012).

Capital Controls Capital controls (which the IMF refers to as "capital flow management tools") are aimed at risks coming from volatile capital flows. Although they have a long history, their use has been controversial. In recent years the IMF has argued that, if macro policies are appropriate, and if the flows are having an adverse impact on financial or macroeconomic stability, the use of these tools can be appropriate, typically in combination with other macroprudential tools (Ostry et al. 2010; IMF 2012b). The arguments are similar to those developed in the earlier discussion of the rationale for foreign exchange intervention. Capital controls and foreign exchange intervention are both complements and substitutes: complements because capital controls decrease the elasticity of flows with respect to relative rates of return, thereby making foreign exchange intervention more powerful; substitutes because both can be used to affect the exchange rate. An advantage of capital controls compared with foreign exchange intervention is that they can be targeted at specific flows, but, precisely because controls are targeted, they are also more exposed to circumvention (e.g., when flows are opportunistically relabeled to that end).

Because capital controls have been used many times in the past, evidence on their effects is more abundant, but still surprisingly inconclusive (Ostry et al. 2010). An often stated conclusion is that controls affect the composition of flows but not their level; this, however, seems unlikely, given the specialization of the different types of investors. If capital controls decrease short-term flows, it is unlikely they will be replaced by long-term flows, one for one. First readings of the experience of Brazil, which has used taxes on capital inflows during the current crisis, varying both the tax rate and the perimeter of the tax over time, are mixed: despite some circumvention, they appear to have slowed down portfolio inflows and limited exchange rate appreciation (for two views, see Jinjarak, Noy, and Zheng 2012; Chamon and Garcia 2013).

C. How to Combine Monetary and Macroprudential Policies?

If macroprudential tools are to play an important role in the future, a central issue is the way in which macroprudential and monetary policies interact: on the one hand, low policy rates affect behavior in financial markets, leading to potentially excessive risk taking. Macroprudential tools, on the other hand, affect aggregate demand through their effects on the cost of credit.

In theory, if both policies worked perfectly—that is, if they could be used to achieve full macroeconomic and financial stability—then macroeconomic stability could be allocated to the monetary authority and financial stability to the macroprudential authority. If a change in the monetary policy stance led to an excessive increase or decrease in risk taking, macroprudential tools could be adjusted accordingly. Similarly, monetary policy could offset any decline in aggregate demand associated with a tightening in macroprudential conditions.

In practice, however, both tools work far less than perfectly. Therefore, one policy cannot be blind to the limitations of the other. To the extent that macroprudential tools work poorly, monetary policy must take into account financial stability, as discussed in the section on monetary policy. Similarly, when monetary policy is unavailable to deal with an individual country's cycle (as under a currency union or an exchange rate peg), macroprudential tools have to contribute to the management of aggregate demand (for a discussion, see IMF 2012c).

In principle, coordination between the two authorities can solve this problem; however, it is likely that each policymaker cares primarily about his or her own objective. If this is the case, separate agencies with different powers and mandates (a central bank, much like those we have now, in charge of monetary policy and tasked with price and output stability, and a financial authority in charge of macroprudential policy and tasked with macrofinancial stability) independently setting monetary and macroprudential policy will typically not end up coordinating on the first-best solution. For example, in a recession, the central bank may cut the policy rate aggressively to stimulate demand. Worried about the effects of a relaxed monetary stance on risk taking, the financial authority may react by tightening macroprudential regulation. Anticipating this response and its contractionary effect on demand, the central bank may cut rates even more aggressively. And so on. The outcome is a policy mix with interest rates that are too low and macroprudential measures that are too tight relative to what a coordinated solution would deliver.

The obvious solution, on paper, to this problem is consolidation: put everything under one roof, which is probably the preferable design. Indeed, beyond the arguments just given, putting the central bank in charge of micro- and macroprudential tools gives it information useful to the conduct of monetary policy (see, e.g., Coeure 2013; see Jácome, Nier, and Imam 2012 for a discussion of institutional arrangements in Latin America). Yet, just as for the consolidation of micro- and macroprudential policies, there are also costs associated with this arrangement.

First, to the extent that macroprudential tools work imperfectly, a central bank with a dual mandate will have a harder time convincing the public that it will fight inflation (and thus anchor expectations) if and when inflation fighting conflicts with the other objective. (This was one of the arguments used earlier for moving prudential supervision out of central banks and giving it to financial stability authorities.)

Second, and perhaps more critical, consolidation raises political economy issues. Central bank independence (achieved through the outsourcing of operational targets to nonelected technocrats) was facilitated by a clear objective (inflation) and relatively simple operational tools (open market operations and a policy rate). The measurable nature of the objective allowed for easy accountability, which in turn made operational independence politically acceptable. The objectives of macroprudential policy are murkier and more difficult to measure, for several reasons. First, there are multidimensional intermediate targets: credit growth, leverage, asset-price growth, and so on. Second is the issue of understanding the relationship of the macroprudential objectives to the financial stability objective. Third, defining financial stability and identifying its desirable level is difficult: a policy rate hike can be defended after the fact by showing that inflation is close to the target and arguably would have exceeded it if tightening had not occurred, whereas a tightening of macroprudential measures that prevents a financial crisis could be attacked afterward as unnecessary. Fourth, the very fact that the macroprudential tool is targeted implies that its use may raise strong, focused political opposition. For example, young households may strongly object to a decrease in the maximum LTV. Because of these features, the independence of macroprudential policy is on weaker ground. And opponents of the idea of a centralized authority worry that political interference with macroprudential policy will undermine the independence of monetary policy. (Again, the UK may be showing the way, by having a Monetary Policy Committee and a Financial Policy committee, both within the Bank of England).

IV. Conclusions

To go back to the issue raised at the start of the discussion, despite significant research progress and policy experimentation in the last two years, the contours of future macroeconomic policy remain vague. The relative roles of monetary policy, fiscal policy, and macroprudential policy are still evolving. We can see two alternative structures developing: at a less ambitious extreme, a return to flexible inflation targeting could be foreseen, with little use of fiscal policy for macroeconomic stability purposes, and limited use of macroprudential instruments as they prove difficult or politically costly to use. At a more ambitious extreme, central banks could be envisaged to have a broad macroeconomic and financial stability mandate, using many monetary and macroprudential instruments, together with a more active use of fiscal policy tools. Where we end up is likely to be the result of experimentation, with learning pains but with the expectation of more successful outcomes.

Note

This paper was written as background for the conference "Rethinking Macroeconomic Policy II," sponsored by the International Monetary Fund, Washington, D.C., April 16–17, 2013. We thank George Akerlof, Markus Brunnermeier, Olivier Coibion, Jorg Decressin, Avinash Dixit, Chris Erceg, Josh Felman, and Jonathan Ostry for useful comments and suggestions.

References

Akitoby, Bernardin, Takuji Komatsuzaki, and Ariel Binder. Forthcoming. "Inflation and Public Debt Reduction in the G7 Economies." International Monetary Fund, Washington, DC.

Ball, Laurence. 2013. "The Case for Four Percent Inflation." Manuscript, Department of Economics, Johns Hopkins University, Baltimore.

Bernanke, Ben. 2011. "The Effects of the Great Recession on Central Bank Doctrine and Practice." Keynote address at the Federal Reserve Bank of Boston's 56th Economic Conference, "Long-Term Effects of the Great Recession," Boston, October 18–19.

Blanchard, Olivier, and Carlo Cottarelli, 2010. "Ten Commandments for Fiscal Adjustment in Advanced Economies." Blogpost, IMF Direct blog, June 24. http://blog-imfdirect.imf.org/2010/06/24/ten-commandments-for-fiscal-adjustment-in-advanced-economies.

Blanchard, Olivier, Giovanni Dell'Ariccia, and Paolo Mauro. 2010. "Rethinking Macroeconomic Policy." *Journal of Money, Credit and Banking* 42: 199–215.

Blanchard, Olivier, and Daniel Leigh. 2013. "Growth Forecast Errors and Fiscal Multipliers." IMF Working Paper 13/1, International Monetary Fund, Washington, DC.

Blanchard, Olivier, David Romer, Michael Spence, and Joseph Stiglitz. 2012. *In the Wake of the Crisis*. Cambridge, MA: MIT Press.

Borio, Claudio, and Ilhyock Shim. 2007. "What Can (Macro-)prudential Policy Do to Support Monetary Policy?" BIS Working Paper 242, Bank for International Settlements, Basel.

Chamon, Marcos, and Marcio Garcia. 2013. "Capital Controls in Brazil: Effective?" Discussion Paper 606, Department of Economics, PUC-Rio, Rio de Janeiro.

Coeure, Benoit, 2013. "Monetary Policy and Banking Supervision." Speech delivered at the Institute for Monetary and Financial Stability, Goethe University, Frankfurt, February 7.

Cottarelli, Carlo, and José Viñals. 2009. "A Strategy for Renormalizing Fiscal and Monetary Policies in Advanced Economies." IMF Staff Position Note 09/22, International Monetary Fund, Washington, DC.

Crowe, Chris, Giovanni Dell'Ariccia, Deniz Igan, and Pau Rabanal. 2011. "Policies for Macrofinancial Stability: Options to Deal with Real Estate Booms." IMF Staff Discussion Note 11/2, International Monetary Fund, Washington, DC.

Dell'Ariccia, Giovanni, Deniz Igan, Luc Laeven, and Hui Tong, with Bas Bakker and Jérôme Vandenbussche. 2012. "Policies for Macrofinancial Stability: How to Deal with Credit Booms." IMF Staff Discussion Note 12/6, International Monetary Fund, Washington, DC.

European Central Bank (ECB). 2012. "Report on the First Two Years of the Macro-Prudential Research Network." Frankfurt, European Central Bank, October. http://www.ecb.europa.eu/pub/pdf/other/macroprudentialresearchnetworkreport201210en.pdf.

Farhi, Emmanuel, and Jean Tirole. 2012. "Collective Moral Hazard, Maturity Mismatch and Systemic Bailouts." *American Economic Review* 102 (1): 60–93.

Gagnon, Joseph, Matthew Raskin, Julie Remache, and Brian Sack. 2011. "The Financial Market Effects of the Federal Reserve's Large-Scale Asset Purchases." *International Journal of Central Banking* 7 (1): 3–43.

International Monetary Fund (IMF). 2008. "The Changing Housing Cycle and the Implications for Monetary Policy," chap. 3 in *World Economic Outlook*. International Monetary Fund, Washington, DC.

International Monetary Fund (IMF). 2010. "Strategies for Fiscal Consolidation in the Post-Crisis World." Fiscal Affairs Department Paper 10/04, International Monetary Fund, Washington, DC.

International Monetary Fund (IMF). 2012a. *Fiscal Transparency: Accountability and Risk.* Fiscal Affairs Department in collaboration with the Statistics Department, International Monetary Fund, Washington, DC.

International Monetary Fund (IMF). 2012b. *The Liberalization and Management of Capital Flows: An Institutional View.* International Monetary Fund, Washington, DC.

International Monetary Fund (IMF). 2012c. *The Interaction of Monetary and Macroprudential Policies.* Washington, DC: International Monetary Fund.

International Monetary Fund (IMF). 2013. "The Dog That Didn't Bark: Has Inflation Been Muzzled or Was It Just Sleeping?," Chap. 3 in *World Economic Outlook*. International Monetary Fund, Washington, DC.

Irwin, Timothy. 2012. "Accounting Devices and Fiscal Illusions." IMF Staff Discussion Note 12/02, International Monetary Fund, Washington, DC.

Jácome, Luis I., Erlend W. Nier, and Patrick Imam. 2012. "Building Blocks for Effective Macroprudential Policies in Latin America: Institutional Considerations." IMF Working Paper 12/183, International Monetary Fund, Washington, DC.

Jinjarak, Yothin, Ilan Noy, and Huanhuan Zheng. 2012. "Capital Controls in Brazil: Stemming a Tide with a Signal?" Working Paper, School of Economics and Finance, Victoria, University of Wellington, NZ.

King, Mervyn, 2012. "Twenty Years of Inflation Targeting." Stamp Memorial Lecture, London School of Economics, London, October 9.

Mauro, Paolo, ed. 2011. *Chipping Away at Public Debt: When Do Fiscal Adjustment Plans Fail? When Do They Work?* Hoboken, NJ: John Wiley & Sons.

Mauro, Paolo, and Mauricio Villafuerte. 2013. "Past Fiscal Adjustments: Lessons from Failures and Successes." *IMF Economic Review* 61 (2): 379–404.

McKay, Alisdair, and Ricardo Reis, 2012. "The Role of Automatic Stabilizers in the US Business Cycle." Manuscript, Department of Economics, Boston University, Boston, and Department of Economics, Columbia University, New York.

Mishkin, Frederic. 2010. "Monetary Policy Strategy: Lessons from the Crisis." Paper presented at the ECB Central Banking Conference, "Monetary Policy Revisited: Lessons from the Crisis," Frankfurt, November 18–19.

Ostry, Jonathan David, Atish R. Ghosh, and Marcos Chamon. 2012. "Two Targets, Two Instruments: Monetary and Exchange Rate Policies in Emerging Market Economies." IMF Staff Discussion Note 12/01, International Monetary Fund, Washington, DC.

Ostry, Jonathan, Atish R. Ghosh, Karl Habermeier, Luc Laeven, Marcos Chamon, Mahvash S. Qureshi, and Annamaria Kokenyne. 2010. "Managing Capital Inflows: What Tools to Use?" IMF Staff Discussion Note 11/06, International Monetary Fund, Washington, DC.

Ostry, Jonathan, Atish Ghosh, and Anton Korinek. 2012. "Multilateral Aspects of Managing the Capital Account." IMF Staff Discussion Note 12/10, International Monetary Fund, Washington, DC.

Perotti, Roberto. 2011. "The 'Austerity Myth': Gain Without Pain?" NBER Working Paper 17571, National Bureau of Economic Research, Cambridge, MA.

Reinhart, Carmen M., and M. Belen Sbrancia. 2011. "The Liquidation of Government Debt." NBER Working Paper 16893, National Bureau of Economic Research, Cambridge, MA.

Saurina, Jesus. 2009. "Dynamic Provisioning: The Experience of Spain." Crisis Response Note 7, World Bank, Washington, DC.

Schaechter, Andrea, Tidiane Kinda, Nina Budina, and Anke Weber. 2012. "Fiscal Rules in Response to the Crisis: Toward the 'Next-Generation' Rules—A New Dataset." IMF Working Paper 12/187, International Monetary Fund, Washington, DC.

Spilimbergo, Antonio, Steven A. Symansky, and Martin Schindler. 2009. "Fiscal Multipliers." IMF Staff Position Note 2009/11. International Monetary Fund, Washington, DC.

Svensson, Lars, 2009. "Flexible Inflation Targeting: Lessons from the Financial Crisis." Speech delivered at De Nederlandsche Bank, Amsterdam, September 21.

Woodford, Michael. 2012. "Methods of Policy Accommodation at the Interest-Rate Lower Bound." Paper presented at the Jackson Hole Symposium, "The Changing Policy Landscape," August 31–September 1.

I

Monetary Policy

1

Many Targets, Many Instruments: Where Do We Stand?

Janet L. Yellen

Thank you to the International Monetary Fund for allowing me to take part in what I expect will be a very lively discussion.[1]

Only five or six years ago, there wouldn't have been a panel on the "many instruments" and "many targets" of monetary policy. Before the financial crisis, the focus was on one policy instrument: the short-term policy interest rate. Although central banks did not uniformly rely on a single policy target, many adopted an "inflation targeting" framework that, as the name implies, gives a certain preeminence to that one objective. Of course, the Federal Reserve has long been a bit of an outlier in this regard, with its explicit dual mandate of price stability and maximum employment. Still, the discussion might not have gone much beyond "one instrument and two targets" if not for the financial crisis and its aftermath, which have presented central banks with great challenges and transformed how we look at this topic.

Let me start with a few general observations to get the ball rolling. In terms of the targets, or, more generally, the objectives of policy, I see continuity in the abiding importance of a framework of flexible inflation targeting. By one authoritative account, about twenty-seven countries now operate full-fledged inflation-targeting regimes.[2] The United States is not on this list, but the Federal Reserve has embraced most of the key features of flexible inflation targeting: a commitment to promote low and stable inflation over a longer-term horizon, a predictable monetary policy, and clear and transparent communication. The Federal Open Market Committee (FOMC) struggled for years to formulate an inflation goal that would not seem to give preference to price stability over maximum employment. In January 2012, the committee adopted a "Statement on

Longer-Run Goals and Monetary Policy Strategy," which includes a 2 percent longer-run inflation goal along with numerical estimates of what the committee views as the longer-run normal rate of unemployment. The statement also makes clear that the FOMC will take a "balanced approach" in seeking to mitigate deviations of inflation from 2 percent and employment from estimates of its maximum sustainable level. I see this language as entirely consistent with modern descriptions of flexible inflation targeting.

For the past four years, a major challenge for the Federal Reserve and many other central banks has been how to address persistently high unemployment when the policy rate is at or near the effective lower bound. This troubling situation has naturally and appropriately given rise to extensive discussion about alternative policy frameworks. I have been very keen, however, to retain what I see as the key ingredient of a flexible inflation-targeting framework: clear communication about goals and how central banks intend to achieve them.

With respect to the Federal Reserve's goals, price stability and maximum employment are not only mandated by the Congress but are also easily understandable and widely embraced. Well-anchored inflation expectations have proven to be an immense asset in conducting monetary policy. They have helped keep inflation low and stable while monetary policy has been used to help promote a healthy economy. After the onset of the financial crisis, these stable expectations also helped the United States avoid excessive disinflation or even deflation.

Of course, many central banks have, in the wake of the crisis, found it challenging to provide appropriate monetary stimulus after their policy interest rate hit the effective lower bound. This is the point where "many instruments" enters the discussion. The main tools for the FOMC have been forward guidance on the future path of the federal funds rate and large-scale asset purchases.

The objective of forward guidance is to affect expectations about how long the highly accommodative stance of the policy interest rate will be maintained as conditions improve. By lowering private-sector expectations of the future path of short-term rates, this guidance can reduce longer-term interest rates and also raise asset prices, in turn, stimulating aggregate demand. Absent such forward guidance, the public might expect the federal funds rate to follow a path suggested by past FOMC behavior in "normal times"—for example, the behavior captured by John Taylor's famous Taylor rule. I am persuaded, however, by the arguments laid out by our panelist Michael Woodford and others suggesting that the policy rate should, under present conditions, be held "lower for longer" than conventional policy rules imply.

I see these ideas reflected in the FOMC's recent policy. Since September 2012, the FOMC has stated that a highly accommodative stance of monetary policy will remain appropriate for a considerable time after the economic recovery strengthens. Since December 2012, the committee has said it intends to hold the federal funds rate near zero at least until unemployment has declined below 6½ percent, provided that inflation between one and two years ahead is projected to be no more than a half percentage point above the Committee's 2 percent longer-run goal, and longer-term inflation expectations continue to be well anchored. I believe that the clarity of this commitment to accommodation will itself support spending and employment and help to strengthen the recovery.

Asset purchases have complemented our forward guidance, and the many dimensions of different purchase programs arguably constitute "many instruments." In designing a purchase program, one must consider which assets to buy: just Treasury securities or agency mortgage-backed securities as well? Which maturities? The Federal Reserve, the Bank of England, and, more recently, the Bank of Japan have emphasized longer-duration securities. At what pace should the securities be purchased? And how long should they be held once purchases cease? Each of these factors may affect the degree of accommodation delivered. Two innovations in the FOMC's current asset purchase program, for example, are that it is open-ended rather than fixed in size like past programs and that the overall size of the program is explicitly linked to seeing a substantial improvement in the outlook for the labor market.

In these brief remarks, I won't thoroughly review the benefits or costs of our highly accommodative policies, emphasizing only that I believe they have, on net, provided meaningful support to the recovery. But I do want to spend a moment on one potential cost—financial stability—because this topic returns us to the theme of "many targets" for central banks. As Chairman Bernanke has observed, in the years before the crisis, financial stability became a "junior partner" in the monetary policy process, in contrast with its traditionally larger role.[3] The greater focus on financial stability is probably the largest shift in central bank objectives wrought by the crisis.

Some have asked whether the extraordinary accommodation being provided in response to the financial crisis may itself tend to generate new financial stability risks. This is a very important question. To put it in context, let's remember that the Federal Reserve's policies are intended to promote a return to prudent risk-taking, reflecting a normalization of credit markets that is essential to a healthy economy. Obviously, risk-taking can go too far. Low interest rates may induce investors to take on too much leverage and reach too aggressively for yield. I don't see pervasive evidence of rapid credit growth, a marked buildup in leverage, or significant asset bubbles that would threaten financial stability, but there are signs that some parties are reaching for yield, and the Federal Reserve continues to carefully monitor this situation.

However, I think most central bankers view monetary policy as a blunt tool for addressing financial stability concerns and many probably share my own strong preference to rely on micro- and macroprudential supervision and regulation as the main line of defense. The Federal Reserve has been working with a number of federal agencies and international bodies since the crisis to implement a broad range of reforms to enhance our monitoring, mitigate systemic risk, and generally improve the resilience of the financial system. Significant work will be needed to implement these reforms, and vulnerabilities still remain. Thus, we are prepared to use any of our many instruments as appropriate to address any stability concerns.

Let me conclude by noting that I have touched on only some of the important dimensions of monetary policy targets and instruments that have arisen in recent years. I look forward to a discussion that I expect will explore these issues and perhaps raise others.

Notes

1. The views I express here are my own and not necessarily those of my colleagues in the Federal Reserve System.

2. See Gill Hammond, *State of the Art of Inflation Targeting*, Centre for Central Banking Studies, CCBS Handbook No. 29 (London: Bank of England, 2012), www.bankofengland.co.uk/education/Documents/ccbs/handbooks/pdf/ccbshb29 .pdf.

3. http://www.federalreserve.gov/newsevents/lectures/the-aftermath-of-the-crisis .htm.

2

Monetary Policy, the Only Game in Town?

Lorenzo Bini Smaghi

In addressing monetary policy's targets and instruments, I would like to focus on how much of the precrisis inflation-targeting frameworks we should keep going forward. There are two dimensions to the issue. The first relates to the ability of the inflation-targeting framework to ensure price stability, in particular during times of market exuberance, which may lead to the buildup of bubbles, whose burst jeopardizes financial stability and thus price stability. In light of experience, a pure inflation-targeting framework, one that ignores financial imbalances, may not allow a proper calibration of monetary policy. The second dimension relates to the postcrisis developments, where the inflation-targeting framework has not provided an appropriate monetary policy stance capable of addressing the challenges that advanced economies are currently facing. The task of cleaning up the mess after the bubble burst is much more complex than what the precrisis conventional wisdom expected.

There is an increasing literature on the first issue, in particular that addressing how to make inflation-targeting frameworks more flexible to incorporate the financial sector and how to broaden the range of tools available to central banks to address financial stability issues so as to prevent credit bubbles. I will therefore concentrate on the second issue, which questions the use of inflation targeting as the appropriate framework for getting out of a crisis like the 2008–2012 one.

Indeed, monetary policy does not currently seem to be as effective as expected. This certainly points to the need to improve economic models that are used for policy analysis. The question is whether central banks should work toward improving the existing models or whether they need to totally change the approach.

Independent of any improvement that might be made in understanding monetary policy, we should not depart from a few fundamental principles, related in particular to assigning policy instruments to targets. Two principles are worth recalling in all circumstances. The first is that each instrument should be assigned to a specific target. The second principle is that the assignment should be based on efficiency; that is, each instrument should be assigned to the target it can achieve most effectively.

These two principles suggest there is no reason to depart in a fundamental way from inflation targeting as the basic analytical framework for monetary policy during and after a crisis. That we do not understand why certain relations that were assumed to hold in the past no longer hold is not a good reason to completely change the policy framework.

The main frustration with the inflation-targeting framework comes from the fact that monetary policy, even when pushed to the extreme of keeping very low interest rates for a prolonged period of time and implementing nonstandard measures, which have enormously increased the size of the central bank's balance sheet, does not seem to be effective in raising growth, whereas inflation remains broadly in line with its target. Indeed, targeting inflation is not a goal in itself but aims at creating the conditions for sustainable growth. If keeping inflation on target is not leading to stronger growth, then what is its worth?

There are two possible reactions to this frustration. The first is to consider that if monetary policy has not been very effective so far in supporting growth, it should become even more expansionary. If the money multiplier, so to speak, is lower than expected, we need more monetary expansion, in all of its forms. The opposite reaction is to consider that perhaps the way in which monetary policy has been conducted so far is not very effective in addressing the problems faced by advanced economies. Trying to push further on this front may actually make monetary policy even less effective and increase the collateral damage over time.

The two hypotheses should be tested. The problem is that we do not seem to have the right analytical model to conduct such an exercise. Indeed, the result will depend on the model that is used to compare the costs and benefits of the two alternatives. A standard neo-Keynesian model, for instance, without a sophisticated financial sector, would probably validate the first hypothesis. But we know that models that ignore the financial sector do not provide a good description of advanced economies. Their uncritical use in the past may actually have been responsible for the policies that led to the crisis.

The key challenge is thus to improve models with a view to acquiring a better understanding of monetary policies' impact on agents' behavior, in particular after the global financial crisis of 2008–2009 and its aftermath. Here I would like to draw an analogy with the state of monetary theory before rational expectations became an accepted part of the economics literature. Standard Keynesian theory of the 1960s assumed that agents would react in a naïve way to monetary authorities' attempt to induce inflation so as to reduce the real value of debts and wages. That theory, however, could not explain why monetary policy was not capable of systematically increasing employment. The reason was that the theoretical model used by the policymakers was misspecified. The old models assumed agents to be naïve, forming their expectations in a backward-looking fashion, whereas in fact they were not. Agents are much more forward-looking than was thought at the time and know that when the economy slows down, the central bank will try to stimulate the economy by creating surprise inflation. They will thus rationally try to protect their income and wealth. If agents have rational expectations, monetary policy becomes less effective. Rational expectations are an extreme assumption, of course, but one that is useful in explaining the limits of traditional models of monetary policy.

Back to the present: we may ask ourselves whether monetary authorities—and economists—are not now making a similar mistake in considering economic agents naïve when in fact they are not. We know in particular—and economic agents know—that there are three ways to get out from a debt overhang. The first is to save your way out, which means low growth for a protracted period of time. The second is default or debt restructuring. The third is inflation.

Economic agents want to understand what objective the central bank pursues when it embarks on exceptional nonstandard measures. Their effectiveness may be very different if the aim is to repair the transmission mechanism of monetary policy when the latter is impaired by inefficiencies or bottlenecks in the financial system, as may be the case, for instance, in the euro area because of the sovereign debt crisis or an undercapitalized banking system, or when the objective is to increase the amount of liquidity in the system with a view to induce investors to diversify into more risky assets so as to stimulate aggregate demand, as may be the case today in Japan and the United States.

In other words, it's different if monetary policy tries to address liquidity problems in specific markets instead of stimulating aggregate demand or repairing solvency problems.

In the first case, monetary policy uses instruments to try to unclog the transmission mechanism, enhancing the correlation between the policy rate and the interest rate to end users. An example is the Securities Market Program implemented by the European Central Bank, whose effects on the money base are sterilized, or the purchase of covered bonds, which represents an attempt to try to revitalize a specific segment of the banking system. The impact on inflation and wealth distribution is limited.

In the second case, the objective of monetary policy is broader, as it tries to enhance its overall effectiveness by influencing the allocation of resources across agents and within financial markets, in particular between creditors and debtors. Quantitative easing and forward guidance are aimed at this second, broader objective. This type of policy is more likely to generate reactions by economic agents, in particular creditors, which may in turn have repercussions for the effectiveness of the policy itself.

Inflation reduces the real value of the debt, and thus redistributes wealth from creditors to debtors. The best way to redistribute wealth ex post is to create unexpected inflation while maintaining low interest rates for a protracted period of time. This is the stock adjustment effect. By reducing the real return on safe assets, this strategy also redistributes wealth through a flow effect, as investors shift their preferences toward riskier investments until inflation picks up and the returns on these assets turn out to be lower than anticipated.

The instruments that are currently used by central banks, such as very low interest rates for a prolonged period of time, forward guidance, and massive balance sheet expansion, are ways to try to tax creditors and subsidize borrowers, either directly by inferring capital losses and gains or indirectly by socializing losses accumulated on central banks' balance sheets. It is another way of trying to do what central banks did in the 1960s by reducing the real value of wages or, to put it in Milton Friedman's terms, to fool some of the people (i.e., creditors) at least some of the time. This is why such a policy is also named "financial repression." Financial repression is actually the optimal way to get out of a debt crisis, much as surprise inflation used to be considered the optimal way to reduce real wages and stimulate employment.

Such a policy assumes, however, that economic agents, in particular creditors, are naïve and do not react to policymakers' attempts to reduce the real value of their assets. This is what the models used by the policy authorities assume. And this is what makes the policy optimal. But it is fair to ask, as some economists did 40 years ago, whether the real world really looks like the models that policymakers use, and whether agents are indeed so naïve as to passively accept financial repression. The fact that monetary policy is not as effective as we thought may suggest that it's not the economic agents who are naïve.

I would like to raise a couple of issues in this respect.

The first is that financial repression is not easy to implement in highly sophisticated financial markets, where it is the task of investors to protect themselves against risk, including especially the risk of being trapped into excessively low returns on investments. Our models may be too simple to capture such behavior.

Second, even when agents are not able to protect themselves and are pushed toward investing in highly risky assets because of a lack of alternatives, that does not mean they are naïve and will take the loss passively when it materializes. Sophisticated investors may know, for instance, that in current market conditions some assets are overpriced, in particular in the fixed income market, but they may still be willing to hold them and even continue to buy them as long as they think that (1) in the short run these assets are nevertheless relatively attractive, and it may be risky to hold positions that are contrarian to the central bank's policy, and (2) they will be the first to sell these assets when the bubble bursts and will therefore contain any loss. We know, however, that not all investors can be first out of the door, and thus some will have to bear large losses, but the rush to the door could be so disorderly that a bursting bubble might be very damaging to economic and financial stability.

One reason why central banks may feel confident in using the old models is that inflation has remained low and inflation expectations are still anchored, despite the very expansionary monetary policies that have been implemented so far.

Here again, one might question whether we have the right model of inflation. Our simple models may not sufficiently take into account the fact that asset prices move more quickly than do goods and service prices. In fact, asset-price bubbles may build up and burst even before goods inflation starts rising. After all, isn't that what happened in 2005–2007? The bubble burst while inflation was still relatively moderate.

We could thus envision a world in which inflation remains low but the accommodative monetary policy of the central bank creates asset-price bubble that may burst even before inflation materializes. The burst itself generates deflationary pressures in the goods markets, which then requires that the central bank keep a very accommodative monetary policy. In such a world, real interest rates that are kept low for too long generate bouts of financial instability, which negatively affects the real economy and justifies keeping rates low for even longer. The relative stability in inflation and in the (low) level of interest rates creates the conditions for instability in the financial system and in the real economy. In other words, it's not monetary conditions that adapt to real and financial conditions but the reverse. Financial conditions and the real economy become more unstable as a result of low and stable inflation, fostered by accommodative monetary conditions.

How far is this description from reality? Doesn't it look very similar to what we have observed over the past decade, with relatively low real rates of interest and more volatile real growth? The models used by central banks to implement monetary policy do not consider these effects. Maybe we just need another financial crisis for such issues to get greater attention.

I would like to make a final point, which also touches upon the structure of this conference, in which the various macro policies are treated separately. If you think about the current discussion about the role of monetary policy—and, in particular, the need for monetary policy to focus more on growth—it is partly obscured by the fact that other policy instruments are subject to severe financial and political constraints. That other instruments are constrained does not justify shifting the responsibility for achieving goals other than price stability to monetary policy without a better understanding of the potential distortions and risks that may be created in the short to medium term. Before abandoning the basic principle that monetary policy should primarily aim at price stability, there should be a sound and transparent analysis of the intertemporal costs that this may entail for society as a whole.

For instance, by conducting aggressive asset purchases and maintaining interest rates at very low levels, the central bank undoubtedly takes away the incentive from the fiscal authorities to implement medium-term fiscal adjustment plans. We have seen this in the euro area. It is also apparent in the United States. The policy of persistently low long-term interest rates removed the incentive from the Obama administration and the US Congress to agree on a medium-term fiscal adjustment plan, and the lack of such a plan creates uncertainty about future taxation, which may hinder firms from investing.

The question should be, are investments more sensitive to the promise of low interest rates for a prolonged period of time or to the medium-term fiscal uncertainty that such low interest rates involuntarily produce?

The low level of long-term rates produced by the bond purchase program also contributes to the illusion, held even among some prominent economists, that there is no need nor pressure for budgetary adjustment.

Another institutional issue relates to the redistributive effects of monetary policy, which are essential for its effectiveness in a post-bubble situation. It might be questioned whether such a sensitive political issue can continue to be dealt with in a semi-disguised way by the central bank only, rather than through the normal democratic decision-making process, which involves, in particular, the parliament.

The crisis has shown how political authorities in our democracies try to postpone painful decisions and act only when they come under market pressure, as a last resort, at the edge of the cliff. By relieving market pressure, the central bank de facto can be led to play a very important political role. It can help governments gain time for implementing their policies, but it can also lead governments to waste time and indefinitely postpone urgent decisions. The central bank can actually be cornered into being "the only game in town."

So, isn't it a bit naïve to assume that when monetary policy starts aiming at other goals, which should be in the realm of the political authorities, the institutional framework underlying the central bank and its independence will not be affected? Isn't it a bit naïve to assume that the distortions that are introduced in the economy as a result of central banks entering other fields than monetary policy can be removed through decisions that can be of a technical nature, that is, decisions that can be made just by the central bank?

In other words, there is a risk that the exit strategy from a monetary policy that produces fiscal or distributional effects will no longer be just a monetary policy issue but a major political one. It is thus, in my view, delusional to think that the debate about the exit from the current policy is over whether the central bank has the instruments to exit such a policy or not. The central bank does have the instruments. Rather, the real question is whether it will have the political ability to decide the exit.

To be blunt, the independence of the central bank is at risk when the central bank enters the field of fiscal, regulatory, and distributional policies.

In my view, it is very dangerous to address such questions as "Should central banks more explicitly target activity? Should central banks target financial stability, and if so, how?" without considering what the role of the other policies should be, in particular fiscal, structural, and supervisory policies. Any unconditional answer to these questions—which would make the central bank the only player left in town—would lead to a time-inconsistent monetary policy because it would create incentives among the other policymakers to act in a way that would lead monetary policy to become ineffective, and would at some point have to be reneged on. This would inevitably lead to a loss of credibility of the central bank. Insofar as all the other policymakers have already lost part of their credibility, the possibility that the central bank may lose it as well should be a concern for society as a whole, not only for the central bank. This issue should be at the heart of the surveillance mandate of international institutions such as the International Monetary Fund.

I will conclude with a few words on whether central banks should care about the exchange rate. It seems to me that central banks actually care too much about the exchange rate, although they will not admit it. In the current environment the exchange rate remains the most powerful channel of transmission of monetary policy. However, this is true only to the extent that other central banks ignore it. Because other central banks will not ignore it, and cannot ignore it in the current environment, monetary policy designed separately by each national central bank will inevitably be suboptimal and lead to excess money creation, and thus fuel the next asset bubble.

This is a typical example of coordination failure. Again, this is an issue that cannot be ignored by international macroeconomic surveillance.

3

Monetary Policy during the Crisis: From the Depths to the Heights

Mervyn A. King

The past five years have been an extraordinary period for central banks. The breadth and scale of our operations have expanded in ways that were previously unimaginable as we responded to a crisis in the banking sector and the wider economy. In monetary policy, we have moved into uncharted territory. But has our notion of what central banks should do, and how, changed? Now is a good time to reflect on where we stand.

I want to focus this discussion on two areas. First, I want to distill what we have learned about the objectives of monetary policy. Second, I want to reflect on the implications of the proliferation of instruments that have been used to meet those objectives.

Objectives

For more than 30 years, the objective of central banks was clear: it was to set monetary policy to achieve long-run price stability. But the events of the past five years have raised questions about how central banks manage the trade-offs between price stability, output stability, and financial stability in order to meet our overall macroeconomic objectives.

Throughout the era of inflation targeting, the importance of the trade-off between output and inflation stabilization in the short term has been well understood. Monetary policy was seen as aiming at a target for inflation in the long run, which was to be achieved by bringing inflation back to target over a suitable time horizon so as to avoid excessive volatility of real variables, such as output and employment. Optimal monetary policy was seen as a choice of how best to navigate the short-run trade-off while ensuring that the long-run objective was met.

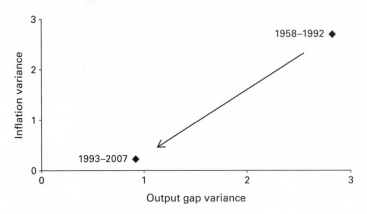

Figure 3.1
UK Inflation and Output Gap Variances.
Source: Office for National Statistics and Bank of England calculations.

Failure to deliver price stability is costly, as the experience of the United Kingdom amply demonstrates. Figure 3.1 shows the variance of inflation and the variance of the output gap in the UK using quarterly data for two periods.[1] Here we may contrast the performance in the 35 years up to 1992 with the first 15 years of inflation targeting. Better policy can take some credit for this improvement, as the anchoring of inflation expectations led to a huge reduction in inflation volatility.

It was tempting to think that we had moved onto the "Taylor frontier," which maps feasible combinations of the smallest variances of the output gap and inflation. The Great Stability appeared to be a permanent break from earlier periods—periods when monetary policy exhibited more unpredictable behavior and left the economy above and to the right of the Taylor frontier (figure 3.2). And in one important sense, it was: the dark days of double-digit inflation were consigned to the past.

But the Great Stability was not representative of a new normal. The variance of the output gap—though not of inflation—has been much higher over the past five years as the financial crisis generated a deep recession (figure 3.3). So what have we learned?

The banking and broader economic crisis has demonstrated that macroeconomic policy can face an additional trade-off between ensuring the soundness of the financial system in the medium term and keeping output in line with potential output and inflation on target in the near term. Such

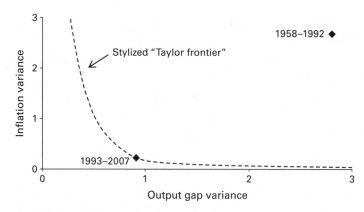

Figure 3.2
The UK's Precrisis Trade-off?

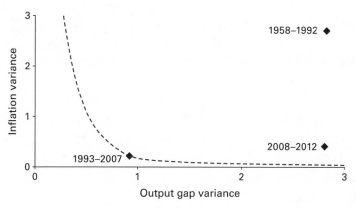

Figure 3.3
The Great Stability and Crisis Periods.

a trade-off arises because financial vulnerabilities can build even while output is growing steadily and inflation is low and stable.

Let me give three examples of the sort of underlying mechanisms in play. First, persistent misperceptions of future spending power may generate a mix of demand that proves to be unsustainable. I believe this was an important factor underlying the crisis. Although output in deficit countries, such as the UK, appeared to be growing at a sustainable rate, that gave a misleading impression of the sustainability of the Great Stability. In fact, the level of domestic demand was too high and the level of net exports correspondingly too weak. Second, as Hyman Minsky described, periods of stability encourage exuberance in credit markets, leading eventually to instability.[2] And third, low short-term policy rates may encourage investors to take on more risk than they would otherwise accept as they "search for yield."

It is arguable that monetary policy paid insufficient heed to the potential impact of such financial vulnerabilities. Financial shocks are costly because their effects can be too rapid for policy easily to offset and because they hit potential supply, thereby creating a trade-off between output and inflation. In other words, the Taylor frontier is less favorable (further from the origin) when account is taken of financial shocks than we might have believed. Taking the entire period of inflation targeting, including the recent past, might give a more accurate indication of where this "Minsky-Taylor" frontier lies than using data for the Great Stability period alone (figure 3.4).

What implications does this have for monetary policy? Possibly none, if we can rely now on macroprudential tools to ensure financial sector resilience. But set those tools to one side for a moment. Monetary policy could be used to reach a point more like *P* in figure 3.5, with less variation in the output gap and more variation in inflation than we have actually experienced over the past 20 years. Put another way, higher interest rates in the run-up to the financial crisis might have reduced the impact of the subsequent bust—at the cost of below-target inflation and below-trend output before the crisis hit.[3]

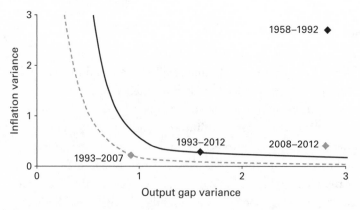

Figure 3.4
The True Trade-off for the UK over 20 Years?

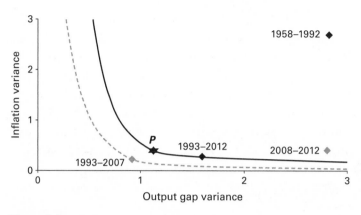

Figure 3.5
A Preferable Outcome?

In practice, new macroprudential tools and better microprudential supervision will improve the possibilities available to monetary policy-makers. Having additional instruments in effect brings about a favorable shift in the Minsky-Taylor frontier (or surface), which defines the possibilities open to policymakers.[4]

Nevertheless, consistent with the new remit[5] given to the Monetary Policy Committee by the UK government last month, the experience of recent years suggests there may be circumstances in which it is justified to aim off the inflation target for a while in order to moderate the risk of financial crises.

Instruments

For institutions generally regarded as conservative or even hidebound, central banks have been remarkably innovative in their creation of new instruments during the crisis. Lowering official interest rates virtually to zero was extraordinary in itself. But the wholesale redesign of frameworks to supply liquidity to the banking system, the expansion of the monetary base by multiples of its precrisis level through the purchase of assets held by the nonbank private sector, and the involvement of central banks in risky credit easing operations have all raised serious questions about the role of central banks—and have even challenged the idea of central bank independence.

Table 3.1 shows just how large the scale of central bank expansion has been. The monetary base has risen by unprecedented proportions as we tried to prevent a collapse of broad money and credit, as happened in the United States during the Great Depression and is happening in Greece today. And central bank balance sheets have risen across the industrialized world, as shown in table 3.2. That expansion has reflected both money creation through asset purchases and lending against collateral. All major central banks have created new ways to lend against collateral.[6] Far from their image as conservative creatures, are central banks at risk of throwing their traditional caution to the wind and ignoring the limits on monetary policy?

Table 3.1
Monetary Base (January 2007 = 100)

	UK	US	Japan	Euro Area
January				
2007	100	100	100	100
2008	113	101	100	109
2009	143	209	104	153
2010	323	244	109	145
2011	304	250	115	140
2012	362	323	132	188
2013	521	336	146	205
Latest	528	359	150	180

Note: Data are month averages for the UK, US, and Japan, and end-of-month for the euro area.
Sources: Bank of England, Federal Reserve, Bank of Japan, European Central Bank.

Table 3.2
Size of Central Bank Balance Sheets

	UK	US	Japan	Euro Area
March 2013 (% nominal GDP)	26	19	34	31
Increase since December 2007 (pp of nominal GDP)	20	12	13	18

Sources: Datastream, Bank of Japan.

Two limits are relevant in current circumstances. First, no matter how much liquidity is thrown at the banking system, lending and the economy will not recover if the banking system is inadequately capitalized and suffering from excessive leverage. That is why the Bank of England's Financial Policy Committee has placed weight on the need for the weaker UK banks to raise capital. It is not surprising that the more strongly capitalized banks in the UK are expanding lending and the poorly capitalized banks are contracting lending.

Second, there are limits on the ability of domestic monetary policy to expand real demand in the face of the need for changes in the real equilibrium of the economy. I do not believe that the present problems in the UK stem only from a large negative shock to aggregate demand. In common with many other countries, the UK's problems also reflect the underlying need to rebalance the economy, requiring a reallocation of resources both within and between nations. It is not simply a question of boosting aggregate demand but of helping to bring about a shift to a new equilibrium. That, in turn, implies the need both for large changes in relative prices, especially between tradable and nontradable goods and services, and a shift in the relative levels of domestic demand at home and overseas. There are, therefore, limits on what any one country's domestic monetary policies can achieve without the support of others.

Despite these limits, circumstances have demanded that central banks take extraordinary measures. Such measures can risk moving into territory more normally associated with fiscal policy and, in doing so, put at risk central banks' hard-won independence. There are, it seems to me, three threats to central bank independence.

First, there is the risk of appearing to promise too much or allowing too much to be expected of central banks. With constraints on other policy instruments, central banks are seen as "the only game in town." But failure to make clear the limits to monetary policy risks disillusionment with central banks and the inevitable political pressure on them that would follow.

Second, at the zero lower bound there is no clear distinction between monetary and fiscal policy. But it is still important to ensure that central banks do not take on to their balance sheets risks to the taxpayer that are properly matters that should be decided by elected politicians. To ensure price stability in the long run, it is vital to maintain the operational independence of a central bank. Any decisions that put taxpayers' money at risk must be made by finance ministries, and central banks must protect their balance sheets by imposing appropriate haircuts on collateral and avoiding the purchase of risky private-sector assets.

Third—and important even when we move away from the zero lower bound—the expansion of central banks' responsibilities to include macroprudential policy and, in the case of the Bank of England, responsibility for regulating the banking system has made independence much harder to define. The deployment of responsibilities outside monetary policy cannot be divorced from the government in the same way as is possible for monetary policy. For example, in the area of financial stability and banking supervision, there will be times when public funds may be put at risk when rescuing or resolving a failing institution—and that decision is properly one for the finance ministry. It is far from straightforward for a central bank governor to be completely independent in terms of monetary policy, somewhat independent in terms of financial stability, and not at all independent in terms of operations that risk taxpayers' money.

The financial crisis has challenged our understanding of the objectives of monetary policy and exposed its limits. And, through the proliferation of instruments and the resulting increase in responsibilities, it has complicated the question of central bank independence. How should we respond to this more complex environment? We must keep sight of three important principles. First, although they should be realistic about what can be achieved, it is right that elected politicians and parliaments decide on the objectives of policy. Second, as we learned in the 1970s, if the central bank is to achieve price stability—its fundamental role—then it must be sufficiently independent. And third, to protect that independence, its limits should be very clearly circumscribed, and central banks should be exceptionally careful with decisions that put public funds at risk.

The challenge remains, as it was 20 years ago, to make "constrained discretion" work in practice. But it has gotten harder.

Notes

I would like to thank Charlie Bean, Alex Brazier, Spencer Dale, Andy Haldane, and Iain de Weymarn for helpful comments and suggestions in preparing this chapter, and in particular Tim Taylor, whom I regard as a coauthor, although he is absolved of any errors in the current draft.

1. The inflation measure used is the quarterly rate of increase of the GDP deflator, defined as the ratio of nominal GDP to real GDP. The output gap is estimated as the difference between the log of real GDP and the trend path of log GDP, derived using the Hodrick–Prescott filter.

2. Hyman P. Minsky, "The Financial-Instability Hypothesis: Capitalist Processes and the Behavior of the Economy," in *Financial Crises: Theory, History, and Policy*, ed. Charles Kindleberger and Jean-Pierre Laffargue (Cambridge: Cambridge University Press, 1982).

3. A more detailed appraisal of this argument is contained in "Twenty Years of Inflation Targeting," a 2012 speech by Mervyn A. King, available at http://www .bankofengland.co.uk/publications/Pages/speeches/2012/606.aspx.

4. A social planner would use both instruments together to pick the welfare-maximizing point on the frontier (or surface), and in the UK, the Monetary Policy Committee is expected to work closely with the Financial Policy Committee, which has the statutory power to deploy macroprudential instruments.

5. The relevant passage in the Monetary Policy Committee's remit states: "Circumstances may also arise in which attempts to keep inflation at the inflation target could exacerbate the development of imbalances that the Financial Policy Committee may judge to represent a potential risk to financial stability. The Financial Policy Committee's macro-prudential tools are the first line of defence against such risks, but in these circumstances the Committee may wish to allow inflation to deviate from the target temporarily, consistent with its need to have regard to the policy actions of the Financial Policy Committee." The full remit is available at http://www.bankofengland.co.uk/monetarypolicy/Documents/pdf/chancellorletter130320r.pdf.

6. Facilities introduced by the Bank of England have included the Discount Window Facility, the Special Liquidity Scheme, Extended Collateral Term Repos, Extended Collateral Long Term Repos, and the Funding for Lending Scheme. The ECB initiated its Long Term Repo Operations. And Federal Reserve facilities include the Term Auction Facility, the Term Assert Backed Securities Loan Facility, the Primary Dealer Credit Facility, the Commercial Paper Funding Facility, the Term Securities Lending Facility, the ABCP Money Market Fund Liquidity Facility, the Money Market Investing Funding Facility, and the Term Discount Window Program.

4

Monetary Policy Targets after the Crisis

Michael Woodford

During the global financial crisis and its aftermath, central banks have undertaken unprecedented actions of many kinds. This raises a natural question: has the crisis revealed that the previous consensus framework for monetary policy was inadequate and should now be fundamentally reconsidered? It is surely true that central banks were not too well prepared for the crisis and that new policies had to be created, to a large extent on the fly. And it would obviously be desirable to try to learn from this experience, to be better prepared for an appropriate response next time and perhaps even to reduce the probability of there being a next time.

This does not mean that all previous conventional wisdom must now be discarded. In particular, it has not been shown that central banks erred in committing themselves to explicit, quantitative inflation targets. Inflation targeting—and the "implicit" inflation targeting that was practiced by some other central banks—has resulted in a high degree of stability in medium-run inflation expectations during the crisis and its aftermath, and this has likely improved the stability of the real economy as well. If the prolonged high unemployment of the past several years had led to a deflationary spiral, our situation would surely have been far worse. That has been a benefit of the Fed's and other central banks' credibility in inflation stabilization in the years prior to the crisis, and it is not something we should want to casually discard.

Nevertheless, it is important to stress that inflation targeting need not mean and should not mean the caricature sometimes given of it, according to which inflation control should be the sole objective of policy at all times because inflation stabilization by itself will be sufficient to guarantee macroeconomic stability. Recent events have obviously cast considerable doubt on this overly simplistic view. However, it's important to remember that this was not the view advocated by most proponents of inflation targeting even before the crisis. Mervyn King famously called that view the "inflation nutter" position in one of his classic early discussions of the theory of inflation targeting[1] and argued instead for a more flexible form of inflation targeting. Other leading proponents of inflation targeting such as Ben Bernanke and Lars Svensson also consistently argued for a flexible conception.[2] They believed it was important to conduct monetary policy in such a way as to maintain medium-run inflation expectations relatively constant at the preannounced target rate but that it was permissible to allow temporary departures of the inflation rate from this medium-run target for the sake of other stabilization objectives. A near-term inflation rate near the target was neither necessary nor sufficient for good policy.

But this doctrine, while sensible as far as it goes, does leave an important question unanswered: What does it mean to conduct policy in the short run in such a way as to ensure that medium-run inflation expectations remain anchored, even though one is not always acting to keep inflation as close as possible to the medium-run target? Inflation-targeting central banks talk a lot about how they try to assess whether inflation expectations are still anchored and whether their internal models still forecast an inflation rate near the target some years in the future, but they are frequently less clear about what it is about the way in which they intend to make policy decisions that would make that a correct expectation.

Vagueness on this point didn't create great difficulties in the 15 years or so of relative macroeconomic stability prior to the global financial crisis. But when larger disturbances occur, the incompleteness of the flexible inflation-targeting doctrine becomes more of a problem. Inflation-targeting central banks have recently been conducting policy in ways that don't seem to be directly dictated by their inflation-targeting framework, but that observation raises questions about whether the framework remains in effect.

In my view, flexible inflation targeting doesn't need to be repudiated as a policy framework, but it does need to be *completed*. Inflation-targeting central banks need to commit themselves not only to a medium-run inflation target but also to criteria for making nearer-term policy decisions that will, among other desiderata, imply that the inflation rate should be near the target if one averages over a sufficient number of years.[3]

As an example of such a criterion, a central bank might commit itself to making short-run decisions that keep nominal GDP as close as possible to a particular target path, even in the nearer term. The target path for nominal GDP could be chosen so that keeping nominal GDP on that path should ensure, over the medium run, an average inflation rate equal to the inflation target. At the same time, it would imply that inflation would not be the sole determinant of short-run policy decisions. For example, a loosening of policy might be appropriate even when inflation is not running below target if insufficient real growth has resulted in a level of nominal GDP below the target path.[4]

Another respect in which the inflation-targeting doctrine prior to the crisis has proven to be incomplete is in its failure to specify how policy should be carried out if aggregate demand remains insufficient to achieve the central bank's stabilization targets, even when the zero lower bound on short-term nominal interest rates is reached, as it has been in many countries over the last few years.

One approach used by several central banks has been "forward guidance," or indications by the central bank that interest rates will remain low in the future, as a substitute for further immediate interest rate cuts. Such announcements do seem to have been able to influence market expectations about future short-term rates and hence able to influence longer-term interest rates and other asset prices. But important questions remain about the form that such forward guidance should take and how the existence of such statements should constrain subsequent policy decisions.

One question is whether forward guidance should take the form of a statement about future policy *intentions,* or if it suffices for the central bank to offer a forecast of its likely future decisions, given the conditions that can be anticipated at present. The idea of merely offering a forecast has had a certain appeal to central bankers since it doesn't tie the hands of the future policy committee. Unfortunately, there is no obvious reason for a mere forecast to be effective in stimulating demand.

For a central bank forecast of future interest rates to change market expectations, it would have to reveal either new information about likely future conditions or new information about the central bank's future policy reaction function. But convincing people that interest rates will remain low for longer than they had previously expected—either because the economic recovery will be slower than previously expected or because deflation is coming, and not because of any change in the central bank's reaction function—should be expected to have a contractionary rather than an expansionary effect on current expenditure.[5]

This is surely not the aim of forward guidance at the zero lower bound. Hence, to be effective, the announcement must communicate a different view of the future reaction function; that is, of the conditions under which policy will or will not be tightened in the future.

But if this is the goal, a mere forecast of future interest rates is not the most effective way to change expectations. If a central bank intends to conduct policy later in a way that is different from what people in the markets would already expect, then it should seek to communicate that intention by talking directly about how future policy decisions will be made.

What kind of statements about future policy decisions would be desirable if that were one's aim? Recently, several central banks have made statements about specific dates until which the policy rate is expected to remain at its lower bound. But while traders and financial markets are certainly interested in hearing about such dates, I don't think a date-based approach makes sense as a way of communicating future policy intentions. It would not make sense, after all, for a central bank to actually bind itself not to consider raising rates before a specific date as far as two years in the future regardless of what may occur in the interim. Hence it is hard for date-based forward guidance to be understood as a genuine communication of policy intentions rather than as a mere forecast.

A better approach would instead specify economic conditions that must be reached in order for it to be appropriate to raise the policy rate. Such a statement should allow market participants to form judgments about the likely length of time for which low rates might continue, but it will imply that the actual liftoff date would depend on future outcomes, as indeed it should.

The recent move of the US Federal Open Market Committee (FOMC) to replace date-based forward guidance with explicit numerical thresholds for economic indicators is a desirable step. The thresholds, however, have had to be determined on an ad hoc basis and do not obviously follow from previously announced policy targets. Nor do they indicate the policy that one should expect the FOMC to follow after the current anomalous period.

Under the version of flexible inflation targeting that I've just proposed, the criterion for liftoff from the zero lower bound could follow from the same target criterion that guides policy decisions at other times. A central bank that seeks to use its policy instruments to keep nominal GDP on a certain, steady growth path could also, when the zero lower bound makes it unable to prevent a sustained shortfall of nominal GDP relative to the target path, commit itself to maintain unusual policy accommodation until nominal GDP can be brought back to that target path, even though this would mean seeking higher than average nominal growth during a transitional period.[6]

An approach of this kind to forward guidance during a zero lower bound episode would have two advantages over the ad hoc approach. First, it would provide an explanation for pursuing unusually aggressive policies in the aftermath of a zero lower bound episode, even as a monetary stimulus began to have effects, and it would do this in a way that should not create doubts about the cumulative increase in prices that might occur before the policy has ended, for the existence of a target path for the level of nominal GDP—a target that has not been raised as a result of the crisis—implies that nominal growth should indeed be capped. And the pursuit of such a temporary policy would remain perfectly consistent with a stated intention to pursue a subsequent approach to policy (namely, keeping nominal GDP near that target path) that should once again deliver an average inflation rate near the long-run inflation target.

The second advantage is that if such a policy were expected to be followed as soon as the zero lower bound was reached, this anticipation should have a stabilizing effect, reducing the distortions associated with the zero lower bound on interest rates. If a decline in nominal GDP growth owing to an inability to cut the policy rate below the zero lower bound were expected to automatically imply faster nominal GDP growth later to undo the shortfall, this anticipation should reduce the size of that initial shortfall.

I believe that confidence that central banks would not allow inflation to drift permanently below their long-run inflation targets has been a stabilizing factor in the recent crisis. In the same way, I believe that had there been an existing commitment to a nominal GDP target path, this would have been an even greater stabilizing factor.

Finally, another question raised by the recent crisis is whether central banks should have paid more attention to the growing risks to financial stability before the crisis. Or, to pose the more practical question of relevance to us now, to what extent should central banks consider risks to financial stability when making monetary policy decisions going forward?

Certainly, this issue can't be dismissed as easily as it often was before the crisis. A popular argument then was that it was difficult to be sure a bubble was forming before it burst and that it was therefore more practical not to consider the question until after the crash, and then use monetary policy to deal with the consequences of the crash. But surely the events of 2008–2009 and their aftermath have dented our confidence regarding how easy it is to "mop up after the crash" with the tools actually available to central banks.

It therefore makes sense going forward to seek to assess potential risks to financial stability before they grow too large, as difficult as that undoubtedly will be. This does not, however, mean that monetary policy should be the only line of defense. To say that monetary policy might have some capacity to restrain the growth of dangerous degrees of leverage doesn't imply that no other measures to restrain such developments should be needed, if only we had a sound monetary policy.

Using monetary policy for this purpose, even under the assumption that it could be fully effective, would surely have costs in terms of decreasing the extent to which monetary policy could simultaneously achieve its usual stabilization objectives. Hence, it behooves us to seek to improve financial regulation, and to develop instruments of macroprudential policy as well. Multiple instruments should increase the extent to which multiple objectives can simultaneously be pursued, and they are much to be desired in this case.

Still, in our current situation, without yet having these alternative policies that can be relied on to fully eliminate the issue of controlling risks to financial stability, how should monetary policy take account of the issue? Simply tracking the outlook for measures of inflation and real activity will not, in general, be sufficient for sound monetary policy decisions. It may well be that under most circumstances, risks to financial stability will be small enough under all of the currently contemplated interest rate decisions for interest rate policy to be set purely on the basis of expected consequences for inflation and output. But one should at least recognize the possibility of exceptions to that situation and keep an eye out for them.

This means that the proposal I've been describing, that interest rate policy be used to keep nominal GDP on a fixed target path, should not be viewed as an absolute rule. It might well be reasonable, under some circumstances, to maintain tighter policy in order to restrain excessive growth of leverage, even if this requires nominal GDP to fall below the target path. But this would not, in my view, make the existence of a nominal GDP target path pointless.

In particular, even in the case of a temporary departure from the nominal GDP target path because of financial stability concerns, it makes sense for the central bank to remain committed to eventually reaching that target path again, through a subsequent period of higher than average nominal growth to make up for the period of insufficient nominal growth.[7] The argument is the same as in the case of the zero lower bound: an expectation that current undershooting of the nominal GDP target path will subsequently be compensated by a period of higher nominal GDP growth should reduce the extent to which a temporarily high policy rate causes nominal GDP to undershoot in the first place.

To the extent that such anticipation effects occur, they should reduce the tension between the goals of restraining risks to financial stability, on the one hand, and maintaining macroeconomic stability on the other. This is another advantage of modifying the understanding of flexible inflation targeting in the more ambitious way I've just sketched.

Notes

1. Mervyn A. King, "Changes in UK Monetary Policy: Rules and Discretion in Practice," *Journal of Monetary Economics* 39 (1997): 81–97.

2. See, for example, Ben S. Bernanke and Frederic S. Mishkin, "Inflation Targeting: A New Framework for Monetary Policy?," *Journal of Economic Perspectives* Spring (1997): 97–116; Ben S. Bernanke et al., *Inflation Targeting* (Princeton, NJ: Princeton University Press, 1999); Lars E. O. Svensson, "Inflation Targeting: Some Extensions," *Scandinavian Journal of Economics* 101 (1999): 337–361; and idem, "Inflation Targeting as a Monetary Policy Rule," *Journal of Monetary Economics* 43 (1999): 607–654.

3. For further discussion of the desirability of such an intermediate target criterion, see Michael Woodford, *Interest and Prices: Foundations of a Theory of Monetary Policy* (Princeton, NJ: Princeton University Press, 2003), chap. 7; idem, "The Case for Forecast Targeting as a Monetary Policy Strategy," *Journal of Economic Perspectives* Fall (2007): 3–24; and idem, "Forecast Targeting as a Monetary Policy Strategy: Policy Rules in Practice," in *The Taylor Rule and the Transformation of Monetary Policy*, ed. E. F. Koenig, R. Leeson, and J. B. Taylor (Stanford, CA: Hoover Institution Press, 2012).

4. A nominal GDP target path can be viewed as a simpler version of the proposal of a target path for an "output-gap-adjusted price level," a proposal that can be shown to represent a theoretical ideal in certain New Keynesian models, as discussed in Michael Woodford, "Optimal Monetary Stabilization Policy," in *Handbook of Monetary Economics*, vol. 3B, ed. B. M. Friedman and M. Woodford (Amsterdam: Elsevier, 2011). On the advantages of a nominal GDP target path as a practical proposal, see Michael Woodford, "Methods of Policy Accommodation at the Interest-Rate Lower Bound," in *The Changing Policy Landscape* (Kansas City: Federal Reserve Bank of Kansas City, 2012); and idem, "Inflation Targeting: Fix It, Don't Scrap It," in *Is Inflation Targeting Dead? Central Banking after the Crisis*, ed. L. Reichlin and R. Baldwin (London: Centre for Economic Policy Research, 2013).

5. For further discussion, see Woodford, "Methods of Policy Accommodation."

6. The way this would work and the advantages of this proposal over the kind of thresholds introduced by the FOMC are discussed further in Michael Woodford, "Forward Guidance by Inflation Targeting Central Banks," http://www.columbia.edu/~mw2230/RiksbankIT.pdf.

7. See Michael Woodford, "Inflation Targeting and Financial Stability," Sveriges Riksbank *Economic Review* 1 (2012): 7–32, for an analytical demonstration that a rule of this kind represents an optimal policy commitment in the context of a simple new Keynesian model with a trade-off among the three goals of inflation stabilization, output gap stabilization, and minimization of the economic distortions associated with financial crises. The rule shown there to be optimal generalizes the optimal policy rule for a new Keynesian model that abstracts from endogenous risks to financial stability; thus, it actually involves a target path for an output-gap-adjusted price level rather than for nominal GDP. Under the optimal commitment, the deterministic target path for this variable is not shifted by variations in financial risk or by the occurrence of financial crises, but temporary departures from the target path are justified in proportion to variations in a "marginal crisis risk" variable. The variant with a constant target path for nominal GDP is intended as an approximation of the optimal rule derived there (which is, however, only exactly optimal under quite specific assumptions).

II
Macroprudential Policy

5

Macroprudential Policy in Prospect

Andrew Haldane

Macroprudential policy is the new kid on the block, perhaps even the next big thing. Hopes are high. Reflecting that, we have new macroprudential agencies and policies popping up all over the world, in both developed and developing economies (see, e.g., Aikman, Haldane, and Kapadia 2013). But that begs the question: What actually is macroprudential policy? How should it be executed? And how effective will it be?

This session is well positioned to answer these questions, coming after the one on monetary policy, because there are direct parallels with, and lessons that can be learned from, monetary policy in the design of a macroprudential framework.

The state of knowledge about macroprudential regimes today is roughly where monetary policy was in the '40s—and if I am being charitable, that would be the 1940s rather than the 1840s. It is easy to forget that 70 years ago there was still a great deal of uncertainty about the key tenets of an optimal monetary policy framework:

- What were appropriate *objectives?*
- What *instruments* should best be deployed?
- What was the appropriate *governance and accountability* framework?

Since then, all three of those design features have been, if not resolved, then much better articulated for monetary policy frameworks.

When it comes to macroprudential policy frameworks, all three features are, if not undefined, then poorly articulated at present. Let me touch briefly on the each of them in turn.

First, *objectives*. Macroprudential is, as its name implies, about the interaction or interface between prudential policy and the macroeconomy.

But how exactly does that translate into a macroprudential objective? In particular, should we think of macroprudential objectives as being:

• To protect the *financial system* from swings and cycles in the real economy? That would give macroprudential policies a purist financial stability objective.

Or, more ambitiously, are macroprudential policies:

• To protect the *real economy* from swings and cycles in the financial system? That would give macroprudential policies a more overtly macroeconomic focus.

Put differently, should macroprudential policy be about providing power to the elbow of the microprudential supervisor? Or is macroprudential policy a legitimately distinct arm of macroeconomic policy, working alongside monetary and fiscal policy?

This question has a direct parallel with the monetary policy debate about appropriate mandates, a debate that to some extent still exists today (see, e.g., Woodford 2012). What is the appropriate balance between a purist price stability mandate, on the one hand, and a dual mandate that also weighs output and employment objectives on the other? Most countries' monetary mandates these days tend to weigh wider (than price stability) objectives.

Existing international experience suggests some important differences in the scope of macroprudential mandates. For example, the recent US stress tests focused on the implications of a severe macroeconomic downturn for US banks' financial resilience. In other words, stress testing provided a macroprudential overlay to—or power to the elbow of—microprudential supervision (Bernanke 2013). This is consistent with a type 1 macroprudential mandate.

By contrast, in the UK the Bank of England's new Financial Policy Committee (FPC) has a statutory macroprudential mandate with a clear lexicographic ordering of objectives. This places financial resilience as the primary objective, but then weighs output and employment stabilization as a secondary objective. There is a dual but ordered mandate—a type 2 mandate.

That mandate has had an important bearing on the actions of the FPC. For example, in the middle of 2012 the FPC *reduced* UK banks' liquidity requirements. This was an overtly countercyclical attempt to stimulate bank lending and output in the wider economy. More recently the FPC has asked UK banks to boost their capital, with an explicit eye to lowering funding and lending rates and thereby supporting the economy. In other words, macroprudential policy has operated as an extra arm of macroeconomic policy.

The macroprudential actions recently undertaken by Brazil, Hong Kong SAR, India, Korea, and Israel, among other countries, are also consistent with a type 2 macroprudential mandate. In each case the objective appears to have been to modulate fluctuations in asset markets—for example, the housing market—and thereby the wider economy. Suffice it to say, internationally the jury is still out on appropriate objectives for macroprudential policies and their scope and ambition.

Second, *instruments*. Here again there is a parallel with the monetary policy debates of a couple of generations ago. Back then, monetary theorists and practitioners actively debated the relative merits of price-based instruments (such as the setting of short-term interest rates) and quantity-based instruments (such as the setting of targets for base money supply or selective use of credit and capital flow controls). In the time since, that debate has settled firmly on the side of price-based instruments, certainly during normal times.

Today, one key strand of the macroprudential debate is whether it should be executed using price-based instruments (such as by setting of capital and liquidity ratios or by taxing certain financial transactions) or quantity-based measures (such as by setting loan-to-value [LTV] or debt-to-income [DTI] limits for mortgages, or margin requirements for secured financing transactions)—or indeed, by a combined toolkit of both.

Existing international macroprudential practices differ sharply on this question. A recent survey by Lim and others (2011) makes clear the extent of these differences, summarized in table 5.1. In the UK, the Bank of England's FPC has expressed a preference for using capital and liquidity tools—price-based instruments—at least when it issues directions to other regulators (Bank of England 2013). This was partly on the grounds that price-based instruments will tend to be less distortionary in their impact on behavior.

On the other hand, a number of emerging markets have instead used LTV or DTI interventions—quantity-based interventions—as their macroprudential instrument of choice (table 5.1). This was done partly on the

Table 5.1
Cross-Country Use of Macroprudential Instruments (2000–2010)

Use	Limits on LTV	Limits on DTI	Capital Requirements	Deposit Reserves	Limits on Credit Level
Individual use	5	2	3	5	2
Used in conjunction with other measures	15	11	8	14	5
Broad	6	5	1	11	1
Targeted	14	8	10	8	6
Fixed	11	7	0	7	3
Time-varying[a]	9	6	11	12	4
Rule	0	0	2	0	0
Discretion	9	6	9	12	4
Coordination with other policies	13	6	8	14	5
No coordination	7	7	3	5	2
Countries that use this instrument	20	13	11	19	7

Note: a. This includes instruments originally used as a response to the cycle, although they were not necessarily reversed in response to credit weakness following the 2008 crisis.
Source: Lim and others (2011).

grounds that these measures are likely to have a more direct and immediate impact on, for example, the housing market or creditor flows. A number of countries have employed both price- and quantity-based macroprudential instruments. Once again, the jury, academically and practically, remains out.

Third, *governance and accountability.* Here there is an interesting difference between monetary and macroprudential policy mandates. Monetary policy is not, by its nature and in normal times, granular; it is, if not blind, then blindfolded to its distributional consequences. Central banks cannot set different interest rates for the north versus south of a currency area, for those with and without a mortgage, for small firms versus large.

Macroprudential policies can do just that—and in practice sometimes have. For example, LTV or DTI interventions have sometimes been targeted at particular regions or cities or loan types. In that role, they are overtly distributional in their impact and, at least in principle, almost infinitely granular. While this can have benefits in targeting selective areas of risk for policy intervention, this comes at a political economy cost. Because of their distributional impact, macroprudential policies raise questions about appropriate governance and democratic accountability.

These tensions are clearly evident in existing governance structures for macroprudential policy around the world. Table 5.2 provides a summary of the governance arrangements for macroprudential policy in a selection of countries. Some regimes have placed the central bank in the driver's seat, as in the UK. Others have the lead role played instead by the Finance Ministry or Treasury as part of a college of regulators, as in the United States.

Table 5.2
Macroprudential Decision-making Frameworks by Country

Governance Arrangement		Examples	
Committee for Action	India, South Africa, Ireland, Czech Republic, Lithuania, Cyprus, Belgium, Greece, Estonia, Malta, United Kingdom, Portugal,[a] Italy,[a] New Zealand,[a] Finland[b]		France, Germany, Bulgaria, Poland, Denmark, Netherlands, Brazil, Hong Kong
Committee for Coordination		Sweden	Spain, US, Canada, Australia
No committee	Singapore, Switzerland	Japan, South Korea, Turkey	China
	Authority lies with central bank	Multiple agencies, *not* including the Ministry of Finance	Multiple agencies, including the Ministry of Finance

Notes: a. Portugal, Italy, and New Zealand are currently discussing their framework. b. In Finland, the macroprudential authority is the banking supervisor, not the central bank.

Even when in the driver's seat, a central bank assuming macroprudential responsibilities is likely to face additional pressures on its independence. A larger set of powers, which have a direct impact on the distribution and levels of GDP, raise important questions about democratic legitimacy. Accountability practices may need to be ratcheted upward accordingly. For central banks, that may be a price worth paying for having an extra degree of macroeconomic freedom, but it is a price nonetheless.

Resolving all of these macroprudential framework questions will take time: for academics, time to conduct research on the efficacy and design of macroprudential policies; for policymakers, time to execute and adapt these policies in the light of experience. As with monetary policy half a century ago, both academics and policymakers have an important role to play in developing an intellectually coherent yet operationally practicable framework for macroprudential policy. Doubtless, as with monetary policy, this will be a slow, evolutionary process of trial and error. But the biggest error we could make would be to not try.

References

Aikman, D., A. G. Haldane, and S. Kapadia. 2013. "Operationalising a Macroprudential Regime: Goals, Tools and Open Issues." *Estabilidad Financiera* [Financial Stability Journal of the Bank of Spain] 24:10–30. http://www.bde.es/f/webbde/ GAP/Secciones/Publicaciones/InformesBoletinesRevistas/RevistaEstabilidad Financiera/13/Mayo/Fic/ref2013241.pdf.

Bank of England. 2013. "The Financial Policy Committee's Powers to Supplement Capital Requirements: A Draft Policy Statement." http://www.bankofengland .co.uk/financialstability/Documents/fpc/policystatement130114.pdf.

Bernanke, B. S. 2013. "Stress Testing Banks: What Have We Learned?" Paper presented at the Federal Reserve Bank of Atlanta Conference, "Maintaining Financial Stability: Holding a Tiger by the Tail," April. http://www.federalreserve.gov/ newsevents/speech/bernanke20130408a.pdf.

Lim, C. H., F. Columba, A. Costa, P. Kongsamut, A. Otani, M. Saiyid, T. Wezel, and X. Wu. 2011. "Macroprudential Policy: What Instruments and How Are They Used? Lessons from Country Experiences." IMF Working Paper 238, International Monetary Fund, Washington, DC.

Woodford, M. 2012. "Methods of Policy Accommodation at the Interest-Rate Lower Bound." Paper presented at the Jackson Hole Symposium, August. http:// www.columbia.edu/~mw2230/JHole2012final.pdf.

6

Macroprudential Policy and the Financial Cycle: Some Stylized Facts and Policy Suggestions

Claudio Borio

This chapter seeks to provide some context for the macroprudential policy debate. The objective is to explore what I consider *the* major source of systemic risk, namely, the financial cycle and its link with systemic financial (banking) crises and the far better known business cycle. I would like to highlight a few stylized facts and then turn to the implications for macroprudential policy.

By "financial cycle" I mean, somewhat loosely, the self-reinforcing interaction between risk perceptions and risk tolerance, on the one hand, and financing constraints on the other that, as experience indicates, can lead to serious episodes of financial distress and macroeconomic dislocations. This is what has also come to be known as the procyclicality of the financial system.

There are three takeaways from my presentation. First, the financial cycle should be at the very core of our understanding of the macroeconomy. To my mind, macroeconomics without the financial cycle is very much like *Hamlet* without the prince. Second, the financial cycle has significant implications for the design and limits of macroprudential policy. And finally, it also has significant implications for the design and limits of other policies, notably monetary and fiscal.

I will address two questions in turn. What are the properties of the financial cycle? I will highlight seven. What are the policy issues it raises? I will highlight four.

I should mention that what I will be presenting is based on research carried out at the Bank for International Settlements (BIS) over the years. But many of the findings are quite consistent with work carried out elsewhere, including at the IMF.[1]

The Financial Cycle: Seven Properties

It is useful to think of the financial cycle as having seven properties.[2]

First, its most parsimonious description is in terms of the joint behavior of credit and property prices. In some respects, equity prices, while so prominent in finance and macroeconomics, can be a distraction. This in turn is related to the next property.

Second, the financial cycle has a much lower frequency than the traditional business cycle.[3] By "traditional business cycle" I mean how economists and policymakers think of the business cycle and measure it. This business cycle has a duration of up to eight years. By contrast, the financial cycle that is most relevant for serious macroeconomic dislocations has since the early 1980s had a duration of 16 to 20 years. It is a medium-term process. This is what we found in a sample of seven advanced economies for which we had good data (Drehmann, Borio, and Tsatsaronis 2012). The point is illustrated for the United States in figure 6.1.

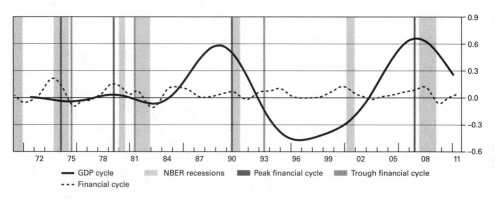

Figure 6.1
Financial and Business Cycles in the United States.
Note: Dark gray and light gray bars indicate peaks and troughs of the combined cycle using the turning-point method. The frequency-based cycle (continuous line) is the average of the medium-term cycle in credit, the credit to GDP ratio and house prices (frequency based filters). The short-term GDP cycle (dashed line) is the cycle identified by the traditional short-term frequency filter used to measure the business cycle. Shaded areas indicate NBER recessions.
Note: The amplitudes of cycles drawn by the dotted and continuous lines are not directly comparable. NBER, National Bureau of Economic Research.
Source: Drehmann, Borio, and Tsatsaronis (2012).

The figure plots the traditional business cycle (dotted line) and the financial cycle (continuous line) as measured through band-pass filters as well as peaks and troughs (vertical lines). The financial cycle is identified by combining the behavior of credit, property prices, and the ratio of credit to GDP.[4] The difference in duration is obvious.

Equities can be a distraction in the sense that their time-series properties are closer to those of GDP in terms of the duration of swings. For example, the stock market crashes of 1987 and 2000 were followed by slowdowns in GDP growth or outright recessions. But the financial cycle as measured by credit and property prices continued to expand, only to turn a few years later (early 1990s and 2007–2008, respectively), bringing the economy down and causing even greater damage. Seen from this longer-term perspective, the early contraction phases in economic activity can thus be considered "unfinished recessions" (Drehmann, Borio, and Tsatsaronis 2012).

Third, peaks in the financial cycle tend to coincide with systemic banking crises or serious strains. This was true for all crises after 1985 in the sample of advanced countries we examined (Drehmann, Borio, and Tsatsaronis 2012). And those crises that occurred well away from the peak were "imported"; that is, they reflected losses on cross-border exposures to financial cycles elsewhere. I recall here, for instance, the losses that German and Swiss banks incurred in the most recent financial crisis from their exposure to the US financial cycle. Not surprisingly, business cycle contractions that coincide with a bust in the financial cycle are much deeper.

Fourth, thanks to the financial cycle, simple leading indicators can identify risks of banking crises fairly well in real time (ex ante)[5] and with a good lead (between two to four years, depending on calibration). The indicators we have found most useful at the BIS are based on the positive deviations of the (private sector) credit-to-GDP ratio and of asset prices, especially property prices, *jointly* exceeding their respective historical trends (e.g., Borio and Drehmann 2009; Borio and Lowe 2002).[6] We may think of these indicators as real-time proxies for the buildup of financial imbalances: The deviations of asset prices provide a sense of the likelihood and size of the subsequent reversal; those of the credit-to-GDP ratio provide a sense of the loss-absorption capacity of the system. These indicators flashed red in the United States in the mid-2000s (figure 6.2).

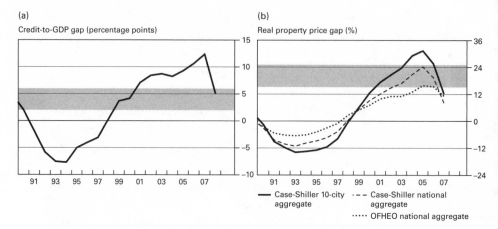

Figure 6.2
Leading Indicators of Banking Crises: Credit and Property Price Gaps, United States.
Note: The shaded areas refer to the threshold values for the indicators: 2 to 6 percentage points for the credit-to-GDP gap (a), and 15 to 25 percent for the real property price gap (b). The real property price gap is the weighted average of residential and commercial property prices with weights corresponding to estimates of their share in overall property wealth. The legend refers to the residential property price component. The estimates for 2008 (a and b) are based on partial data (up to the third quarter). OFHEO, Office of Federal Housing Enterprise Oversight.
Source: Borio and Drehmann (2009).

There is also growing evidence that cross-border credit often outpaces purely domestic credit during such financial booms (e.g., Borio, McCauley, and McGuire 2011; Avdjiev, McCauley, and McGuire 2012).[7]

Fifth, and for much the same reasons, the financial cycle also helps in constructing estimates of sustainable output that, compared with traditional potential output estimates, are much more reliable in real time, as well as statistically more precise (Borio, Disyatat, and Juselius 2013). None of the current methods, ranging from full-fledged production function approaches to simple statistical filters, spotted that output was above its potential sustainable level ahead of the financial crisis. In recent work, we have found that incorporating information about the behavior of credit and property prices allows us to do just that.

Figure 6.3 illustrates this for the United States by comparing our estimates of the output gaps (the so-called "finance-neutral" gap) with those

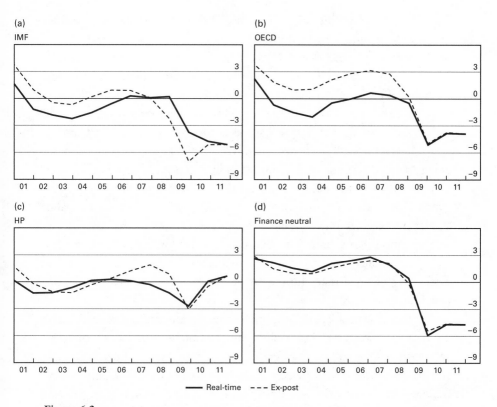

Figure 6.3
US Output Gaps: Full-Sample (ex post) and Real-Time (ex ante) Estimates (in percentage points of potential output).
Notes: a. International Monetary Fund. b. Organisation for Economic Co-operation and Development. c. Hodrick-Prescott filter. d. Finance-neutral estimate of Borio and others (2013). These are linear estimates of financial gaps; the nonlinear estimates, which should better capture the forces at work, would show an output gap that is considerably larger in the boom and smaller in the bust.
Source: Borio, Disyatat, and Juselius (2013).

from the IMF and OECD, based on more full-fledged model approaches and with a popular statistical filter (the Hodrick–Prescott filter).

The traditional estimates made in real time during the economic expansion that preceded the crisis indicated that the economy was running below, or at most close to, potential (continuous lines in the corresponding panels). Only after the crisis did the estimates reveal, though to varying degrees, that output had been above its potential sustainable level (dotted lines). By contrast, the finance-neutral measure sees this all along (panel d in figure 6.3, continuous line). And it hardly gets revised as time unfolds (the continuous and dotted lines are persistently very close to each other in panel d). One reason why production function and similar approaches miss the unsustainable expansion is that they draw on the notion that inflation is the only signal of unsustainability. But, as we know, ahead of the crisis it was the behavior of credit and property prices that signaled that output was on an unsustainable path; inflation remained low and stable.

Sixth, and critically, the amplitude and length of the financial cycle are regime dependent: They are not and cannot be a kind of cosmological constant. Arguably, three key factors support financial cycles: financial liberalization, which weakens financing constraints; monetary policy frameworks focused on near-term inflation control, which provide less resistance to the buildup of financial imbalances as long as inflation remains low and stable; and positive supply-side developments (e.g., the globalization of real economy), which fuel the financial boom while at the same time putting downward pressure on inflation. It is not a coincidence, therefore, that financial cycles have doubled in length since financial liberalization in the early and mid-1980s and that they have become especially virulent since the early 1990s (see figure 6.1).

Finally, busts of financial cycles go hand-in-hand with balance sheet recessions.[8] In this case, compared with other recessions, debts and capital stock overhangs are much larger, the damage to the financial sector is much greater, and the policy room for maneuver is much more limited as policy buffers—prudential, monetary, and fiscal—get depleted. Evidence also indicates that balance sheet recessions result in permanent output losses (growth may return to its long-run precrisis rate, but output does not regain its precrisis trajectory) and usher in slow and long recoveries. Why? I suspect it reflects the legacy of the previous boom and the subsequent financial strains.

The Financial Cycle: Four Observations about Macroprudential Policy

How should prudential policy address the financial cycle? The financial cycle requires that prudential policy have a systemic, or macroprudential, orientation. This means addressing the procyclicality of the financial system head-on, or what has come to be known as the time dimension of macroprudential policy; this is the dimension that relates to how system-wide or systemic risk evolves over time (e.g., Crockett 2000; Borio 2011; Caruana 2012a).[9]

The general principle is quite simple to describe but quite difficult to implement: it is to build up buffers during financial booms so as to draw them down during busts. This has two objectives. It would make the system more resilient and better able to withstand the bust. And, ideally, it would constrain the financial boom in the first place, thereby reducing at its source the probability and intensity of the bust. Note that these two objectives are very different; the second is much more ambitious than the first. I will return to this point later.

Let me now highlight four observations about macroprudential policy. They are all intended to manage expectations about its effectiveness and to set a realistic benchmark about what it can and cannot do—and this from someone who has been a strong advocate of the approach for more than a decade now and who continues to be one. The reason is that the financial cycle is a hugely powerful force.

First Observation
Beware of macro stress tests as early warning devices in tranquil times (Borio, Drehmann, and Tsatsaronis 2012). To the best of my knowledge, none of them flashed red ahead of the recent crisis.[10] Their relentless message was "the system is sound."

There are two reasons for this.

The first has to do with our risk measurement technology. Our current models are unable to capture convincingly the fundamental nonlineari-ties and associated feedback effects that are at the core of the dynamics of financial distress. In essence, no matter how hard you shake the box, little falls out. This shifts the burden to the required size of the shocks, which becomes unreasonably large and, therefore, is discounted by policymakers. The deeper point here is that the essence of financial instability is that normal-sized shocks cause the system to break down. An unstable system is not one that would break down only if hit by a huge shock, such as an outsized recession. An unstable system is *fragile*. As empirical evidence indicates, crises break out close to the peak of the financial cycle, well before GDP has plunged into a deep recession or asset prices have collapsed.

The second reason has to do with the context, or what might be called the "paradox of financial instability" (Borio 2011). Initial conditions are unusually strong just before financial strains emerge. Credit and asset prices have been surging ahead; leverage measured at market prices is artificially low; profits and asset quality look especially healthy; and risk premia and short-term volatilities are extraordinarily compressed. Taken at face value, these signals point to low risk when in fact they are signs of high risk taking. The system is most fragile when it looks strongest. And this point is reached after years of solid and relentless expansion, typically alongside widespread financial innovations. Under these conditions, the temptation to believe that this time things are really different is extraordinarily powerful (Reinhart and Rogoff 2009).

Bottom line: at worst, macro stress tests can lull policymakers into a false sense of security. That said, if properly designed, they can be an effective tool for crisis management and resolution—a tool to promote balance sheet repair. After all, the crisis has already broken out, nonlinearities have revealed themselves, and hubris has given way to prudence. "Properly designed" means that the authorities need to have the will to shake the system hard, need to start the tests from very realistic asset valuations, and should put in place the necessary liquidity and solvency backups.

Second Observation
Beware of network analysis as a tool to detect vulnerabilities (Borio, Drehmann, and Tsatsaronis 2012). As a source of vulnerabilities, bilateral links (counterparty exposures) matter far less than common exposures to the financial cycle.

Network analysis views the financial system as a web of connections linking institutions. It then models systemic risk by tracing the knock-on effects of the default of one institution on the rest along those interconnections. The larger the portion of the system that fails, the larger is the systemic risk.

The main problem is that, as empirical evidence confirms, given the size of the interconnections, it is too hard to get large effects. The reason is simple: mechanical exercises abstract from behavior. A financial crisis is more like a tsunami that sweeps away all that gets in its way than it is like a force knocking down one domino after another. The main force driving it is indiscriminate behavioral responses. This also explains why the failure of small and seemingly innocuous institutions can trigger a major crisis. Small institutions do not matter because of what they are but because of what they signal about the rest. They signal shared vulnerabilities; they are the canary in the coal mine. When the financial cycle turns, the failure of the first institution can shake previously seemingly unshakable convictions and trigger a paradigm shift.

That said, this does not imply that information about bilateral exposures has little value. Much like macro stress tests, it can be very valuable in crisis management as a tool to identify pressure points and understand where and how best to intervene. But for this to be the case, the information has to be quite granular and very up to date (Borio 2013).

Third Observation

Beware of overestimating the effectiveness of macroprudential policy (Borio 2011; Caruana 2012a). There are two sets of reasons here as well, which in some ways echo those that explain the limitations of stress tests.

The first set is technical. The tools are more effective in strengthening the resilience of the financial system (the first objective mentioned above) than in constraining financial booms (the second and more ambitious objective). To be sure, some instruments are more effective than others. For instance, it stands to reason, and it seems to be confirmed by empirical evidence, that ceilings on loan-to-value and debt-to-income ratios have more bite than capital requirements (e.g., CGFS 2012). After all, capital is cheap and plentiful during booms. But for typical calibration of the tools, it would be imprudent to expect a strong impact. Moreover, and critically, all such tools are vulnerable to regulatory arbitrage. And the longer they stay in place, the easier arbitrage becomes.

The second set of reasons has to do with political economy. Compared with monetary policy, it is even harder to take away the punch bowl when the party gets going. The lags between the buildup of risk and its materialization are very long, certainly longer than those between excess demand and inflation (I recall here how long the financial cycle is compared with the business cycle). For some of the tools, the distributional effects are more prominent and concentrated. And while there is a constituency against inflation, there is hardly any against the inebriating feeling of getting richer. All this puts a premium on sound governance arrangements and on maintaining a right balance between rules and discretion.

Fourth Observation
Beware of overburdening macroprudential policy (e.g., Caruana 2011, 2012b; Borio 2012a, 2012b). This follows naturally from the previous observation. The financial cycle is simply too powerful to be tackled exclusively through macroprudential policy or indeed prudential policy more generally, be it micro or macro. Macroprudential policy needs the active support of other policies.

What does this mean in practice? For monetary policy, it means leaning against the buildup of financial imbalances even if near-term inflation remains under control (exercising the "lean option").[11] Monetary policy sets the universal price of leverage in a given currency. In contrast to macroprudential tools, it is not vulnerable to regulatory arbitrage: you can run but you can't hide. For fiscal policy, it means being extra-prudent, recognizing the hugely flattering effect of financial booms on the fiscal accounts. This is because of the overestimation of potential output and growth (see figure 6.3), the revenue-rich nature of financial booms owing to compositional effects, and the contingent liabilities needed to address the subsequent bust.

As an important aside, a big open question is how macroprudential frameworks should address sovereign risk. These frameworks were originally designed with private-sector vulnerabilities in mind, linked to the financial cycle. But such cycles leave in their wake seriously damaged sovereigns, which can all too easily sap banks' strength. Moreover, as history indicates, sovereigns may cause banking crises quite independently of private-sector excesses. At a time when the sovereigns' creditworthiness is increasingly in doubt, much more attention should be devoted to this issue.

Against this broad backdrop, is there a risk that adjustments in policy frameworks are falling short? Ostensibly, this was the case before the crisis, but what about since then? My answer is that the risk should not be underestimated.

Progress has been uneven across policies (Borio 2012b).

Prudential policy has adjusted most. A major shift from a micro- to a macroprudential orientation has taken place in regulation and supervision. Here we may recall the adoption of a countercyclical capital buffer in Basel III (BCBS 2010; Drehmann, Borio, and Tsatsaronis 2011) and, more generally, the efforts under way to implement full-fledged macroprudential frameworks around the world (CGFS 2012). That said, expectations about what these frameworks can deliver are running too high, and there is a question of whether enough has been done with respect to instruments, their calibration, and governance arrangements. Moreover, more could and should have been done to repair banks' balance sheets in some jurisdictions.

Monetary policy has adjusted less. To be sure, there has been some shift toward adopting the lean option, but the will to exercise it has been quite limited. The temptation to rely exclusively on the new macroprudential tools has been very powerful, to avoid disturbing monetary policy. And it is worth asking whether the limitations of monetary policy as a means to tackle financial busts have been fully appreciated.

Fiscal policy has adjusted least. There is as yet little recognition of the hugely flattering effects of financial booms on the fiscal accounts and of the big risks that busts pose for the sustainability and even the effectiveness of fiscal policy.

Bottom line: there is a real risk that policies are not sufficiently mutually supportive. And, critically, they are not sufficiently symmetric between financial booms and busts. They tighten too little during booms, with the serious danger that buffers get depleted during busts. This poses a huge constraint on the room for maneuver—one that becomes tighter over successive cycles. Policy horizons are simply too short—not commensurate with the duration of the financial cycle (Borio 2012b).

Conclusion

There is a need to bring the financial cycle back into macroeconomics. Macroeconomics without the financial cycle is very like *Hamlet* without the prince. This raises huge analytical challenges that the profession is just beginning to tackle.

The financial cycle has major implications for macroprudential policy and beyond. I have highlighted four observations: Beware of macro stress tests as early warning devices. Beware of network analysis as a tool to identify financial vulnerabilities. Beware of the limitations of macroprudential policy. And beware of overburdening it.

Has enough been done to adjust policy frameworks? Not quite. In the case of macroprudential policy, more and better can be done with respect to the calibration and activation of the instruments. In the case of monetary policy, more can be done with respect to the exercise of the lean option. And in the case of fiscal policy, there is a need to recognize the hugely flattering effect that financial booms have on the fiscal accounts.

So much for prevention and how to address the financial boom; what about the question of how to address the bust? If anything, here the questions are even bigger and more controversial, while progress has been more limited (Borio 2012a, 2012b). There is a serious risk, in particular, that the effectiveness of monetary and fiscal policy is overestimated and of a new, more insidious, form of time inconsistency. But that is another story.

Notes

The views expressed in this chapter are my own and not necessarily those of the Bank for International Settlements.

1. The references are almost exclusively to BIS work, especially recent work, although the institution's support of macroprudential policy goes back a long way (e.g., Clement 2010). That work contains extensive references to the literature.

2. This section draws in particular on Borio (2012a).

3. The qualification "traditional" is important. The data also reveal longer swings in GDP, which are closer to those for the financial cycle. See Drehmann, Borio, and Tsatsaronis (2012).

4. Although the changes in amplitude over time in the business and financial cycles are meaningful, because the financial cycle combines different series, it is

not possible to draw inferences about the relative amplitude of the two cycles from the graph in figure 6.1. See Drehmann, Borio, and Tsatsaronis (2012) for a discussion of the technical issues involved.

5. Real-time or ex ante refers to an estimate that is based only on information available at the time the estimate is made.

6. Not surprisingly, these trends are consistent with the average length of the financial cycle (see Drehmann, Borio, and Tsatsaronis 2011).

7. All this casts doubt on the view that current account imbalances were a cause of the financial crisis. For an in-depth discussion of this issue, see Borio and Disyatat (2011).

8. Koo (2003) seems to have been the first to use such a term. He employs it to describe a recession driven by nonfinancial firms' seeking to repay their excessive debt burdens, such as those left by the bursting of the bubble in Japan in the early 1990s. Specifically, he argues that the objective of financial firms shifts from maximizing profits to minimizing debt. The term is used here more generally to denote a recession associated with the financial bust that follows an unsustainable financial boom. But the general characteristics are similar, in particular the debt overhang. That said, we draw different conclusions about the appropriate policy responses, especially with respect to prudential and fiscal policy (see Borio 2012a).

9. There is also a cross-sectional dimension, which relates to how risk is distributed in the financial system at a point in time (see, e.g., Crockett 2000; Borio 2011).

10. Even the Financial Stability Assessment Program for Iceland, released in August 2008, concluded that "stress tests suggest that the system is resilient"; see IMF (2008, 8).

11. The existence of a "risk-taking" channel of monetary policy, whereby changes in interest rates (and other monetary policy tools) influence risk perceptions and risk tolerance, strengthens the case for an active role for monetary policy. It is not, however, a necessary condition for it. See Borio and Zhu (2011).

References

Avdjiev, S., R. McCauley, and P. McGuire. 2012. "Rapid Credit Growth and International Credit: Challenges for Asia." BIS Working Paper 377, Bank for International Settlements, Basel, April. http://www.bis.org/publ/work377.pdf.

Basel Committee for Banking Supervision (BCBS). 2010. *Guidance for National Authorities Operating the Countercyclical Capital Buffer.* Basel: Bank for International Settlements, December. http://www.bis.org/publ/bcbs187.htm.

Borio, C. 2011. "Implementing a Macroprudential Framework: Blending Boldness and Realism." *Capitalism and Society* 6 (1): art. 1. http://papers.ssrn.com/sol3/papers.cfm?abstract_id=2208643.

Borio, C. 2012a. The Financial Cycle and Macroeconomics: What Have We Learnt? BIS Working Paper 395, Bank for International Settlements, Basel,

December. http://www.bis.org/publ/work395.htm. Forthcoming in the *Journal of Banking & Finance*.

Borio, C. 2012b. "On Time, Stocks and Flows: Understanding the Global Macro-economic Challenges." Lecture at the Munich Seminar series, CESIfo-Group and *Süddeutsche Zeitung*, October 15. http://www.bis.org/speeches/sp121109a.htm. Forthcoming in the *NIESR Review*.

Borio, C. 2013. "The Global Financial Crisis: Setting Priorities for New Statistics." BIS Working Paper 408, Bank for International Settlements, Basel, April. http://www.bis.org/publ/work408.htm. Forthcoming in the *Journal of Banking Regulation*.

Borio, C., and P. Disyatat. 2011. "Global Imbalances and the Financial Crisis: Link or No Link?" BIS Working Paper 346, Bank for International Settlements, Basel, May. http://www.bis.org/publ/work346.htm.

Borio, C., and P. Disyatat, and M. Juselius. 2013. "Rethinking Potential Output: Embedding Information about the Financial Cycle." BIS Working Paper 404, Bank for International Settlements, Basel, February. http://www.bis.org/publ/work404.htm.

Borio, C., and M. Drehmann. 2009. "Assessing the Risk of Banking Crises: Revisited." *BIS Quarterly Review*, March, 29–46. http://www.bis.org/publ/qtrpdf/r_qt0903e.pdf.

Borio, C., M. Drehmann, and K. Tsatsaronis. 2012. "Stress-testing Macro Stress Testing: Does It Live Up to Expectations?" BIS Working Paper 369, Bank for International Settlements, Basel, January. http://www.bis.org/publ/work369.htm. Forthcoming in the *Journal of Financial Stability*.

Borio, C., and P. Lowe. 2002. "Assessing the Risk of Banking Crises." *BIS Quarterly Review*, December, 43–54. http://www.bis.org/publ/qtrpdf/r_qt0212e.pdf.

Borio, C., R. McCauley, and P. McGuire. 2011. "Global Credit and Domestic Credit Booms." *BIS Quarterly Review*, September, 43–57. http://www.bis.org/publ/qtrpdf/r_qt1109f.pdf.

Borio, C., and H. Zhu. 2011. "Capital Regulation, Risk-taking and Monetary Policy: A Missing Link in the Transmission Mechanism?" *Journal of Financial Stability*, December. Also available as BIS Working Paper 268, Bank for International Settlements, Basel, December 2008. http://www.bis.org/publ/work268.htm.

Caruana, J. 2011. "Monetary Policy in a World with Macroprudential Policy." Speech delivered at the SAARCFINANCE Governors' Symposium, Kerala, India, June 11. http://www.bis.org/speeches/sp110610.htm.

Caruana, J. 2012a. "Dealing with Financial Systemic Risk: The Contribution of Macroprudential Policies." Panel remarks at the Central Bank of Turkey/G20 Conference on Financial Systemic Risk, Istanbul, September 27–28. http://www.bis.org/speeches/sp121002.htm.

Caruana, J. 2012b. "International Monetary Policy Interactions: Challenges and Prospects." Speech delivered at the CEMLA-SEACEN conference, "The Role of Central Banks in Macroeconomic and Financial Stability: The Challenges in an

Uncertain and Volatile World," Punta del Este, Uruguay, November 16. http://www.bis.org/speeches/sp121116.htm?ql=1.

Clement, P. 2010. "The Term 'Macroprudential': Origins and Evolution." *BIS Quarterly Review,* March, 59–67. http://www.bis.org/publ/qtrpdf/r_qt1003h .htm.

Committee on the Global Financial System (CGFS). 2012. *Operationalising the Selection and Application of Macroprudential Instruments,* publication 48. Basel: Bank for International Settlements, December. http://www.bis.org/publ/cgfs48 .htm.

Crockett, A. 2000. "Marrying the Micro- and Macroprudential Dimensions of Financial Stability." BIS Speeches, Bank for International Settlements, Basel, September 21. http://www.bis.org/review/r000922b.pdf.

Drehmann, M., C. Borio, and K. Tsatsaronis. 2011. "Anchoring Countercyclical Capital Buffers: The Role of Credit Aggregates." *International Journal of Central Banking* 7 (4): 189–239. Also available as BIS Working Paper 355, Bank for International Settlements, Basel, November. http://www.bis.org/publ/work355 .htm.

Drehmann, M., C. Borio, and K. Tsatsaronis. 2012. "Characterising the Financial Cycle: Don't Lose Sight of the Medium Term!" BIS Working Paper 380, Bank for International Settlements, Basel, November. http://www.bis.org/publ/work380 .htm.

International Monetary Fund (IMF). 2008. "Iceland: Financial Stability Assessment: Update." Monetary and Capital Markets and European Departments, International Monetary Fund, Washington, DC, August 19. http://www.imf.org/external/pubs/ft/scr/2008/cr08368.pdf.

Koo, R. 2003. *Balance Sheet Recession.* Singapore: John Wiley & Sons.

Reinhart, C., and K. Rogoff. 2009. *This Time Is Different: Eight Centuries of Financial Folly.* Princeton, NJ: Princeton University Press.

7

Macroprudential Policy in Action: Israel

Stanley Fischer

Macroprudential policy or supervision relates to the behavior of the financial system as a whole, with a focus on systemic interactions, systemic indicators, and systemic risk. The consequences of the Lehman Brothers bankruptcy are the archetype of the result of systemic risk. Macroprudential supervision and policy are directed at monitoring these risks and using available tools to reduce the risks and the consequences of their occurrence.

However, the word "macroprudential" is used in a variety of senses, and it is not clear that we all mean the same thing when we use the term. In this chapter I discuss mainly the Israeli economy and what we have done that might be called macroprudential supervision, or macroprudential policy implementation. At the end of the chapter I briefly raise the question of whether all the actions that are called macroprudential are indeed that.

Israel: The Institutional Setting

Monetary and macroprudential policies in Israel are coordinated via the Bank of Israel—and the bank's ability to coordinate is entirely the result of institutional features, in the creation of which thinking about macroprudential issues had practically no role. I served as governor of the Bank of Israel from May 2005 until June 2013, and hope to offer some insights from this perspective.

In our institutional setup, bank supervision is located in the central bank. Its purposes and structure are defined in a law (Banking Ordinance 1941) that is separate from the Bank of Israel law. The supervisor of banks reports to the governor of the bank—"reports to" in the sense that the governor can instruct the supervisor as to what to do, and has to sign off on significant measures. This line of reporting, in which the governor can instruct the supervisor of banks—subject, of course, to being in conformity with the law relating to bank supervision—appears to be unusual.

Monetary policy decisions are made by the Monetary Policy Committee (MPC), which has six members, three of whom are not employees of the Bank of Israel. In the event of a tied vote, the governor has a double vote. The Bank of Israel law does not give the MPC the authority to instruct the supervisor of banks. Even though the new Bank of Israel law was passed in April 2010, as understanding about the importance of macroprudential issues was strengthening, at that time we did not think of the need to coordinate macroprudential policy with monetary policy.

We have a Financial Stability Unit in the Research Department, which does good work. Once a quarter there is a special meeting of the MPC devoted to financial stability. The Financial Stability Unit, in collaboration with the Department of Bank Supervision and the Markets Department (which is responsible for the bank's operations in both the shekel and foreign exchange markets), prepares and presents to the MPC a comprehensive report on financial stability.

Apart from the quarterly report, members of the MPC may request information on recent developments in the banking sector or other parts of the financial system from the relevant departments. Further, when the bank supervisor is planning actions relevant to, or has information about, financial stability, he or she will be invited to brief the MPC on those topics. The members of the committee are entitled to ask all the questions they want and to offer advice, but they do not make any decisions about the actions of the supervisor of banks.

In practice there is informal cooperation between the bank supervisor and the MPC, and there is a great deal of information provision to the MPC by the supervisor. But there is no formal coordination between the MPC and the supervisor: The channel of coordination goes through the governor, who is both chairman of the MPC and the person to whom the supervisor of banks reports.

One difficulty in this regard is that the Banking Ordinance 1941, which determines the responsibilities of the supervisor of banks, does not relate to macroprudential issues. The supervisor's primary responsibility is to maintain the stability of the banking system. On occasion the bank supervisor has rejected a request to implement measures that would be useful from the viewpoint of monetary policy but that he judged to be inconsistent with his mandate.

Given the institutional setup in which bank supervision is housed in the central bank and in which the banks are the predominant financial institutions, coordination between monetary policy and macroprudential supervision operates reasonably well. However, there are other regulators of the financial system, notably the commissioner of the capital markets, the insurance and savings and insurance supervisor within the Ministry of Finance, and the chairman of the Israel Securities Authority (ISA), the equivalent of the Securities and Exchange Commission in the United States. The ISA is an independent institution, more closely associated with the Treasury than with any other institution.

The actions of the other two financial regulators are also relevant to the stability of the financial system. The three supervisors work well together. They have a committee that meets regularly, at which time they exchange information. The fact that each supervisor is a professional seems to enable them to cooperate in identifying systemic risks, discussing what needs to be done, and exchanging information about what is going on in each of the areas for which they're responsible.

Getting joint action is typically harder, but the information is there and would, in all likelihood, be available to those who would need it in the event of a crisis. The new law (passed in 2010) allows the Bank of Israel to act as lender of last resort to nonbank financial institutions, and we are allowed to demand any information we need from any financial institution, even, if necessary, before the institution needs liquidity or lender-of-last-resort assistance from the Bank of Israel.

In addition, we have tried—and we continue to try—to establish a high-level financial stability committee (FSC) anchored in law. That process is not going well. The first key issue is the relative roles of the finance minister and the bank's governor; and the second is that understandably none of the supervisors wants to be subject to any decision or action of the high-level committee that would require them to do anything they would not otherwise want to do.

We may be en route to solving the problem of the relative roles of the finance minister and the governor, using a framework parallel to that of the Bank of Israel law: The law specifies that so long as a financial institution needs only liquidity assistance, the Bank of Israel can handle the problem on its own; but as soon as the insolvency of a financial institution has to be dealt with, the Treasury has to be involved. Thinking along those lines, we hope it will be possible that in normal times, when the central bank is providing no more than liquidity assistance, the governor will chair the FSC, and when we are involved with solvency issues, the finance minister will be the chair.

With regard to the second issue, the powers of the FSC with respect to the three supervisors, it may be possible to rely on the principle of "comply or explain." Under this approach, the FSC could suggest that a particular supervisor do something. He will then either do it or, if he cannot or does not want to do it, he can explain why.

This sounds simple, but the question arises whether such recommendations will be made public. The supervisors oppose the recommendations being made public; they argue that if the recommendations are made public, the FSC will in effect be using the public to force actions on them that they may not want to take. So the second issue, that of the powers of the FSC, is not resolved. No doubt, in a perfectly operating system, we would all sit down and work it out and come up with a solution. But these are important officials, and each has a valid interest in maintaining his independence—and I'm sure if I was an independent regulator, I would also want to maintain my independence.

In practice, there would be no way of keeping such recommendations from the public. There is a public information law. Further, this is the sort of recommendation that would be likely to leak. So for the moment we seem to be stuck on the issue of the powers of a possible FSC.

What are we doing on macroprudential issues in the Bank of Israel? We monitor the stability of the banking and insurance sectors. Those are the sectors to which we will have to supply liquidity if and when the time comes. We have data on the banks from within the Bank of Israel, and we are receiving data on the insurance companies. We use stress tests to try to detect points of vulnerability in these institutions or in the financial system. In addition, we analyze the risks in the portfolios of institutional investors who are moving increasingly into lending, which means they are becoming a shadow banking system.

We monitor developments in financial markets to try to detect potential problems that might emerge there. We have a variety of indicators for assessing financial stability, among them a radar chart for the entire financial sector.

With regard to the stress tests, we are using contingent claims analysis, about which members of both the Article IV mission and the Financial Sector Assessment Program (FSAP) team educated us. I have some questions about this, because the contingent claims analysis assumes that the stock market got it right at some point, and uses stock market data to identify and quantify risks—and there could be a big gap between what the stock market is signaling and the objective situation; that is, irrational exuberance.

What will we do if we see developments in sectors outside our areas of supervision that threaten financial stability? We would of course first try to work with the relevant supervisors. But if that does not succeed, we would have to mobilize the supervisors of the supervisors and other senior members of the government to try to get the appropriate actions implemented. In that regard, I note that although there was no formal system of coordination among the Bank of Israel, the Treasury, and the Office of the Prime Minister during the period of intense crisis in 2009 and 2010, cooperation was in practice close and effective.

The Problem of House Prices

Now that I have described the institutional structure for macroprudential supervision, let me give one example of its use to deal with a problem, which is our housing market.

Earlier in this conference, Allan Meltzer asked why the extraordinary measures implemented by the Fed and other central banks seem to have had so little effect on real activity, or in other words, why the transmission mechanism of monetary policy seems to have broken down. I believe that in most cases in which it has broken down, it is because the financial system broke down. In practically every country where the financial system remained intact, the transmission mechanism operated well, with activity and asset prices remaining sensitive to monetary policy. Since almost every country has cut interest rates significantly to prevent large-scale capital inflows and consequent appreciations of the currency, as interest rates have fallen, housing demand and house prices have risen sharply in countries that did not have a financial crisis. This happened in Singapore, in Hong Kong SAR, in Korea, in Australia, in Norway, in Germany, in Israel, and elsewhere.

House prices and rents in Israel have gone up significantly since 2008. Since January 2008, nominal housing prices have risen 73 percent, and real housing prices have risen by a little over 50 percent. Rents have gone up 35 percent in nominal terms and about 19 percent in real terms. These are large increases.

Here I would like to note a fact, to which I will return later: Israeli households are not very indebted. The Israeli household debt-to-income ratio is lower than that of Germany, which is the lowest among the major countries, and far below that of the United States. Further, loan-to-value (LTV) ratios on mortgages are low, on average about 53 percent. Following recent changes in regulations, no one can obtain a mortgage with an LTV ratio of more than 75 percent, and most mortgages have an LTV ratio of 60 percent or less.

There has been a great deal of press and popular interest in Israel in the question of whether there is a bubble in house prices. I have tried to educate the press, and tell journalists that a bubble is a feature that has a technical definition and that one can test for it. Olivier Blanchard did fundamental work on this issue long ago, as did others.

Nonetheless, the question of whether we are in a process that meets the technical definition of a bubble is not really useful. Rather, the useful question is whether prices are going up too fast. The fact that two years in a row prices rose more than 16 percent each year is an indication that prices were going up too fast.

So we have tried to deal with the problem. The macroprudential measures we have undertaken are listed in table 7.1; additional measures undertaken by the supervisor of banks are listed in table 7.2. In July 2010 we required the banks, which are the main providers of housing finance, to make additional provisions for housing loans with high LTV ratios. A bit later we required them to increase the capital held against floating interest rate loans that were granted with a high LTV ratio.

In May 2011, we imposed a constraint that was unquestionably the most effective of the various macroprudential measures we have

Table 7.1
Measures to Deal with House Price Increases

July 2010	Requirement for banks to make additional provisions for housing loans with high loan-to-value (LTV) ratios
October 2010	Requirement for a higher capital provision for floating interest rate loans granted with a high LTV ratio
May 2011	Limiting the adjustable-interest-rate component of housing loans to 1/3 of the total loan
November 2012	Limiting the LTV ratio in housing loans: up to 75% for first-home buyers, up to 50% for investors, up to 70% for those upgrading their homes
February 2013	Change of the risk weights for capital charge, and increase in the allowance for credit losses in respect of housing loans

Note: For additional measures implemented by the supervisor of banks, see *Israel's Banking System—Annual Survey, 2010* (Jerusalem: Bank of Israel, April 10, 2011), p. 46 (http://www.boi.org.il/en/NewsAndPublications/RegularPublications/Pages/skira10_skira10e.aspx).

Table 7.2
Residential Mortgage Market: Additional Precautionary Measures

• Detailed reporting requirements on residential mortgage loans, including LTV ratio, payment to income ratio, etc.

• Collecting and analyzing stress test results conducted by the banks on their residential mortgage portfolios.

• Banking supervision department also conducts stress tests in order to identify vulnerabilities in the housing-loan portfolio of the banks (work in process).

• Enhanced supervision of bank practices (off-site and on-site) and monthly monitoring of developments in the consumer market and residential mortgage loan markets.

• Cooperation with the Ministry of Finance and the Ministry of Construction and Housing concerning the residential housing market and its potential impacts on financial stability.

Note: The measures listed in the table are undertaken on a regular basis and have been modified and strengthened over the period since 2008.

introduced. At that time, banks were providing mortgage financing through a mortgage linked to the Bank of Israel interest rate, which was then 3 percent, and the margin on those loans, through competition among banks, had declined to 0.6 percent. So households could obtain financing through a floating rate mortgage, at a nominal interest rate of 3.6 percent, indexed to the Bank of Israel interest rate. The macroprudential measure we imposed was to limit the amount of a mortgage that could be financed through that instrument to one-third of the financing of any loan. That step had a significant impact on the demand for mortgages, and on the demand for housing.

More recently, in November 2012, we limited the LTV ratios on mortgages. That set of measures contained one element not fully consistent with risk management: we allowed first-home buyers to have a 75 percent LTV ratio, and that was included for political reasons. We had earlier (in October 2010) come under considerable pressure because "we were not allowing young couples to buy housing" when we had raised the capital ratio on high LTV loans. So, in November 2012, we allowed first-time buyers a slightly higher LTV ratio—75 percent—and we reduced the LTV ratio particularly for investors (defined as those buying a second apartment).

Finally (so far), in February 2013, we changed the risk weights for mortgages. This came at the initiative of the supervisor, who was becoming worried about the stability of the banks if housing prices started to go down.

Now I want to discuss two issues, the first relating to the fact that house prices continue to rise. We have imposed many measures, and they have not yet done the job. Evidently the measures we have imposed have not been strong enough to reduce the demand for housing sufficiently to stop prices rising.

The issue of how strong the macroprudential measures should have been is a difficult one. Fundamentally, we have two sources of growth in the economy. One is the construction sector, and the other is exports. Our mandate provides that so long as inflation is under control, we should also try to support growth and reduce unemployment, and we have consistently taken that obligation seriously, as we must. Exports have been under constant pressure because of the effect of capital inflows on the exchange rate. Exports amount to 37.5 percent of GDP, with value added of 26 percent of GDP. Exports are critical to growth, and we accordingly are restricted in the use of the interest rate as a means of reducing the demand for housing.

Construction activity amounts to about 8 percent of the business sector GDP, and we have to be careful not to kill the housing market. We could have been much tougher in the various constraints we imposed, but we did not want to take the risk of overdoing the restraining effect of our macroprudential measures. Further, although housing prices have been rising fast, Israeli households are not, by international standards, highly indebted.

So, maybe we have done too little in imposing these measures, but at this stage our knowledge of how macroprudential measures work is far from precise. At some point, after further research, our knowledge should become more accurate. In the meantime, we will approach the use of macroprudential policies in the area of housing with care and with gradualism.

Central Bank Independence

The second issue I want to discuss was raised by Olivier Blanchard in the material sent to speakers at the conference. If central banks are in charge of monetary policy, financial supervision, and macroprudential policies, should we rethink central bank independence?

The reason to raise this issue is that while there are good reasons to insulate the interest rate decision from political control, that may be less true with regard to macroprudential policies. Certainly we at the Bank of Israel have been subjected to far more criticism over some of the macroprudential measures we have imposed than over our standard monetary policy measures. The natural tendency of economists would be to say that if the government wants to favor one group or another's access to housing, it should simply subsidize their housing through the budget. The government might well respond that the central bank is typically critical of subsidies, and that the central bank has the means to solve the issue.

The answer to Olivier's question is yes, we should reconsider some aspects of central bank independence for central banks that are also macroprudential supervisors. As noted above, central bank independence in interest rate setting, which is a classic role of the central bank, at least over the past 20 years, remains essential. But we should recognize that changes in the interest rate have distributional effects. When we raise the interest rate we affect housing prices and the exchange rate, among other variables and sectors. We and the public have gotten used to that, and tend to accept it as a neutral use of monetary policy, which it is not.

Further, flexible inflation targeting leaves a central bank with a lot of choice about the trade-off between inflation and growth at any moment. That choice too has distributional effects, including on unemployment. Much of the public and political pressure exerted on central banks over the years has related to the impact of their monetary policies on growth and unemployment, as well as on inflation. We and the public have over the course of time persuaded ourselves that we can leave that trade-off to the central banks, and that is widely accepted.

So if that is widely accepted, why should we worry so much about the fact that macroprudential policy has clearly defined distributional effects? I believe we have to worry because politicians worry about those distributional effects. That means they will push harder on us to take their preferences in this area into account—and we need to figure out how best to react to that.

I'd like to make one other point here, that coordination between macroprudential policies and monetary policy is necessary. There is in our profession, I believe, an invalid, quasi-Adam Smith theorem that reappears with alarming frequency. The invalid Adam Smith theorem is, if each institution is given one target to achieve, and if each seeks to reach that target, the outcome is a social optimum. The assignment is "one target per institution."

The outcome of such a process is unlikely to be that each institution achieves its target, for there are bound to be trade-offs among the goals of the different institutions. So the question becomes, who will coordinate and decide on the trade-offs? That issue is rarely examined explicitly, but it is a question that needs to be answered.

I do not accept the view that having the same institution be responsible for, say, monetary policy and macroprudential policies would produce an unresolvable conflict in the central bank. The trade-off exists, and somebody has to deal with it. The central bank would likely have the advantage that it would understand the trade-off and its implications, and make a decision that takes all this into account.

Further, it can deal with any such trade-off, as the Bank of England has started to do. Their Monetary Policy Committee (MPC) continues to operate as it has since it was set up, and as MPCs in many countries do, in a manner independent of politics. In addition, the Bank of England now has a Financial Policy Committee, in which government representatives are present as observers.

Some of my colleagues say, well, the central bank, or the governor, cannot be independent in one role and dependent in another. I think you can be. I do not see the presence of government observers in one committee as impinging on the independence of decisions in another committee.

Concluding Comments

In conclusion, I return to the issue of whether all the measures that we describe as macroprudential are that. Are the measures we have used in trying to keep housing prices from rising too fast truly macroprudential? Certainly, there is a genuine fear that if housing prices continue to rise, and if at some later date they fall rapidly, we will have problems in the banking system. Thus, one of the motives for our actions is undoubtedly macroprudential.

But I think there is something else going on, which we ought to recognize. Monetary policy has effects on many relative prices and economic sectors. It may be that what we are doing is finding an additional instrument to deal with some aspect of the business cycle, or of monetary policy, and that we are now using two policy instruments to target two variables.

That is awkward, for it takes us back to what central banks used to do in the 1960s and the 1970s, intervening on too broad a front in too ambitious an attempt to fine-tune the economy. That way we lose the simplicity of the use of the interest rate instrument, and we risk making monetary policy too complicated and ultimately less effective.

There is a question of what are pure macroprudential instruments. One view is that the only truly macroprudential tool is countercyclical capital requirements. I doubt that, because there are other instruments aimed at ensuring financial stability, such as control over LTV ratios.

Finally, I have not discussed foreign exchange intervention as macroprudential. As I read the literature, foreign exchange intervention is sometimes discussed as macroprudential, and you can make a case for why that might be so, because, depending on how capital flows come in, they could create sources of financial instability in the financial system itself. But foreign exchange intervention as most countries have used it is in fact primarily a way of trying to affect the exchange rate to avoid damaging exports. I do not believe that is truly a macroprudential intervention.

Now that we better understand the potential consequences of adverse systemic interactions, we are almost certain to increase our use of macroprudential policies in the future. Over the years we will need to develop our understanding of what macroprudential policy is, what the most useful macroprudential tools are, and how they work. We have made considerable progress in the period since 2008, but much more remains to be done to develop their full potential, and to recognize the limitations of this new set of instruments.

8

Korea's Experiences with Macroprudential Policy

Choongsoo Kim

Korea has good experience in using macroprudential policies to address financial risks in the housing and foreign exchange markets. These two markets have been key sources of the systemic risk in Korea, given their high market volatility and susceptibility to bubbles, and with the significant potential to wreak havoc on the broader economy in case of market dislocation. Indeed, after a precipitous fall during the 1997–1998 financial crisis, house prices rose at a rapid pace in the first half of the 2000s, aided by a strong expansion of credit to households. Similarly, the foreign exchange (FX) market experienced an extended period of large inflows and exchange rate appreciation prior to the global financial crisis, both of which then reversed sharply after the crisis.

It was considered inappropriate to contain the looming financial risks in the housing or FX market by using monetary policy alone, which affects the broader economy and therefore may be too blunt a tool to address localized financial risks. A more targeted policy was called for, in addition to monetary policy, to achieve both price and financial stability. As such, Korea resorted to macroprudential policies while at the same time adjusting the stance of monetary policy—but with an eye on the developments in the broader economy.

For housing market risks, loan-to-value (LTV) and debt-to-income (DTI) regulations were deployed with a view to limiting the volume of bank financing of home purchases. Since their respective introductions in 2002 and 2005, these tools have been adjusted in a broadly counter-cyclical manner. With respect to FX-related risks, Korea learned valuable lessons from the global financial crisis about the danger of currency and maturity mismatches. As capital inflows resumed in 2009 and afterward on the back of the highly accommodative monetary policy in advanced countries, there was a need to prevent such mismatches from developing again in the banking sector. To that end, macroprudential measures were imposed, including leverage caps on FX derivatives positions and a macroprudential stability levy on noncore FX liabilities of banks.

This chapter reviews Korea's experiences in using macroprudential policies, evaluates their effects, and discusses remaining challenges in the design and implementation of macroprudential policies.

Background

Korea's housing market had gone through a dramatic price adjustment in the aftermath of the 1997–1998 financial crisis, possibly overcorrecting its previous price increases. It began to recover in the early 2000s, but the pace of recovery soon accelerated (figure 8.1). House prices increased at an annual average rate of 8.9 percent during the period of 2000–2002. Underlying such steep increases in house prices was households' greatly improved access to bank financing for home purchases, combined with self-fulfilling market expectations of further price increases.[1] Household loans, including bank mortgage loans, increased at an annual average rate of 13.9 percent during the same period.

With the sharp increases in house prices and mortgage loans, there were growing concerns over potential overheating in the housing market and related financial vulnerabilities that could translate into systemic risk. Bank financing for home purchases was in large part offered in the form of variable-rate bullet loans (with a maturity of three years or less) that are vulnerable to rollover risks, particularly if house prices fall. Although monetary policy had been tightened from 2005 to 2007, partly to cool down the overheated housing market, its effects remained limited as the rapid pace of house price increases continued.

Capital flows to Korea—in particular, bank flows—have been volatile and procyclical on the back of high trade and financial openness (figures 8.2 and 8.3). For instance, about half of the bank borrowings that had flowed in over the two-year period immediately before Lehman Brothers' collapse flowed out within just five months after the crisis hit. Moreover, large currency and maturity mismatches emerged on the balance sheets of banks—particularly foreign bank branches—in the mid-2000s (figure 8.4).

(a)

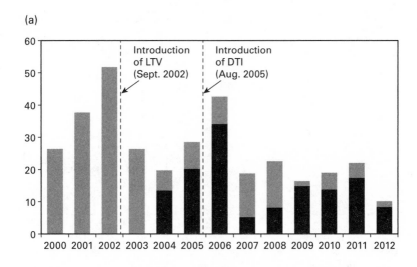

(b)

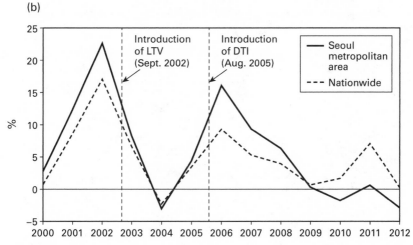

Figure 8.1
Household Loans and House Prices. a. Changes in household/home mortgage loans (US $ billion). Dark bars represent changes in home mortgage loans (no data available before 2004). b. Rate of increase (%) in house prices (year over year). *Source:* Bank of Korea.

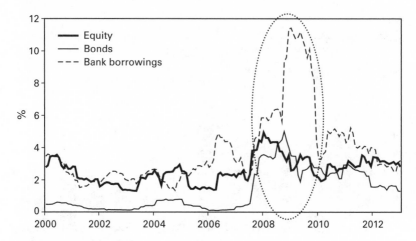

Figure 8.2
Capital Flow Volatility.
Note: Shown is the 12-month moving standard deviation of capital flows as a percentage of GDP (annualized).
Source: Bank of Korea.

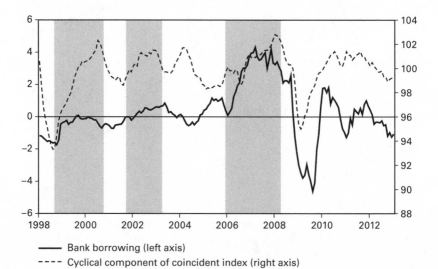

Bank borrowing (left axis)
Cyclical component of coincident index (right axis)

Figure 8.3
Bank Borrowings and the Business Cycle.
Note: Shown is the 12-month moving average of bank borrowings (US $ billion).
Shaded area indicates cyclical upswings.
Source: Bank of Korea.

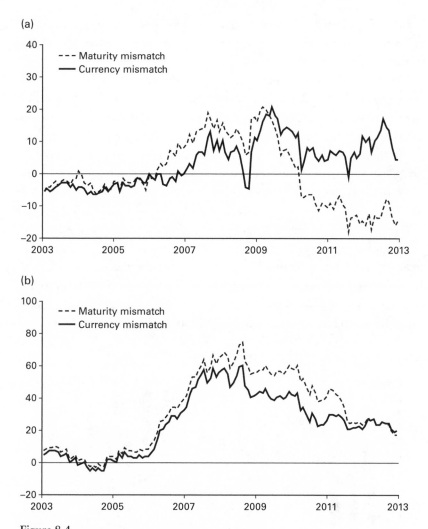

Figure 8.4
Currency and Maturity Mismatches (US $ billion).
a. Domestic banks. b. Foreign bank branches. Currency mismatches are calculated as foreign liabilities minus foreign assets. Maturity mismatches are calculated as short-term foreign liabilities minus short-term foreign assets.
Source: Bank of Korea.

For the entire banking sector, currency and maturity mismatches peaked at US $68 billion and US $85 billion, respectively, just before the global financial crisis.

The main driver of such mismatches was the swollen hedging demand from major shipbuilders amid strong market expectations of currency appreciation. Shipbuilders and other exporters sold dollars forward to banks. Then banks hedged their overbought position by foreign currency borrowings, mostly at short maturity. The consequence was a surge in banks' short-term external debt and rollover risks. The global financial crisis was a testing ground for such risks, and Korean banks failed the test.

Capital inflows resumed from the second half of 2009 on the back of ample global liquidity and the two-speed recovery between advanced and emerging economies (figures 8.5 and 8.6). Although it was a welcome development for economic recovery, policy concerns were raised as to the implications for financial stability, for short-term external borrowings by banks began to rise again and portfolio inflows also surged.

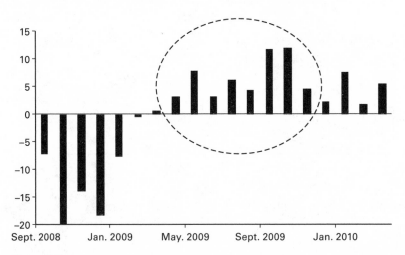

Figure 8.5
Net Non-Foreign Direct Investment Capital Flows (US $ billion).
Source: Bank of Korea.

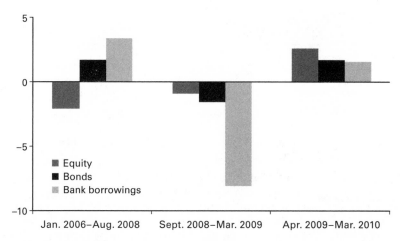

Figure 8.6
Pre- and Post-crisis Capital Flows (Monthly Average, US $ billion).
Source: Bank of Korea.

Macroprudential Policy Measures

Housing Sector–Related Measures

Two major policy instruments were used, LTV and DTI regulations. They were introduced in September 2002 and August 2005, respectively, in the midst of a housing market boom. They have since been adjusted in a broadly countercyclical manner, tightened or relaxed as warranted by cyclical developments in housing markets and bank lending (table 8.1 and figure 8.7).

LTV ratios were adjusted a total of nine times (tightened six times and relaxed three times) within a 40 percent to 70 percent range, and they were also differentiated depending on loan structure and across areas, with tighter standards applied where the real estate market was thought to be plagued by speculation. DTI ratios were similarly adjusted a total of eight times (tightened six times and relaxed two times) within a 40 percent to 75 percent range, and were also differentiated according to borrower characteristics such as marital status, house price, and geographic location of the property, among others.

Table 8.1
Major Changes in LTV and DTI Regulations

Measures	Time	Policy
LTV	Sep. 2002	Limiting of LTV ratio to less than 60%
	Mar. 2004	Raising of LTV ratio cap for installment loans (60% → 70%)
	July 2009	Lowering of LTV ratio cap for Seoul metropolitan area (60% → 50%)
DTI	Aug. 2005	Limiting of DTI ratio to less than 40% for unmarried borrowers of age 30 or younger and for married borrowers with existing loans by spouse for home purchase in speculative areas
	Nov. 2006	Expansion of the list of DTI-regulated areas to cover speculation-prone districts in Seoul metropolitan area
	Sep. 2009	Further expansion of the list of DTI-regulated areas to include nonspeculative districts in Seoul metropolitan area
	Aug. 2010	Temporary suspension of DTI regulations on nonspeculative districts in Seoul metropolitan area

Note: DTI, debt to income; LTV, loan to value.
Source: Bank of Korea.

Foreign Exchange–Related Measures
Specific measures to address FX risks were designed reflecting new thinking and evidence concerning the underlying causes of the global financial crisis and Korea's past experiences as well. Two policy measures were imposed on banks: (1) leverage caps on banks' FX derivatives positions, which required banks to limit their FX derivatives position at or below a targeted level (specified as a percentage of a bank's equity capital of the previous month), and (2) a macroprudential stability levy (MSL) on the noncore FX liabilities of banks.[2]

Leverage caps were first introduced in October 2010 at 250 percent for foreign bank branches and 50 percent for domestic banks. Since then they have been tightened twice, in July 2011 and January 2013, and are presently at 150 percent and 30 percent respectively for foreign bank branches and domestic banks (figure 8.8). The MSL was first imposed on banks in August 2011 and has remained unchanged. The levy rate varies from 2 basis points to 20 basis points, with a lower levy being applied to longer-maturity liabilities (figure 8.9).

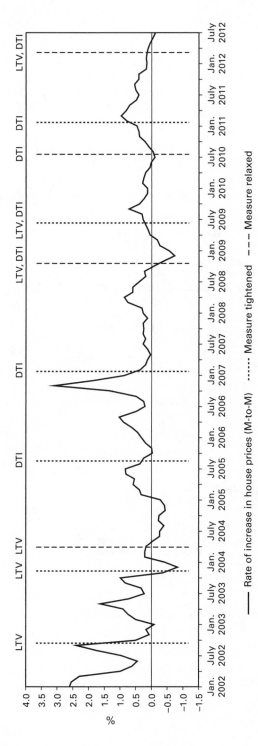

Figure 8.7
Changes in LTV and DTI Regulations and Rate of Increase in House Prices.
Source: Bank of Korea, Kookmin Bank.

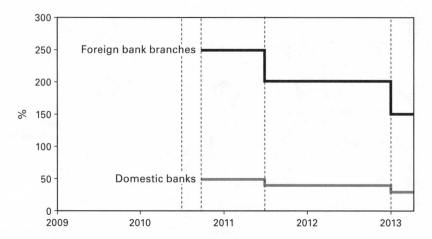

Figure 8.8
Leverage Caps on FX Derivatives Position (as a % of capital).
Note: The leverage was first announced in June 2010. In October 2010 the cap was 50% for domestic banks and 250% for foreign banks. Two subsequent adjustments were made, in July 2011 (to 40% and 200%) and January 2013 (to 30% and 150%).
Source: Bank of Korea.

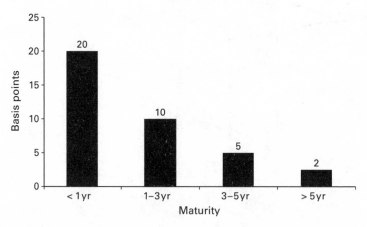

Figure 8.9
Macroprudential Stability Levy: Basis Points by Maturity.
Source: Bank of Korea.

Policy Effects

Cursory Look

A cursory look at financial and economic indicators suggests that the macroprudential policies deployed thus far have produced the intended policy effects on house prices, mortgage lending by banks, and capital flows, at least in the short run.

Looking through a four-quarter window centered on the date of policy change, a tightening of LTV or DTI regulations tends to be associated with a statistically significant decline in the speed at which house price and/or mortgage lending increases (figure 8.10).

Specifically, the rate of increase in house prices fell on average by 1.7 percentage points after LTV regulations were tightened and by 0.8 percentage points after DTI regulations were tightened, compared with the corresponding rate of increases during the pretightening two-quarter

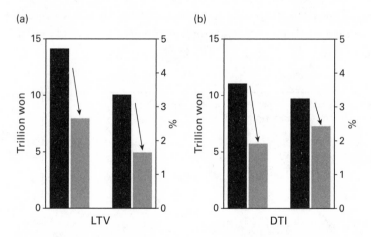

Figure 8.10
Effects of Housing Sector–Related Policy Measures.
a. Potential effects of LTV. b. Potential effects of DTI. From left to right, the first bar is the volume of increase in mortgage loans before tightening (left axis); the second bar is the volume of increase in mortgage loans after tightening (left axis); the third bar is the rate of increase in house prices before tightening (right axis); the fourth bar is the rate of increase in house prices after tightening (right axis). The data are in quarterly frequency and span the period from Q2 2003 to Q3 2011.
Source: NICE Credit Information Service DB, Kookmin Bank.

period. Similarly measured effects on the volume of mortgage loans are also significant: the volume of increase in mortgage lending fell on average by 43.9 percent (6.2 trillion won) after LTV regulations were tightened and by 44.4 percent (4.9 trillion won) after DTI regulations were tightened.

Macroprudential policies targeted for FX risks also appear to have worked well by and large, although limited data availability (owing to the short history of policy implementation) constrains statistical analysis. As regards the effects of leverage caps, banks, particularly foreign bank branches, have reduced their FX derivatives position and hence short-term borrowings by a significant amount since May 2010, when the introduction of leverage caps was first announced (figures 8.11 and 8.12).[3] MSL is a cost to banks and, therefore, ceteris paribus, shrinks the arbitrage margin (figure 8.13). A preliminary estimate suggests that the total levy collected could be as large as 12 percent of net profits for foreign bank branches while being less than 1 percent for domestic banks (figure 8.14). This is not surprising insofar as domestic banks' funding is predominantly in local currency while foreign bank branches fund mostly in foreign currency.

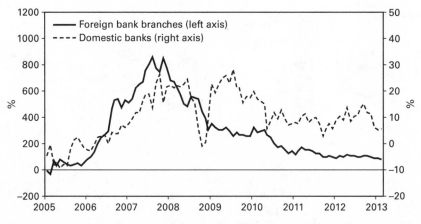

Figure 8.11
Total FX Derivatives Position (% of bank capital).
Source: Bank of Korea.

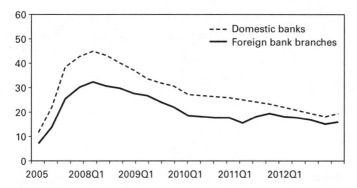

Figure 8.12
FX Derivatives Position, Related to Shipbuilders (US $ billion).
Note: Annual data for periods prior to 2008.
Source: Bank of Korea.

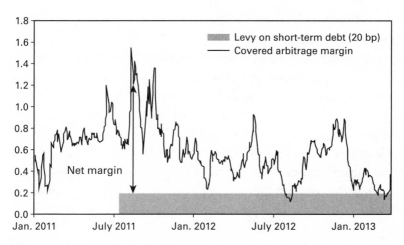

Figure 8.13
Incentives for Arbitrage Transaction (Foreign Bank Branches, Percentage Points).
Note: Incentives are measured as the interest rate differential (3 months) minus
the swap rate (3 months).
Source: Bank of Korea.

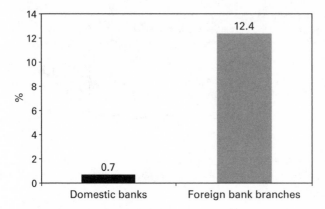

Figure 8.14
Levy as a Percentage of Net Profits (as of end 2012).
Note: Profits are Bank of Korea staff estimates.
Source: Bank of Korea.

The maturity structure of external debt has also improved, particularly in the case of foreign bank branches following the introduction of leverage caps and MSL (figure 8.15). During the two-year period after mid-2010, foreign bank branches' short-term borrowings decreased by US $35 billion, while their long-term borrowings increased by US $20 billion. To be specific, foreign bank branches have resorted more to long-term inter-office borrowings in order to reduce their MSL and also to increase their forward buying capacity in response to a tightening of leverage caps on FX derivatives position.[4] Consequently, foreign bank branches reduced short-term borrowings as a share of total external borrowings from 93 percent to 58 percent during the period of 2010–2012.

Formal Analysis

A more formal empirical analysis is undertaken to gauge the policy effects on targeted risks and variables. It should be noted at the outset, however, that the analysis presented below is highly preliminary and subject to many caveats associated with the difficulty of unknown counterfactuals and limited data availability. Nevertheless, the empirical results appear promising for the effectiveness of macroprudential policies in achieving financial stability.

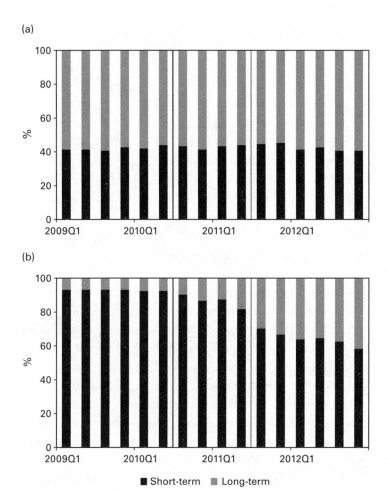

Figure 8.15
Maturity Composition of External Debt (%).
a. Domestic banks. b. Foreign bank branches.
Note: Black and gray vertical lines indicate the dates of the introduction of the leverage cap and the stability levy, respectively.
Source: Bank of Korea.

Effects of LTV and DTI Regulations

A two-variable panel vector autoregression (PVAR) is estimated for the rate of increase in house prices and the volume of bank mortgage loans, controlling for the effects of LTV and DTI regulations and other relevant policies (see appendix 8.1 for model specification and the full estimation results). Monetary policy tightening is estimated to have the intended effects, while higher capital gains taxes also appear to have discouraged the demand for mortgage loans but raised house prices, suggesting a higher tax incidence on home buyers than on home sellers (which is partly attributable to the fact that the housing market was a seller's market rather than a buyer's market when high expectations of capital gains prevailed).

The coefficients of LTV and DTI dummies are negative, as expected, and highly significant in most cases; some DTI dummies included in the equation for mortgage loan growth are estimated imprecisely, indicating that LTV regulations may have been more effective than DTI regulations, at least in Korea. Moreover, the estimated coefficients suggest that tighter LTV regulations (with a lower cap on LTV ratios) have stronger cooling effects on house prices and mortgage lending by banks. Last but not least, the actual effects of LTV and DTI regulations might be even stronger than estimated if the possible upward endogeneity bias in the estimated coefficients (stemming from an endogenous response of policies to developments in housing markets and bank lending) is taken into consideration.

The cumulative effects of LTV and DTI regulations on house prices and mortgage lending are simulated by using the estimated PVAR model. According to the results of a dynamic simulation, house prices and the outstanding stock of mortgage loans would have been 75 percent and 137 percent higher than their respective actual levels by the second quarter of 2012 if there had been no regulations in place throughout the sample period (table 8.2 and figure 8.16).[5] Although the estimated policy effects, especially those on mortgage loans, may appear somewhat larger than one might expect, they are not unreasonable in the context of the galloping pace of credit expansion observed in many housing booms of emerging economies.[6]

Effects of Leverage Caps and MSL

The policy effects of leverage caps and the MSL are estimated by using a Bayesian VAR model for banks' foreign borrowings and other related

Table 8.2
Simulated Mortgage Loans and House Prices by Scenario

	Level				Ratio		
	Actual (A)	No LTV in Place (B)	No DTI in Place (C)	Neither LTV Nor DTI in Place (D)	(B–A)/A	(C–A)/A	(D–A)/A
Mortgage loans[a]	312.0 (2.2%)	702.0 (4.5%)	325.0 (2.3%)	739.1 (4.6%)	125.0%	4.2%	136.9%
House prices[b]	139.8 (0.9%)	241.9 (2.4%)	141.6 (1.0%)	244.8 (2.5%)	73.0%	1.3%	75.1%

Notes: a. In trillion won. b. Q1 2003 = 100. Figures in parentheses indicate quarterly average growth rates over the period of Q1 2003 to Q2 2012.

financial variables such as VIX[7] (see appendix 8.2 for model specifications and estimated impulse responses). The basic assumption is that leverage caps are quantitative restrictions and thus affect directly banks' foreign borrowings, whereas MSL affects banks' foreign borrowings mainly through changes in funding cost or net returns.[8] The estimated model was then used to produce two conditional forecasts of banks' foreign borrowings, one with macroprudential policies (policy scenario) and the other with no macroprudential policies (no policy scenario). The difference between the two scenarios is taken as the estimate of policy effects.

Leverage caps are estimated to have contributed to improving the maturity structure of banks' foreign liabilities. For foreign bank branches, leverage caps are estimated to have reduced short- and long-term foreign borrowings by about 0.6 percent and 0.2 percent of annual GDP, respectively, in cumulative terms over the one-year horizon from their introduction (figure 8.17). For domestic banks, the effects are estimated to be only one-tenth of those for foreign bank branches. Such a difference between foreign bank branches and domestic banks is not surprising since leverage caps were binding for the former at the time of their introduction but not for the latter.

The estimated effects of MSL on the maturity structure of banks' foreign liabilities are smaller than those of leverage caps but nonetheless

(a)

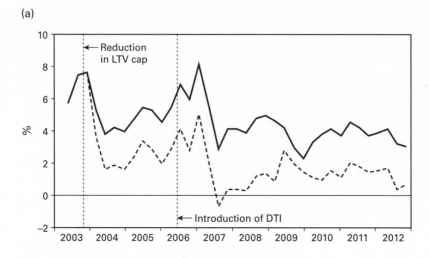

(b)

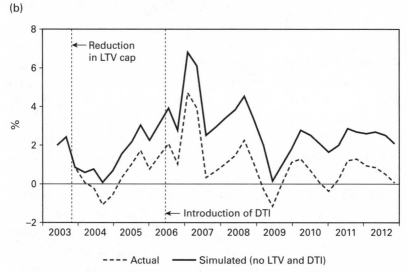

---- Actual   ——— Simulated (no LTV and DTI)

Figure 8.16
Growth Rates of Mortgage Loans and House Prices (Actual vs. Simulated, %).
a. Mortgage loans. b. House prices.
Source: Bank of Korea.

a. Foreign bank branches

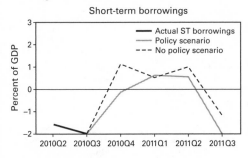

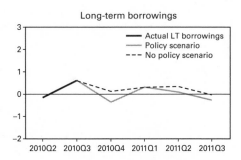

b. Domestic banks

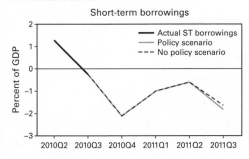

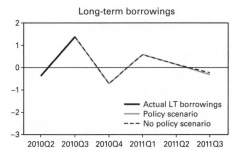

Figure 8.17
Impact of Leverage Caps on External Borrowings (% of GDP).
Note: Gray lines (dashed lines) refer to conditional forecasts under policy scenario (no policy scenario); solid black lines indicate actual values.
Source: Bank of Korea.

moderate in light of the fact that the levy rate was set at fairly low levels. In cumulative terms over the one-year horizon, MSL reduced short-term borrowings of domestic banks and foreign bank branches alike by about 0.2 percent of annual GDP with no discernible impact on long-term borrowings (figure 8.18).

Implications for Systemic Risk

Evidence for the effectiveness of macroprudential policies may have positive implications for systemic risk. Indeed, LTV and DTI regulations seem to have had significant effects in mitigating the credit risk of mortgage loans. For instance, delinquency rate and value-at-risk tend to fall after LTV or DTI regulations are tightened, and vice versa (figure 8.19). DTI

a. Foreign bank branches

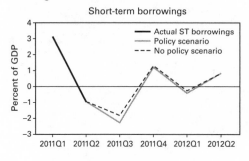

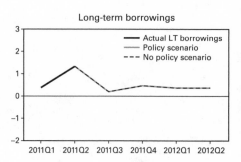

b. Domestic banks

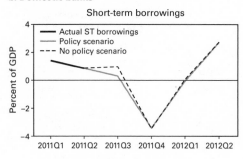

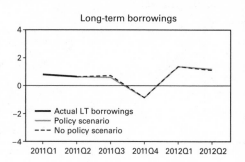

Figure 8.18
Impact of MSL on External Borrowings (% of GDP).
Notes: Gray lines (dashed lines) refer to conditional forecasts under policy scenario (no policy scenario); black lines indicate actual values. MSL, macroprudential stability levy.
Source: Bank of Korea

regulations, introduced in late 2005, also appear to have affected the composition of mortgage loans. The share of installment loans in total mortgage loans was less than 40 percent at end-2005. It began to rise from 2006 and stood at 65 percent by 2012 (figure 8.20). The rising share of installment loans indicates the reduced rollover risks faced by borrowers and thus less default risk on mortgage lending.

But macroprudential policies may not always help reduce systemic risk. For instance, the share of long-term mortgage loans with a maturity of 10 years or longer has been on the rise since DTI regulations came into effect in late 2005. Accordingly, the duration of mortgage loans increased from 3.8 years to 5.5 years over the period of 2006–2012 (figure 8.21). Although a higher share of installment loans may help reduce default risk,

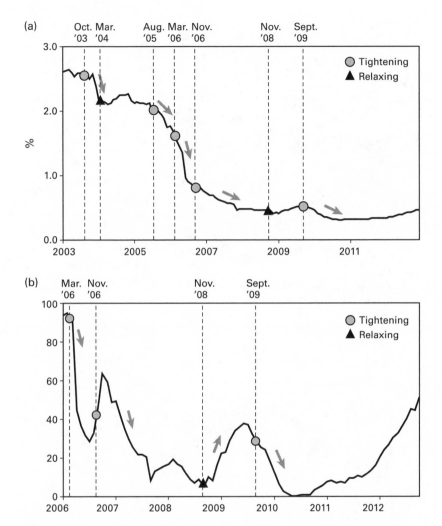

Figure 8.19
Credit Risk of Mortgage Loans.
a. Delinquency rate (%). b. Value-at-risk. Value-at-risk is normalized to lie between 0 and 100.
Source: Bank of Korea.

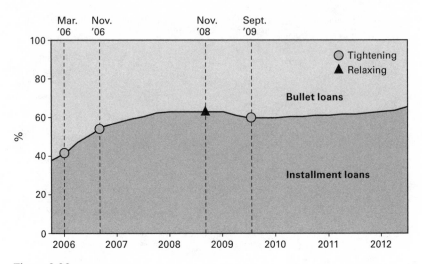

Figure 8.20
Share of Installment Loans (%).
Source: Bank of Korea.

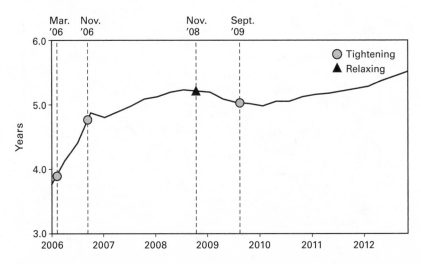

Figure 8.21
Weighted Average Duration of Mortgage Loans, 2006–2012 (years).
Source: Bank of Korea.

the longer duration of mortgage loans may have increased banks' interest rate and liquidity risks.

Concluding Remarks

Preliminary evidence for Korea seems to offer strong support for the usefulness and effectiveness of macroprudential policies as a tool to achieve and ensure macrofinancial stability. LTV and DTI regulations have helped stabilize housing markets and keep credit expansion under proper control. Similarly, macroprudential policies targeting FX risks, such as leverage caps and the bank levy, appear to have contributed to improving the maturity structure of external debt owed by banks and reducing the likelihood of sudden stops.

Several policy issues and lessons are emerging from Korea's experiences. First, country-specific circumstances may matter in important ways for the effectiveness of macroprudential policies. For instance, the powerful role played by LTV and DTI regulations in Korea seems to have been aided by the large presence of short-term bullet mortgage loans, which are treated as new loans whenever rolled over. Second, the policy authorities should bear in mind and exercise vigilance concerning a variety of unintended consequences. LTV regulations could become procyclical if adjustments in LTV caps lag far behind house-price movements. Although DTI regulations have induced banks to offer more long-maturity installment loans, banks' funding maturity has failed to increase accordingly resulting in larger maturity mismatch and higher interest rate and liquidity risk as well.

Third, the issue of policy circumvention should be taken seriously because it could increase or even create systemic risk, not to mention undermine policy effectiveness. As LTV and DTI regulations were focused on banks, mortgage lending by (less regulated and less well-capitalized) nonbanks increased rapidly. Last but not least, more research is called for to answer how best to combine macroprudential and monetary policies.

Appendix 8.1

Estimating the Effects of LTV and DTI Regulations: Panel VAR

Data and Specification   A panel vector autoregression (PVAR) is estimated for house prices and the volume of mortgage lending by banks (both seasonally adjusted), controlling for the effects of LTV and DTI regulations. The sample used for the analysis is a balanced panel that covers 43 areas over the period of Q2 2003 to Q2 2012. The specification of the PVAR is as follows:

$$X_t = A_0 + A_1 X_{t-1} + BP_{t-1} + CZ_{t-1} + e_t,$$

where X is a vector of endogenous variables (house price and mortgage lending), P is a vector of policy variables, and Z represents other controls, such as nominal GDP and dummies for speculative areas and the global financial crisis. Policy variables considered include the overnight call interest rate (as a proxy for monetary policy stance), dummies for LTV and DTI regulations, and dummies for capital gains tax policy (see table A8.1).

As LTV regulations were first introduced with a cap set at 60 percent and have been in place throughout the entire sample period and across all areas, the estimated coefficients of LTV dummies included in the VAR, LTV4 and LTV5, capture the policy effects relative to the baseline case of the LTV ratio being capped at 60 percent. For DTI regulations, three dummies—DTI4, DTI5, and DTI6—are used in the VAR as the sample includes the periods and/or areas in which no DTI regulations were in place. Therefore, their coefficients reflect policy effects relative to the baseline case of no DTI regulations. LTV dummies are constructed based

Table A8.1
Description of Variables in Table A8.2

Name	Description
Loan	Quarterly growth rate of mortgage loans (s.a., %)
House price	Quarterly growth rate of house prices (s.a., %)
NGDP	Quarterly growth rate of nominal GDP (s.a., %)
LTV4, LTV5	LTV4 (LTV5) equals 1 if the LTV cap is 40% (50%), 0 otherwise
DTI4, DTI5, DTI6	DTI4 (DTI5, DTI6) equals 1 if the DTI cap is 40% (50%, 60%), 0 otherwise
Call	Overnight call interest rate (%)
Tax	Tax equals 1 if capital gains tax rate is 50%, 0 otherwise
SPA	SPA equals 1 if the region is designated as a speculative area, 0 otherwise
CS	CS equals 1 for the period of Q4 2008 to Q3 2009, 0 otherwise

Note: s.a., seasonally adjusted data.

on the cap level applied to mortgage loans of 3- to 10-year maturity, which account for the bulk of mortgage lending by banks (the LTV cap for loans with a maturity of 10 years or longer was set to 70 percent but appears to be nonbinding). DTI dummies are relatively free from the coverage issue because DTI regulations are applied uniformly except for the first 10-month period, when DTI regulations were applied only to large mortgage loans exceeding 600 million won.

Estimation Results

The model is estimated using the generalized method of moments (GMM). The overidentifying restrictions are not rejected for both equations if the Hansen test (which is more heteroskedasticity-consistent) is used. The estimated coefficients of LTV and DTI dummies are statistically significant and have the expected sign in most cases, although some DTI coefficients are imprecisely estimated in the equation for mortgage lending. Monetary tightening (as captured by the call interest rate) turns out to have been effective in curbing the housing boom and bank lending. The tax policy appears to have reduced mortgage loan growth but increased house prices.

Appendix 8.2

Estimating the Effects of Leverage Caps and MSL: Bayesian VAR

The baseline model for the estimation is a four-variable Bayesian VAR model:

$$Y_t = \Phi_0 + \sum_{j=1}^{p} \Phi_j Y_{t-j} + e_t,$$

where Y is a vector of foreign borrowings by domestic banks or foreign bank branches and other financial variables (OFVs) that are deemed to have an influence on FX risks. For domestic banks, OFVs include the FX derivatives position ratio (as a percentage of bank capital), VIX (Volatility Index), and borrowing spread over Libor. For foreign bank branches, OFVs include the same variables except that the borrowing spread over Libor is replaced by the covered interest parity deviation (CID).

The sample used for the estimation is in quarterly frequency and spans the period from Q1 2003 to Q2 2012. Use of quarterly data is dictated by

Table A8.2
Estimation Results

	Loan	House price
Loan	0.228***	0.042**
	(0.027)	(0.020)
House price	0.052	0.477***
	(0.038)	(0.024)
NGDP	−0.373***	0.079**
	(0.056)	(0.039)
Call	−0.251**	−0.255***
	(0.104)	(0.069)
Tax	−1.650***	0.781***
	(0.352)	(0.225)
LTV4	−3.157***	−1.587***
	(0.805)	(0.468)
LTV5	−2.056***	−0.954***
	(0.389)	(0.248)
DTI4	−0.346	0.178
	(0.323)	(0.189)
DTI5	0.128	−0.370
	(0.335)	(0.233)
DTI6	−0.191	−1.241***
	(0.552)	(0.379)
SPA	2.211**	1.694***
	(0.867)	(0.493)
CS	−0.880***	−0.819***
	(0.252)	(0.167)
Constant	5.152***	0.679*
	(0.602)	(0.385)
Observations	1,505	1,505
No. of areas	43	43
Sargan stat. (p value)	590.4(0.863)	1,458.9(0.001)
Hansen J-stat. (p value)	40.8(0.999)	41.1(0.999)

Note: *, **, and *** refer to 10%, 5%, and 1% significance level respectively.

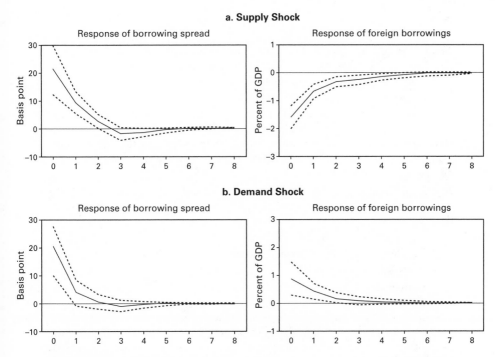

Figure A8.1
Impulse Responses to Supply and Demand Shocks.
Notes: Estimation results are for domestic banks. Solid lines indicate median values of impulse responses, broken lines indicate 68 percent probability bands.
Source: Bank of Korea.

the availability of disaggregated data on foreign borrowings by domestic banks and by foreign bank branches (for a robustness check, however, the model is also estimated using monthly data on proxy variables).

Four structural shocks of the model are identified by using both sign and exclusion restrictions as suggested by economic theory and institutional features. First, a global risk perception shock (or an innovation to VIX) is assumed to be orthogonal to other structural shocks. Second, a supply shock (or push factor) is assumed to move price (borrowing spread or CID) and quantity (foreign borrowings) in the opposite direction. Third, a demand shock (or pull factor) moves price and quantity in the same direction. Finally, a shock to the FX position ratio is assumed to be exogenous and orthogonal to contemporaneous shocks to price and quantity variables, capturing changes in the FX position ratio unrelated to foreign borrowings.

Notes

The author especially thanks Jun Il Kim, Jong Ku Kang, Hoon Kim, Seung Hwan Lee, Namjin Ma, Changho Choi, and Yong Min Kim at the Bank of Korea for their helpful contributions and assistance.

1. After the 1997 financial crisis, domestic banks shifted their business strategy to household lending from corporate lending. The deregulation of the banking industry, the privatization of the Housing and Commercial Bank in 1996 (whose main business was long-term home mortgage lending), and the reduced loan demand by large corporations induced commercial banks to aggressively enter the mortgage loan market.

2. The "global banking glut" view expounded by Shin (2012), as opposed to the global savings glut view, was instrumental in the design and implementation of the MSL.

3. At the time of policy announcement, the average FX leverage ratio of foreign bank branches exceeded 260 percent of equity capital. The same ratio fell sharply to 87 percent by January 2013.

4. For foreign bank branches, part of their long-term borrowings (with a maturity longer than a year) from their head offices is recognized as bank capital (known as Capital B) and exempt from the MSL. Because leverage caps are defined as a percentage of bank equity capital, higher Capital B *ceteris paribus* enables foreign bank branches to buy dollars forward in greater amounts. Capital B of foreign bank branches increased to 16 trillion won by end-March 2012, up from 6.1 trillion won at end-March 2010.

5. For the effects of LTV regulations, the scenario of "no regulations" refers to the case with LTV cap at 60 percent being in place (see appendix 8.1 for greater details).

6. An omitted variable bias is another possibility for the larger estimated policy effects, which warrants further scrutiny in future studies.

7. VIX implies volatility in S&P 500 stock index option prices.

8. Specifically, the borrowing spread over Libor is used as a proxy for domestic banks' borrowing costs whereas the covered interest parity deviation (CID) is used as a proxy for foreign bank branches' net returns. These two price variables are chosen in view of their centrality to banks' foreign asset and liability management.

Reference

Shin, Hyun-Song. 2012. "Global Banking Glut and Loan Risk Premium." *IMF Economic Review* 60:155–192.

III
Financial Regulation

9

Everything the IMF Wanted to Know about Financial Regulation and Wasn't Afraid to Ask

Sheila Bair

I was honored when the IMF asked me to moderate the "Financial Regulation" panel at this year's "Rethinking Macro Policy II" conference. And while naturally I delivered one of the more enlightening and thought-provoking policy discussions of the conference, I did fail in my duties as moderator to make sure the panelists covered all the excellent questions our sponsors submitted to us. Of course, this was to be expected, as panelists at these types of events almost never address the topics requested of them (I certainly never do) but rather, like presidential candidates, answer the questions they want to answer. However, accepting responsibility for my mismanagement, I will now step up and answer those questions myself.

1. Does anybody have a clear vision of the desirable financial system of the future?

Yes, me. It should be smaller, simpler, less leveraged, and more focused on meeting the credit needs of the real economy. And we should ban the speculative use of credit default swaps from the face of the planet.

2. Is the ATM the only useful financial innovation of the last 30 years?

No. If bankers approach the business of banking as a way to provide greater value at less cost to their customers (and that might pose difficulties), technology provides a virtual gold mine for product innovations. For instance, I am currently testing a prepaid, stored-value card that lets me do virtually all my banking on my iPhone. It tracks expenses, tells me when I've blown my budget, and lets me temporarily block use of the card when my daughter, unbeknownst to me, has pulled it out of my wallet to buy the latest jeans from Aeropostale. The card, aptly called Simple, was engineered by two techies in Portland, Oregon. (Note to megabanks: Ditch the pinstripes for Dockers and flip-flops. The techies are coming for you next.)

3. Does the idea of a safe, regulated core set of activities and a less safe, less regulated noncore set make sense?

No.

The idea of a safe, regulated core set of activities with access to the safety net (deposit insurance, central bank lending) and a less safe, more regulated noncore set of activities that do not under any circumstances have access to the safety net—that makes sense.

4. How do the different proposals (Volcker rule, Liikanen's regulations, Vickers's ring-fencing) score in that respect?

Put them all together and you are two-thirds of the way there. The Volcker rule acknowledges the need for tough restrictions on speculative trading throughout the banking organization, including restrictions on trading of securities and derivatives in the so-called "casino bank." Liikanen and Vickers acknowledge the need to firewall insured deposits around traditional commercial banking and force market funding of higher-risk casino banking activities. Combining them would give us a much safer financial system.

But none of these proposals fully addresses the problem of excessive risk taking by nonbank financial institutions like AIG. Title I of the Dodd-Frank Wall Street Reform and Consumer Protection Act empowers the Financial Stability Oversight Council to bring these kinds of shadow banks under prudential supervision by the Fed. Of course, that law was enacted three years ago, and for nearly two years now the regulators have promised that they will be designating shadow banks for supervisory oversight "very soon." This was repeated most recently by Treasury Secretary Jack Lew on May 22, 2013, before the Senate Banking Committee (but this time he really meant it). For some reason, the Fed and the Treasury Department were able to figure out that AIG and GE Capital were systemic in a nanosecond in 2008 when bailout money was at stake, but when it comes to subjecting them to more regulation now, well, hey, we need to be careful here.

5. How much do higher capital ratios actually affect the efficiency and profitability of banks?

You don't have to be very efficient to make money by using a lot of leverage to juice profits, then dump the losses on the government when things go bad. In my experience, the banks with the stronger capital ratios are the ones that are better managed, do a better job of lending, and have more sustainable profits over the long term, with the added benefit that they don't put taxpayers at risk and keep lending during economic downturns.

6. Should we go for very high capital ratios?

Yep. I've argued for a minimum leverage ratio of 8 percent, but I like John Vickers's 10 percent even better.

7. Is there virtue in simplicity—for example, simple leverage rather than capital ratios—or will simplicity only increase regulatory arbitrage?

The late Pat Moynihan once said that there are some things only a PhD can screw up. The Basel Committee's rules for risk weighting assets are exhibit A.

These rules are hopelessly overcomplicated. They were subject to rampant gaming and arbitrage prior to the crisis and still are. (If you don't believe me, read Senator Levin's report on the London Whale.) A simple leverage ratio should be the binding constraint, supplemented with a standardized system of risk weightings to force higher capital levels at banks that take undue risks. It is laughable to think that the leverage ratio is more susceptible to arbitrage than the current system of risk weightings, given the way risk weights were gamed prior to the crisis, for example, by moving assets to the trading book, securitizing loans to get lower capital charges, wrapping high-risk collateralized debt obligations in credit default swap protection to get near-zero risk charges, blindly investing in triple A securities, loading up on high-risk sovereign debt, repo financing. . . . Need I go on?

8. Can we realistically solve the too-big-to-fail problem?

We have to solve it. If we can't, then nationalize these behemoths and pay the people who run them the same wages as everyone else who works for the government.

9. Where do we stand on resolution processes, both at the national level and across borders?

Good progress has been made, but not enough. Resolution authority in the United States could be operationalized now, if necessary, but it would be messy and unduly expensive for creditors. We need thicker cushions of equity at the megabanks, minimum standards for both equity and long-term debt issuances at the holding company level to facilitate the Federal Deposit Insurance Corporation's single-point-of-entry strategy, and—most important—regulators who make clear that they have the guts to put a megabank into receivership. The industry says it wants to end too big to fail, but they aren't doing everything they can to make sure resolution authority works smoothly. For instance, industry groups like the International Swaps and Derivatives Association could greatly facilitate international resolutions by revising global standards for swap documentation to recognize the government's authority to require continued performance on derivatives contracts in a Dodd-Frank resolution.

10. Can we ever hope to measure systemic risk?

Yes. It's all about interconnectedness, which megabanks and regulators should be able to measure. Ironically, interconnectedness is encouraged by those %$#@& Basel capital rules for risk weighting assets. Lending to IBM is viewed as five times riskier than lending to Morgan Stanley. Repos among financial institutions are treated as extremely low risk, even though excessive reliance on repo funding almost brought our system down. How dumb is that?

We need to fix the capital rules. Regulators also need to focus more attention on the credit exposure reports that are required under Dodd-Frank. These reports require megabanks to identify and quantify for regulators how exposed they are to each other. Megabank failure scenarios should be factored into stress testing as well.

(Since these questions are related to financial regulation, I will not opine on measuring systemic risk building as a result of loose monetary policy.)

11. Are banks in effect driving the reform process?

It sure seems that way.

12. Can regulators ever be as nimble as the regulatees?

Yes. Read Roger Martin's *Fixing the Game* (Harvard Business Review Press, 2011). Financial regulators should look to the NFL for inspiration.

13. Given the cat-and-mouse game between regulators and regulatees, do we have to live with regulatory uncertainty?

Simple regulations that focus on market discipline and skin-in-the-game requirements are harder to game and more adaptable to changing conditions than rules that try to dictate behavior. For instance, thick capital cushions will help ensure that whatever dumb mistakes banks may make in the future (and they will), there will be significant capacity to absorb the resulting losses. Unfortunately, the trend has been toward complex, prescriptive rules that smart banking lawyers love to exploit. The industry generally likes the prescriptive rules because they always find a way around them, and the regulators don't keep up.

You can see that dynamic playing out now, where the securitization industry is seeking to undermine a Dodd-Frank requirement that securitizers take 5 cents of every dollar of loss on mortgages they securitize. They say risk retention is no longer required because the Consumer Bureau has promulgated mortgage lending standards. But these rules are pretty permissive (no down payment requirement and a whopping 43 percent debt-to-income ratio), and I'm sure that the Mortgage Bankers Association is already trying to figure out ways to skirt them.

Rules dictating behavior can sometimes be helpful, but forcing market participants to take the losses from their risk taking can be much more effective. One approach tells them what kinds of loans they can make. The other says that whatever kind of loans they make, they will take losses if those loans default.

10

Regulating Large Financial Institutions

Jeremy C. Stein

I will focus my remarks on the ongoing regulatory challenges associated with large, systemically important financial institutions, or SIFIs. In part, this focus amounts to asking a question that seems to be on everyone's mind these days: Where do we stand with respect to fixing the problem of "too big to fail" (TBTF)? Are we making satisfactory progress, or it is time to think about further measures?

I should note at the outset that solving the TBTF problem has two distinct aspects. First, and most obvious, one goal is to get to the point where all market participants understand—with certainty—that if a large SIFI were to fail, then the losses would fall on its shareholders and creditors, and taxpayers would have no exposure. However, this is only a necessary condition for success, not a sufficient one. A second aim is that the failure of a SIFI must not impose significant spillovers on the rest of the financial system, in the form of contagion effects, fire sales, widespread credit crunches, and the like. Clearly, these two goals are closely related. If policy does a better job of mitigating spillovers, it becomes more credible to claim that a SIFI will be allowed to fail without government bailout.

So where do we stand? I believe two statements are simultaneously true. We've made considerable progress with respect to SIFIs since the financial crisis. And we're not yet at a point where we should be satisfied.

The areas of progress are familiar to many. Higher and more robust capital requirements, new liquidity requirements, and stress testing all should help to materially reduce the probability of a SIFI finding itself at the point of failure. And if, despite these measures, a SIFI does fail, the orderly liquidation authority (OLA) in Title II of the Dodd-Frank Wall Street Reform and Consumer Protection Act now offers a mechanism for recapitalizing and restructuring the institution by imposing losses on shareholders and creditors. In the interest of brevity, I won't go into a lot of detail about OLA. But my board colleague, Jay Powell, talked in depth about this topic in a speech last month, and I would just register my broad agreement with his conclusion—namely, that the Federal Deposit Insurance Corporation's (FDIC's) so-called single-point-of-entry approach to resolution is a promising one (see Powell 2013). The Federal Reserve continues to work with the FDIC on the many difficult implementation challenges that remain, but I believe this approach gets the first-order economics right and ultimately has a good chance to be effective.

Perhaps more to the point for TBTF, if a SIFI does fail, I have little doubt that private investors will, in fact, bear the losses—even if this leads to an outcome that is messier and more costly to society than we would ideally like. Dodd-Frank is very clear in saying that the Federal Reserve and other regulators cannot use their emergency authorities to bail out an individual failing institution. And as a member of the board, I am committed to following both the letter and the spirit of the law.

Still, we are quite a way from having fully solved the policy problems associated with SIFIs. For one thing, the market still appears to attach some probability to the government bailing out the creditors of a SIFI; this can be seen in the ratings uplift granted to large banks based on the ratings agencies' assessment of the probability of government support. While this uplift seems to have shrunk to some degree since the passage of Dodd-Frank, it is still significant.[1] All else equal, this uplift confers a funding subsidy to the largest financial firms.

Moreover, as I noted earlier, even if bailouts were commonly understood to be a zero-probability event, the problem of spillovers remains. It is one thing to believe that a SIFI will be allowed to fail without government support; it is another to believe that such failure will not inflict significant damage on other parts of the financial system. In the presence of such externalities, financial firms may still have excessive private incentives to remain big, complicated, and interconnected, because they reap any benefits—for example, in terms of economies of scale and scope—but don't bear all the social costs.

How can we do better? Some have argued that the current policy path is not working and that we need to take a fundamentally different approach.[2] Such an alternative approach might include, for example, outright caps on the size of individual banks or a return to Glass-Steagall–type activity limits.

My own view is somewhat different. While I agree that we have a long way to go, I believe that the way to get there is not by abandoning the current reform agenda but rather by sticking to its broad contours and ratcheting up its forcefulness on a number of dimensions. In this spirit, two ideas merit consideration: (1) an increase in the slope of the capital-surcharge schedule that is applied to large complex firms and (2) the imposition at the holding company level of a substantial senior debt requirement to facilitate resolution under Title II of Dodd-Frank. In parallel with the approach to capital surcharges, a senior debt requirement could also potentially be made a function of an institution's systemic footprint.

To illustrate my argument, let us take as given the central premise of those who favor size limits, namely, that society would be better off if the distribution of banks were not so skewed toward a handful of very large institutions. (To be clear, I am using the word "size" as shorthand for the broader concept of an institution's systemic footprint, which in addition to size might reflect complexity, interconnectedness, and global span of operations.) In other words, let's simply posit that a goal of regulation should be to lean against bank size, and ask: What are the best regulatory tools for accomplishing that goal? As in many other regulatory settings, this question can be mapped into the "prices-versus-quantities" framework laid out by Martin Weitzman nearly 40 years ago.[3] Here a size cap is a form of quantity regulation, whereas capital requirements that increase with bank size can be thought of as a kind of price regulation, in the sense that such capital requirements are analogous to a progressive tax on bank size.[4]

A key challenge with quantity-based regulation is that one has to decide where to set the cap. Doing so requires a regulator to take a strong stand on the nature of scale and scope economies in large financial firms. Moreover, even if one reads the empirical literature as being quite skeptical about the existence of such economies beyond a certain point in the size distribution—a proposition that itself is debatable—the most that such large-sample studies can do is to make on-average statements about scale and scope economies.[5] These studies still leave open the possibility of considerable heterogeneity across firms, and that some firms are able to add considerable value in a given line of business by being very big—even if the average firm in the population is not. And such heterogeneity alone is enough to create significant drawbacks to quantity-based regulation.

Consider the following example. There are three banks, A, B, and C. Both A and B have $1 trillion in assets, whereas C is smaller, with only $400 billion in assets. Bank A actually generates significant economies of scale so that it is socially optimal for it to remain at its current size. Banks B and C, by contrast, have very modest economies of scale, not enough to outweigh the costs that their size and complexity impose on society. From the perspective of an omniscient social planner, it would be better if both B and C were half their current size.

Now let's ask what happens if we impose a size cap of, say, $500 billion. This size cap does the right thing with respect to bank B, by shrinking it to a socially optimal size. But it mishandles both banks A and C, for different reasons. In the case of A, the cap forces it to shrink when it shouldn't, because given the specifics of its business model, it actually creates a substantial amount of value by being big. And in the case of C, the cap makes the opposite mistake. It would actually be beneficial to put pressure on C to shrink at the margin—that is, to move it in the direction of being a $200 billion bank instead of a $400 billion one—but since it lies below the cap, it is completely untouched by the regulation.

Suppose instead we attack the problem by imposing capital requirements that are an increasing function of bank size. This price-based approach creates some incentive for all three banks to shrink, but lets them balance this incentive against the scale benefits they realize by staying big. In this case we would expect A, with its significant scale economies, to absorb the tax hit and choose to remain large, while B and C, with more modest scale economies, would be expected to shrink more radically. In other words, price-based regulation is more flexible in that it leaves the size decision to bank managers, who can then base their decisions on their own understanding of the synergies—or lack thereof—in their respective businesses.

This logic can be thought of as supporting the approach taken by the Basel Committee on Banking Supervision in its rule imposing a common equity surcharge on designated global systemically important banks. The exact amount of the surcharge will range from 1 percent to 2.5 percent and will depend on factors that include a bank's size, complexity, and interconnectedness, as measured by a variety of indicator variables.[6] These progressive surcharges are effectively a type of price-based regulation and therefore should have the advantages I just noted.

However, a proponent of size caps might reasonably reply, "Fine, but how do I know that these surcharges are actually enough to change behavior—that is, to exert a meaningful influence on the size distribution of the banking system?" After all, the analogy between a capital requirement and a tax is somewhat imperfect because we don't know exactly the implicit tax rate associated with a given level of capital. Some view capital requirements as quite burdensome, which would mean that even a 2 percent surcharge amounts to a significant tax and, hence, a strong incentive for a bank to shrink, while others have argued that capital requirements impose only modest costs, which would imply little incentive to shrink.[7]

This uncertainty about the ultimate effect of a given capital-surcharge regime on the size distribution of banks could potentially tip the balance back in favor of quantity-based regulation, like size caps. And indeed, if we were faced with a static, once-and-for-all decision, I don't think economic reasoning alone could give us a definitive answer as to whether caps should be preferred to capital surcharges. This ambiguity is in some sense the central message of Weitzman's original analysis.

One way to resolve this tension is to refrain from putting ourselves in the position of having to make a once-and-for-all decision in a setting of substantial uncertainty. Rather, it might be preferable to try to learn from the incoming data and adjust over time, particularly since the recent changes to capital regulation already on the books may represent an informative experiment. In my view, this observation about the potential for learning tips the balance in favor of capital surcharges. For example, the capital-surcharge schedule proposed by the Basel Committee for globally important systemic banks may be a reasonable starting point; however, if after some time it has not delivered much of a change in the size and complexity of the largest of banks, one might conclude that the implicit tax was too small and should be ratcheted up.[8] In principle, this turning-up-the-dials approach feels to me like the right way to go: It retains the flexibility that makes price-based regulation attractive while mitigating the risk that the implicit tax rate will be set too low. Of course, I recognize that its gradualist nature presents practical challenges, not least of which is sustaining a level of regulatory commitment and resolve sufficient to keep the dials turning so long as this is the right thing to do.

Before wrapping up, let me briefly mention another piece of the puzzle that I think is sometimes overlooked but that strikes me as having the potential to play an important complementary role in efforts to address the TBTF problem, namely, corporate governance. Suppose we do everything right with respect to capital regulation and set up a system of capital surcharges that imposes a strong incentive to shrink on those institutions that don't create large synergies. How would the adjustment process actually play out? The first step would be for shareholders, seeing an inadequate return on capital, to sell their shares, driving the bank's stock price down. And the second step would be for management, seeking to restore shareholder value, to respond by selectively shedding assets.

But as decades of research in corporate finance have taught us, we shouldn't take the second step for granted. Numerous studies across a wide range of industries have documented how difficult it is for managers to voluntarily downsize their firms, even when the stock market is sending a clear signal that downsizing would be in the interests of outside shareholders. Often, change of this sort requires the application of some external force, be it from the market for corporate control, an activist investor, or a strong and independent board.[9] As we move forward, we should keep these governance mechanisms in mind and do what we can to ensure that they support the broader regulatory strategy.

Notes

This chapter was originally delivered on April 17, 2013, as remarks at the International Monetary Fund's "Rethinking Macro Policy II" conference. The thoughts that follow are my own. They are not necessarily shared by my colleagues on the Federal Reserve Board. I am grateful to members of the board staff, Michael Gibson, Michael Hsu, Nellie Liang, and Mark Van Der Weide, for their advice.

1. For example, in June 2012, Moody's described its ratings process for JP Morgan Chase as follows: "JP Morgan's ratings benefit from three notches of uplift from the standalone credit assessment at the bank level, and from two notches of uplift at the holding company, reflecting Moody's assumptions about a very high likelihood of support from the US government for bondholders or other creditors in the event such support was required to prevent a default. . . . The negative outlook on the parent holding company reflects Moody's view that government support for US bank holding company creditors is becoming less certain and less predictable, given the evolving attitude of US authorities to the resolution of large

financial institutions, whereas support for creditors of operating entities remains sufficiently likely and predictable to warrant stable outlooks" (Moody's Investors Service 2012, pp. 11–12 of the pdf version). Also see similar statements by Moody's in the same document for Bank of America (pp. 4–5) and Citibank (p. 7).

2. See Fisher (2013), who said: "We recommend that the largest financial holding companies be restructured so that every one of their corporate entities is subject to a speedy bankruptcy process, and in the case of the banking entities themselves, that they be of a size that is 'too small to save.' Addressing institutional size is vital to maintaining a credible threat of failure, thereby providing a convincing case that policy has truly changed" (paragraph 40).

3. See Weitzman (1974). Haldane (2010) also uses Weitzman's framework to talk about price-versus-quantity regulation in the TBTF context. It should be noted that there are various hybrid approaches that are neither pure quantity nor pure price regulation. For example, Tarullo's (2012) discussion of limits on uninsured liabilities is not a rigid size cap, since it does not constrain an institution's absolute size, to the extent that it is able to adjust its funding mix.

4. To be clear, this taxation aspect of capital requirements is not their only appeal, or even their primary one. Even if it were almost costless to impose higher capital requirements on bigger banks—so that doing so provided essentially no disincentive to bank size—it might still be a good idea to do so for purely prudential reasons. In other words, capital requirements serve as both a prudential buffer and a tax, and can be a useful regulatory tool for both reasons.

5. See Hughes and Mester (2011) for a recent contribution to the literature on scale economies in banking.

6. See BCBS (2011) for a description of the methodology.

7. For different estimates of the costs of capital requirements to banks, see Baker and Wurgler (2013), Admati and others (2011), and Hanson, Kashyap, and Stein (2011).

8. Again, it should be emphasized that the underlying problem is not simply an institution's size but rather its systemic footprint—which, in addition to sheer size, is related to its complexity, interconnectedness, and global span of operations.

9. Jensen (1993) is a classic treatment of the issues.

References

Admati, Anat R., Peter M. DeMarzo, Martin F. Hellwig, and Paul Pfleiderer. 2011. "Fallacies, Irrelevant Facts, and Myths in the Discussion of Capital Regulation: Why Bank Equity Is *Not* Expensive." Working paper, Graduate School of Business, Stanford University, Stanford, CA, and the Max Planck Institute for Research on Collective Goods, Bonn. http://gsbapps.stanford.edu/researchpapers/library/RP2065R1&86.pdf.

Baker, Malcolm, and Jeffrey Wurgler. 2013. "Would Stricter Capital Requirements Raise the Cost of Capital? Bank Capital Regulation and the Low Risk Anomaly." Working paper, Harvard Business School, Cambridge, MA, and NYU

Stern School of Business, New York. http://people.stern.nyu.edu/jwurgler/papers/Bank%20Capital%20Regulation.pdf.

Basel Committee on Banking Supervision (BCBS). 2011. "Global Systemically Important Banks: Assessment Methodology and the Additional Loss Absorbency Requirement." Bank for International Settlements, Basel, November. http://www.bis.org/publ/bcbs207.pdf.

Fisher, Richard W. 2013. "Ending 'Too Big to Fail.'" Speech delivered at the Conservative Political Action Conference, National Harbor, MD, March 16. http://www.dallasfed.org/news/speeches/fisher/2013/fs130316.cfm.

Haldane, Andrew G. 2010. "The $100 Billion Question." Speech delivered at the Institute of Regulation & Risk, Hong Kong, March 30. http://www.bis.org/review/r100406d.pdf.

Hanson, Samuel G., Anil K. Kashyap, and Jeremy C. Stein. 2011. "A Macroprudential Approach to Financial Regulation." *Journal of Economic Perspectives* 25 (1): 3–28. http://www.people.hbs.edu/shanson/hanson_kashyap_stein_JEP.pdf.

Hughes, Joseph P., and Loretta J. Mester. 2011. "Who Said Large Banks Don't Experience Scale Economies? Evidence from a Risk-Return-Driven Cost Function." Working Paper 11-27, Federal Reserve Bank of Philadelphia, Philadelphia, PA, July. www.phil.frb.org/research-and-data/publications/working-papers/2011/wp11-27.pdf.

Jensen, Michael C. 1993. "The Modern Industrial Revolution, Exit, and the Failure of Internal Control Systems." *Journal of Finance* 48 (3): 831–880. http://onlinelibrary.wiley.com/doi/10.1111/j.1540-6261.1993.tb04022.x/full.

Moody's Investors Service. 2012. "Moody's Downgrades Firms with Global Capital Markets Operations." Press release, Moody's Investors Service, New York, June 21. www.moodys.com/research/Moodys-downgrades-firms-with-global-capital-markets-operations--PR_248989?WT.mc_id=BankRatings2012.

Powell, Jerome H. 2013. "Ending 'Too Big to Fail.'" Speech delivered at the Institute of International Bankers 2013 Washington Conference, Washington, DC, March 4. http://www.federalreserve.gov/newsevents/speech/powell20130304a.htm.

Tarullo, Daniel K. 2012. "Industry Structure and Systemic Risk Regulation." Speech delivered at the Brookings Institution Conference, "Structuring the Financial Industry to Enhance Economic Growth and Stability." Brookings Institution, Washington, DC, December 4. http://www.federalreserve.gov/newsevents/speech/tarullo20121204a.htm.

Weitzman, Martin L. 1974. "Prices vs. Quantities." *Review of Economic Studies* 41 (October): 477–491. http://scholar.harvard.edu/files/weitzman/files/prices_vs_quantities.pdf.

11

The Contours of Banking and the Future of Its Regulation

Jean Tirole

Aftermaths of banking, sovereign, and other crises often look alike: after years of neglect and quasi-laissez-faire leading to a crisis, policymakers and scholars work assiduously on new schemes that will prevent the next crisis. While this constitutes a useful reaction, the process also reflects political immediacy as much as a long-term perspective. The title of the conference, "Rethinking Macro Policy II: First Steps and Early Lessons," modestly but rightly reminds us of the limits of our knowledge in these areas.

This chapter briefly discusses three kinds of reforms in the making in financial regulation: structural reforms (among which I would include governance and the interaction with shadow banking), solvency and liquidity regulation, and institutional/supervisory reforms.

Before I begin, two preliminary remarks are in order. First, we need to step back a moment and think about why the banking sector is regulated in the first place, regardless of its degree of competition. There are multiple reasons for regulation. The most universal one is to protect depositors, or the deposit insurance fund and the taxpayer, if deposits are explicitly or implicitly covered. The state represents the interests of depositors, who do not have the expertise, the information, or the incentive to monitor the balance sheet and off-balance-sheet activities of their banks. This "representation hypothesis" explains why even tiny banks, without market power and systemically unimportant, are supervised, and why pension funds and insurance companies are subject to similar prudential requirements.[1] It also explains why investment banks, with no retail investors, have so far been left unregulated or lightly regulated.

The representation hypothesis, however, does not account for the recent bailout of the investment banks and of AIG's holding in the United

States or that of Long-Term Capital Management (LTCM) in 1998. Nor does it explain the current emphasis on regulating systemically important financial institutions (SIFIs). Systemic risk is often invoked as an argument for paying close attention to financial institutions, and so the representation and systemic risk rationales are related. When large institutions fail, unpaid liabilities (counterparty risk) and fire sales create externalities on the prudentially regulated sector and may put at risk some retail banks or insurance companies.[2] These externalities are, to be certain, highly endogenous. Were retail banks, for instance, to have limited counterparty exposure to institutions outside the prudentially regulated sector, the ex post case for rescuing institutions in the latter sector would be much weaker. I return to this point later.

The second preliminary remark is that we need to make progress on a general equilibrium view, and not only for the standard macroprudential reasons. Making balance sheets safer is a laudable goal in light of the recent experience, but it cannot be the only consideration. Otherwise, prudential regulation would be a rather simple matter: it would suffice to impose very high capital requirements, demand CoCos—contingent convertible bonds[3]—in large amounts, or require banks to invest only in German bunds. There is a demand for the safe, liquid instruments created by the banks' liability side, as illustrated in the theory of aggregate liquidity, but so far the latter has been poorly connected to prudential regulation analysis. There is also an incidence of banking regulation on the volume of credit to the economy, as well as implications for the incentives of managers and shareholders.

Structural Reforms

The rationale for separating retail from investment banking is to insulate basic banking services—and thereby the trilogy of depositors, the guarantee fund, and taxpayers—from investment banking risks. It is a simple refusal to engage in cross-subsidies and thereby promote value-decreasing marginal investment banking services.

In a sense, structural reform, coming on top of the Basel III prudential regulation, is an admission that society will always lose in the prudential regulation cat-and-mouse game; prudential regulation ought to be capable at the very least of duplicating structural reforms (which often are a special case of prudential regulation without separation but with infinite weights on some assets or activities) and should in theory do better. Thus, either regulators are not trusted to choose and enforce less extreme risk weights, or there is a feeling that outright prohibition has very different effects from high risk weights. Under the latter hypothesis, a specificity of banking is that the mouse moves really fast; indeed, there are few industries in which the balance sheet can be changed substantially within a matter of days. The banking industry, at least in its most "innovative" segments, is highly complex, and asymmetric information with the regulator is paramount. There is latency in conforming to capital and liquidity requirements, which, if very risky instruments are available, may give scope for gambling for resurrection when the bank is underwater.

The various proposals for structural separation have been described and commented on carefully elsewhere.[4] Here I will make just a few remarks on the economics of such rules to point out where our knowledge ought to be improved on.

For the sake of illustration, let's consider the Vickers rule.[5] In essence, it creates a ring-fenced subsidiary (the retail bank) with a limited scope of activities: It can lend only to households and nonfinancial firms and trade high-quality securities. It can hedge the risk on corresponding exposures—the Independent Commission on Banking (ICB)[6] report calls this the "Treasury function." All other activities are not allowed within the ring-fenced bank but can be performed by the rest of the bank (the investment bank). The ring-fenced bank has operational independence and is prohibited from providing support to the investment bank.

As the ICB report emphasizes, ring-fencing is no substitute for capital adequacy and liquidity requirements. Actually, the report calls for higher capital adequacy requirements for ring-fenced banks than now prevail, which amounts to saying that even the ring-fenced bank may not be that safe.

The Vickers rule has a number of desirable properties, one of which is the facilitation of resolution. As in the case of prudential regulation, this argument is some kind of admission that the requirement of a living will (i.e., the provision by a bank of detailed information on how authorities can dismantle the bank and proceed through an orderly resolution) will not function properly or at least needs to be reinforced by structural separation.

Although the aims of structural separation are well grounded, there are nonetheless serious concerns that the rule may not achieve its purposes. Here are a few potential reasons, on which economists should probably do more research:

• The retail bank can build large macro risks on its retail book, such as real estate risk (think of Irish, Spanish, and US banks), or through rather simple financial products offered to retail customers, such as guarantees of minimum returns on investment portfolios (as granted by some European banks). Indeed, a number of recent failures had to do with institutions then abiding by the separation requirements, primarily-retail banks and large investment banks.

• The ICB report recognizes that such risks exist and, accordingly, allows the retail bank to hedge. Hedging is a well-known double-edged sword. If not carefully monitored, it can enable institutions to (voluntarily or involuntarily) increase risk. Here I recall that JP Morgan's trader "London Whale" was actually using very risky credit default swaps as part of the hedging function.

• It must not be the case that authorities feel compelled to rescue the investment bank. There might be two reasons for such a rescue. One is reputation risk for the retail bank, although this argument cuts both ways (i.e., the investment bank might feel compelled to rescue the retail bank). Another is more standard: In 2008 the US government bailed out all investment banks (except Lehman Brothers), as well as AIG, because it was concerned about systemic risk.[7] Direct and indirect exposures of retail regulated entities to failing entities, as well as the possibility of fire sales, probably contributed to this very unfortunate outcome.[8]

Relationship to Shadow Banking

The level playing field in the shadow banking sector (the unregulated sector that performs maturity transformation and, because of the absence of retail liabilities, has no access to public sector enhancements such as central bank liquidity and deposit insurance) has been destroyed in two opposite ways. First, in the case of integrated banks, retail deposit activities and public sector enhancements may unduly cross-subsidize investment banking activities; this is a key rationale for introducing structural separation. Second, non-integrated investment banks and other shadow banking players can avail themselves of massive access to taxpayer money, as we saw in 2008.[9]

As of today, the exact tightening of rules for shadow banking is still uncertain (Adrian and Ashcraft 2012). Particularly prominent in the last few years have been the proposals for regulating SIFIs. While I agree with the premises and purpose of this reform, I have reservations. First, in an environment characterized by complex products and balance sheets and fragmented information, it is rather hard to identify systemically important actors.[10] Would AIG have been deemed systemically important? LTCM? Second, there are currently too few regulators to oversee retail institutions; carefully overseeing investment banks, hedge funds and other potential SIFIs would require a substantial expansion in regulatory resources. Besides, activities keep migrating; tomorrow new entities (such as energy companies, which already are active in financial markets) might expand their financial involvement in response to a tight regulation of investment banks and hedge funds. This migration issue compounds the difficulty of achieving widespread financial regulation with scarce resources.

While the jury on this issue is clearly out, my own, nonmainstream view is that rather than attempting ubiquitous regulation, it might be preferable to insulate prudentially regulated entities (retail banks, insurance companies, pension funds) from counterparty risk with unregulated financial entities. That would contribute to bringing to a halt the soft budget constraint enjoyed by a number of unregulated entities, which secure cheap refinancing thanks to the expectation that they will be rescued by public money if push comes to shove. A faster migration toward the use of centralized exchanges (which need to be prudentially regulated) and further disincentives for prudentially regulated entities to use over-the-counter (OTC) markets would be desirable in this respect.

The Vickers rule is a step toward this insulation strategy: the retail bank will have limited exposure to its own investment bank. The extension of the rule to the insulation from the impact of failures of non-affiliated entities remains a question mark, as exposures may reside in the Treasury function through OTC transactions; to be sure, the rule's proponents seem sympathetic to the use of central counterparty clearing houses (CCPs) in the CCP/OTC debate.[11]

Asset Income Runs

Structural separation is an instance of asset income run; that is, the compartmentalization of the balance sheet through the earmarking of specific assets to specific lenders. While structural separation is demanded by authorities and is meant to protect retail depositors and taxpayers against certain types of risks on the asset side, asset income runs are usually carried out by private lenders. To this extent, earmarking has always existed: repos (whose use increased tremendously when legal uncertainty concerning the effectiveness of the earmarking guarantee was lifted) and covered bonds are cases in point. And in rough times, asset income runs in various guises (shortening of maturity structure, higher collateral demands) increase. This is particularly the case today.

Earmarking specific assets to specific liabilities has two benefits (and, to pursue the analogy, both benefits are mentioned by structural separation proponents to make their case). First, it facilitates resolution. Relatedly, lenders need to ascertain only the value of the specific asset that is matched with their liability and not the quality of the entire balance sheet, a possibly daunting task for the lender; by contrast, asserting the value of a single asset (say, of a government security) may be a no-brainer. Alternatively, the lenders may bring their specialized knowledge to assess the value of the collateral; they thereby certify a piece of the balance sheet.

Earmarking also has costs. First, it is known that there may be less adverse selection or less moral hazard on a bundle than on individual assets.[12] Second, and currently very much to the point, it creates more scope for a rat race, in which each lender tries to obtain priority over other lenders.[13] Indeed, one of the current concerns is that the Deposit Insurance Fund would face an empty shell when trying to collect, after all good assets have been collateralized with private lenders; put differently, such asset income runs make bail-ins infeasible. One would therefore expect in the near future more prudential moves toward limiting asset income runs; a case in point is the recent Australian decision to limit to 8 percent the fraction of assets that can be used to create covered bonds.

Prudential Regulation Reforms

This is no place to review the very extensive discussions and alterations concerning various aspects of regulatory reform: capital adequacy, countercyclical buffers, treatment of derivatives, and so on. Similarly, I cannot cover the many questions remaining today, including the future of internal models or the homogenization and coordination of resolution processes. I will content myself with a few light remarks concerning an innovation of the current reforms: the introduction of liquidity requirements into the Basel process, with two ratios in the making—the liquidity coverage ratio (LCR) and the net stable funding ratio (NSFR). Reflections on the former are more advanced; the LCR will become operative in 2019 (with a light version for 2015).

The LCR will be based on stress tests: banks must claim access to a sufficient buffer of high-quality liquid assets to be able to face outflows during a month. The NSFR will relate longer-term funding to longer-term liquidity.

The academic contributions on liquidity have helped clarify the need for a liquidity requirement on top of a solvency one. They have emphasized three main rationales: agency, microeconomic externalities, and macroprudential concerns. The agency rationale has a standard prudential flavor and relates to the need for constraining a specific form of risk taking: engaging in an excessively unbalanced maturity transformation by not hedging against short-term shocks, market collapse, or increases in interest rates. The externalities rationale is to prevent propagation to other financial institutions through counterparty risk or fire sales. The third rationale also takes up on the first one and emphasizes the strategic complementarities in balance sheet mismatches. Authorities (first monetary, then fiscal) are more tempted to bail out the financial sector if more of its members have engaged in dangerous levels of maturity transformation; the classic example of a collective bailout is the massive transfer of wealth from savers to borrowers during times of low interest rates.[14]

Where, in my view, academic research falls behind is in providing guidance on technical but important issues in liquidity regulation. Should liquid assets receive risk weights in liquidity ratios as general assets do in capital ratios? (It would seem so.) Should central-bank-eligible assets, which are liquid by definition, be counted as liquid assets, given that the choice of what counts as liquidity in the computation of the liquidity ratio and central banks' choice of acceptable collateral are two (imperfectly substitutable) public sector interventions in the provision of aggregate liquidity? Could the focus on a certain horizon give rise to detrimental cliff effects and gaming strategies (e.g., automatic rollover/substitution of liabilities with maturity just above the horizon)? To what extent should the buffer be usable? How do we incorporate general equilibrium considerations and country specificities? For example, countries differ in their stock of government debt and in the amount of retail deposits, which will be deemed largely more stable than wholesale deposits under the LCR regulation. Also, the implications of bank distress differ across countries according to the indebtedness of the country itself or the autonomy of the monetary policy. Should asset quality be assessed through ratings, as is currently proposed, despite the Dodd-Frank Act hostility to ratings? This list is far from exhaustive.

This discussion points to a blatant need for academic research in the area. Over the past 20 years economists have made much progress in conceptualizing liquidity, but they have not yet reached the point at which their theories can be operationalized for prudential purposes. At best, the new knowledge suggests educated guesses, but this is insufficient.

Strengthening Regulatory Institutions: Europe's Banking Union

Regulation is pretty hopeless without good supervision. I will therefore conclude with a few words on a specific institutional matter, Europe's nascent banking union. My hunch here is that Europe in this area is definitely moving in the right direction, and yet the new institutions are not only incomplete with respect to resolution and deposit insurance but also are unlikely to function well as currently designed.

There are three rationales for abandoning domestic regulation. The first is expertise. In the cat-and-mouse game discussed earlier, it is rather unlikely that there will be adequate expertise in the 27 national supervisors; pooling resources may enable regulators to have access to more expertise. Second, there are strong cross-border externalities of a bank failure in Europe, including the impact on foreign counterparties and borrowers, the effect on the foreign deposit insurance scheme (for subsidiaries, although not for branches), ring-fencing, and appropriation of liquidity. Third, bank failures may increase government debt and later force Europe to rescue the country itself. The Maastricht Treaty did not integrate the fact that private bank debt can become public debt.

Despite the recent move to create a supranational supervisor located at the European Central Bank (ECB), there are still strong concerns that national interests remain powerful under the new system. In my view, there is a need to provide the key national supervisors in each country with a European mission and status. Otherwise, there is a real danger that information will be withheld from the ECB precisely when such information should be acted on to trigger early intervention or resolution. Such a European status would also make the board less captured by national interests. We have observed how decision-making bodies composed primarily of national representatives can be quite ineffective at taking difficult decisions; a case in point is the Economic and Financial Affairs Council (Ecofin) in the run-up to the European crisis.

Europe's banking union is still by and large missing a resolution authority. The Competition Directorate currently substitutes for such an authority but only for some aspects; it makes bailouts more difficult and tries to prevent the distressed banks' use of government funds to gamble for resurrection. But it does not have any money to create bad banks or facilitate purchase and assumption. In the future, we will need the treatment of individual failures to be financed by a deposit insurance fund collecting fees from insured institutions. Systemic failures will require a strengthening of the European Stability Mechanism's firing power.

The creation of a European deposit insurance scheme should be made feasible by credible, European-oriented supervision. At this stage, though, losses on underwater legacy assets could imply substantial cross-subsidies among countries under a mutualized deposit insurance scheme. Putting these assets into bad banks that become the property of countries is fair, and starting again with a clean slate can make common deposit insurance happen. To be certain, these bad assets will worsen the countries' financial situation. But in a restructuring situation, there is no distinction to be made between public debt due to profligacy and public debt due to negligence in prudential supervision.

Notes

I am grateful to the conference participants and discussants, and to Joshua Felman for helpful responses to the ideas developed in this chapter.
1. See Dewatripont and Tirole (1994) for a more detailed argument on the representation hypothesis.

2. Another common source of systemic risk created by bank failures is the creation of sovereign risk through bailouts and recessions, as dramatically illustrated by the recent examples of Spain, Ireland, and Cyprus.

3. CoCos, or contingent convertible bonds, are bonds that are converted into equity contingent on the occurrence of a specified event, such as an insufficient capital adequacy ratio.

4. See, for example, Vickers (2012).

5. As John Vickers noted during the conference, the US Volcker rule has some drawbacks, which led Europeans (most notably the U.K. Independent Banking Commission, chaired by John Vickers, and the Liikanen Commission, at the European level) to look for different approaches to insulating retail banking from investment banking (Liikanen 2012). In a nutshell, the Volcker rule rules out proprietary trading, the ownership of private equity and hedge funds, and activities leading to a conflict of interest. At the same time, it allows hedging, the proprietary trading of US government securities, underwriting, and market-making. (Note that market-makers' inventory risk is in essence proprietary trading and that underwriting is the sale of a put option.)

6. See ICB (2011).

7. The AIG insurance company was relatively healthy, as well as ring-fenced relative to the investment bank. Thus, we are discussing the bailout of an investment bank rather than of a prudentially regulated entity.

8. This is not an exhaustive list. For example, one might think of rescues of shadow banks that lend to politically sensitive entities.

9. Traditional banking activities are more and more performed by a variety of players, such as hedge funds or special purpose vehicles (SPVs). For instance, hedge funds lend to mid-caps.

10. Each regulator knows only about his or her own jurisdiction. Domestic turf issues, national interests, and mere overload impose limits on the sharing of information among regulators.

11. Links can also occur through fire sales and wholesale funding (although there will be restrictions on the latter), and not just derivative transactions. This insulation from the nonretail sector would not be complete, although it would be seriously reduced.

12. See, for example, Diamond (1984) and Farhi and Tirole (2013).

13. See, for example, Bizer and DeMarzo (1992) and Brunnermeier and Oehmke (2013).

14. See Farhi and Tirole (2012). The transfer and concomitant diversion of savings to other uses is not the only cost. Low short-term rates encourage future maturity mismatches and therefore a continued fragility of the financial sector. Furthermore, institutions that have committed to certain returns for their customers are highly incentivized to gamble for resurrection (in the parlance of finance, to reach for yield).

References

Adrian, T., and A. B. Ashcraft. 2012. "Shadow Banking: A Review of the Literature." Federal Reserve Bank of New York Staff Report 580, Federal Reserve Bank of New York, New York, October. http://www.newyorkfed.org/research/staff_reports/sr580.pdf.

Bizer, D. S., and P. M. DeMarzo. 1992. "Sequential Banking." *Journal of Political Economy* 100:41, 61.

Brunnermeier, M., and M. Oehmke. 2013. "The Maturity Rat Race." *Journal of Finance* 68 (2): 483–521.

Dewatripont, Mathias, and Jean Tirole. 1994. *The Prudential Regulation of Banks.* Cambridge, MA: MIT Press.

Diamond, D. 1984. "Financial Intermediation and Delegated Monitoring." *Review of Economic Studies* 51:393–414.

Farhi, E., and J. Tirole. 2012. "Collective Moral Hazard, Maturity Mismatch and Systemic Bailouts." *American Economic Review* 102:60–93.

Farhi, E., and J. Tirole. 2013. "Liquid Bundles." Faculty paper, Department of Economics, Harvard University, Cambridge, MA, and Toulouse School of Economics, Toulouse, France. http://files.conferencemanager.dk/medialibrary/51432ddb-bbe3-4327-85f4-be3493077470/images/liquid_bundles_07_08_13.pdf.

Independent Commission on Banking (ICB). 2011. "Final Report: Recommendations." European Corporate Governance Institute, London, September. http://www.ecgi.org/documents/icb_final_report_12sep2011.pdf.

Liikanen, E., and the High-Level Expert Group on Reforming the Structure of the EU Banking Sector. 2012. "Final Report of the High-Level Expert Group on Reforming the Structure of the EU Banking Sector." European Commission, Brussels, October 2. http://ec.europa.eu/internal_market/bank/docs/high-level_expert_group/report_en.pdf.

Vickers, J. 2012. "Some Economics of Banking Reforms." Discussion Paper 632, Department of Economics, Oxford University, Oxford.

12

Banking Reform in Britain and Europe

John Vickers

To start, we need concrete progress with the too-important-to-fail conundrum. We need a global level discussion of the pros and cons of direct restrictions on business models.

—Christine Lagarde, Toronto, October 25, 2012

An international discussion on the structure of banking has taken a long time to get going. In the United States, the structural debate since the global economic crisis of 2008–2009 has focused on how to implement the Volcker rule, which prohibits banks from engaging in proprietary trading that is not customer-related. In the United Kingdom, the discussion has concentrated on ring-fencing—the separation within banking groups of retail and investment banking. France and Germany are developing the mild hybrid of ring-fencing some proprietary trading. The first international consideration of structural reform was the Liikanen (2012) report for the European Union, which, like the UK approach, recommended separation, within bank holding companies, between deposit banking and trading.

How are these structural reform initiatives related? What do they seek to achieve? This chapter considers these questions, but first it puts structural reform in the context of banking reform more generally.

Structural Reform in Context

The case for structural reform of banks is not that it solves the too-important-to-fail conundrum by itself. Rather, it is that structural reform is an element in the optimal policy package, at the heart of which must also be a much greater capacity by banks to absorb losses.

A pure structuralist argument might run as follows: (1) retail banking is low risk and essential, (2) investment banking is risky and inessential, and (3) separating the two confines the public safety net to the low-risk and essential activities, leaving market forces to discipline risk taking in investment banking.

If only things were so simple! In reality, unless defined so narrowly as to exclude all lending, retail banking, contrary to the first proposition, is risky. Lending involves credit risk, much of which is linked to property values, which can go down as well as up. And as to the second proposition, even if investment banking is separated fully from retail banking, the occurrence of investment banking risks can, through various channels, jeopardize essential banking services.

Banking reform—both for retail and for investment banking—must therefore have greater loss absorbency at its core. The crisis exposed a double problem with banks' loss absorbency. First, banks had nowhere near enough equity capital—so far too much leverage—for the risks they were running. Second, after the thin equity layer had gone, bondholders bore remarkably little loss. They would bear losses in a bankruptcy, but to preserve continuity of essential services, governments staved off bankruptcy by providing taxpayer support. So bondholders generally came out whole, with the public purse bearing losses that the bondholders should have taken. Moreover, where depositor preference is absent, in a bankruptcy, bondholders would have legal rights to be treated on par with ordinary depositors.

Under the Basel III agreement, which is to be implemented by 2019, banks will need to maintain equity capital of at least 7 percent of risk-weighted assets, or up to 9.5 percent for banks of global systemic importance. But risk weights, which were such a failure in the run-up to the crisis, are typically well below unity, so these ratios allow bank balance sheets still to be a large multiple of equity capital. A backstop limiting leverage to 33 times capital is proposed to address this issue.[1]

In a commonsense view, 33 is a lot of leverage, and way above corporate norms in the rest of the economy. Remember too that this is for the *post*-reform world. It is true that many banks were much more leveraged pre-crisis, so the Basel III capital reforms, which also address issues about risk weights, represent a fundamental shift from where things were. But given the scale of the crisis their intended destination is hardly ambitious, and might not be reached if implementation falls short. It is seriously open to question whether it is wise to operate market economies with banking systems as lowly capitalized as the Basel reforms will still allow.[2]

A partial remedy to this problem might come from bail-in debt. This is debt that is required to be converted to equity, or be wiped out, once low capital triggers are breached. Thus the regulator "bails in" bondholders rather than, as tended to happen in the crisis, taxpayers bailing them out. But for this to be credible, the debt subject to regulatory bail-in needs to be unsecured, to have significant time (e.g., at least a year) to maturity so as not to be prone to run risk, and to be junior to other debt, particularly retail deposits. And for bail-in debt to make a major contribution to loss absorbency, banks need to have enough of it in addition to equity (or else far more equity than the Basel minima). The international debate has so far been silent on how much bail-in debt to require, which is currently an important missing piece of international policy on loss absorbency.

Against this background, what can structural policy—forms of separation between retail and investment banking—add? There are three potential contributions. First, structural reform can help contain, but cannot wholly prevent, kinds of within-bank contagion from investment banking shocks to vital retail services, the continuous provision of which is an economic and social imperative. An external shock, such as that in 2008 from US subprime mortgages and related derivatives, directly jeopardized ordinary domestic High Street banking in universal banks lacking internal structure (e.g., RBS). Separation provides an internal firebreak, together with independent loss absorbency for retail banking. Separation also creates the possibility of different loss-absorbency requirements for retail and for investment banking.

Second, separation helps crisis management and resolution. Unlike in 2008–2009, it would allow policymakers to pursue different policies for retail and investment banking rather than an indiscriminate policy for the entirety. Thus, separation helps resolvability, which is universally acknowledged to be an essential ingredient of banking reform. Indeed, it is hard to see how resolution plans for large and complex institutions can be credible without ex ante separation measures.[3] For related reasons, separation can assist bank supervision in normal times.

Third, by curtailing the implicit taxpayer guarantee, separation together with higher loss-absorbency requirements improves ex ante disciplines on risk taking. In particular, if investment banking can no longer be funded by (government-insured) retail deposits, it will face more risk-reflective funding costs, just as it should, and government funding costs will benefit correspondingly. Depending on the design of separation, this in turn should promote lending to the real economy being funded by, among other things, deposits, including insured retail deposits.

Structural Reform Options

In broad terms the structural reform of banks involves two issues. One is where to draw the line (or multiples lines) between different kinds of banking activity. The other is how strong the separation should be.

United States

The United States provides a useful benchmark for comparing current reform efforts in Britain and Europe. From 1933 through the 1990s, US law had the Glass-Steagall *prohibition* of affiliation between deposit-taking banks and companies "engaged principally" in securities business. This provided for total separation between retail/commercial banking and investment banking. Over time, regulatory permissiveness and market developments led to the effective erosion of the prohibition, ahead of its repeal in 1999. Since then, affiliation has been allowed, but a substantial body of law provides for regulation of how deposit-taking banks may and may not deal with their investment banking affiliates, notably section 23A of the Federal Reserve Act and its implementing Regulation W. These regulations were not always applied strictly in the past, and the Dodd-Frank Act of 2010 makes provision for them to be tightened.

Thus, the repeal of the Glass-Steagall prohibition was not a move from separation to unstructured universal banking. On the contrary, it was a move to universal banking with structural regulation.

The Volcker rule, which is also and famously part of the Dodd-Frank legislation, is an *addition* to that kind of structural regulation. Like the Glass-Steagall legislation of old, it is a prohibition. Its aim is to prevent institutions that do banking from engaging in speculative proprietary trading—that is, trading that is not customer-related. The rule likewise prohibits substantial bank ownership of hedge funds and private equity. Its purpose is not to prohibit banking groups from doing customer-related proprietary trading such as market-making, which is among the exemptions from the rule. It has, however, proved difficult to distinguish in practice between kinds of proprietary trading, and implementation of the rule is behind schedule.[4]

Britain

Britain had a bad banking crisis, and is suffering severe economic and fiscal consequences, in part because of the size of its banks in relation to the economy—roughly five times its annual GDP. In response, the UK is enacting a far-reaching reform program, following the report of the Independent Commission on Banking (ICB 2011).[5]

The ICB was asked to make recommendations on structural measures—"including the complex issue of separating retail and investment banking functions"—and "related non-structural measures" to promote financial stability and competition. Competition was another casualty of the crisis but is not considered further here beyond noting that the too-important-to-fail conundrum, if unsolved, is a problem for competition as well as for financial stability and the public finances.

As to the related nonstructural measures, the ICB focused on loss absorbency and recommended higher-than-Basel capital requirements for the major retail banks, accordingly tighter leverage caps, quantified requirements for primary loss-absorbing capacity (e.g., long-term unsecured debt subject to bail-in powers) on top of the equity requirement, and depositor preference for insured deposits.

On structural reform, the ICB considered a range of options and recommended ring-fencing, requiring that retail banking be conducted in an entity separate from investment banking, with self-standing equity and other loss-absorbing capacity, and appropriately independent governance. The retail entity could be part of a wider banking group but with tight restrictions on its dealings with, and exposures to, the rest of the group.

On where to draw the line between retail and investment banking, the ICB approach was to identify (1) core retail activities, the continuous provision of which is essential, which can be carried out only in a ring-fenced entity, and (2) prohibited activities, which cannot be carried out in the ring-fenced entity (but are permitted in the rest of the group). Deposits and overdrafts to individuals and small businesses are core activities. Prohibited activities include trading (not just proprietary trading in the

Volcker sense), underwriting, derivatives (other than hedging retail risks), lending to other kinds of financial institution, and much overseas business outside the European Economic Area. A wide swath of commercial banking—for example, mortgage lending and lending to larger nonfinancial corporates—is neither core nor prohibited in these terms. In the ICB approach, banks and their customers are free to decide whether or not to conduct such business from the retail entity. In that sense, the fence is flexible. But it is strong with respect to independence between the ring-fenced entity and the rest of a banking group to which it may belong.

The ICB considered but did not recommend total separation between retail and investment banking. That would entail considerably higher costs, and for an uncertain financial stability gain. There are circumstances in which total separation would protect retail banking from external shocks more surely than would ring-fencing. But equally there are situations in which total separation would be detrimental to financial stability. It would create a stand-alone intercorrelated domestic banking sector without recourse to support from elsewhere in banking groups in the event of a domestic crisis, such as a property crash. Such crises are perfectly possible, and might well be more acute if diversification has been lost.

Neither did the ICB favor the Volcker rule as an alternative to ring-fencing. It would have applied to a very small proportion of UK bank balance sheets and by itself would have gone nowhere near far enough, in the ICB's analysis, to shield retail banking and the public finances from investment banking risks. Yet it would have been complex to implement.

The UK government has accepted the ICB recommendations, including those pertaining to competition, in very large part,[6] and a banking reform act has been passed by Parliament.[7] The draft legislation has been scrutinized by the Parliamentary Commission on Banking Standards, which was established in the summer of 2012 following the London interbank offered rate (LIBOR) scandal. Among other things, that commission has proposed strengthening ring-fencing and its durability by way of "electrification"—reserve powers for regulators, subject to a framework of accountability, fully to separate individual institutions, and even the sector as a whole, in the event that ring-fencing were being undermined. The Parliamentary Commission has also examined the case for *adding* a form of the Volcker rule to ring-fencing but concluded against legislating for that now, partly in the light of claims by the British banks that they do not engage in such proprietary trading anyway.

The casual observer might think that UK reform, with ring-fencing, is on a different track from reform in the United States, which is adopting the Volcker rule. But this is to overlook the fact that the United States already has, and is strengthening, a framework of separation between deposit banks and their investment banking affiliates within bank holding companies. Thus, the truer picture is one of UK-US *convergence*—on structured universal banking. The United States moved from separation to structured universal banking as the Glass-Steagall prohibition eroded and was finally repealed. It is adding a Volcker rule to that model. The UK is legislating for structured universal banking against a background of a lack of structure. (For the UK there would be little gain but some cost in adding a Volcker rule as well.) Thus, the UK and the United States have come from different directions to a broadly similar place.

Europe

The EU is moving forward with a variety of financial sector reforms, notably in directives on capital requirements to implement Basel III and on bank recovery and resolution.[8] The question of EU-wide structural reform was opened up in 2012 by the creation by Commissioner Barnier of the high-level expert group chaired by Erkki Liikanen, governor of the Bank of Finland.

The recommendations in the Liikanen (2012) report have much in common with the UK reforms outlined above, even though the group's remit was pan-EU. It recommended that for banks above certain size thresholds, trading should be separated from deposit banking, but the two kinds of activity can coexist within bank holding companies. In addition, there should be powers to require further separation if judged necessary for resolvability. It also made a number of recommendations on loss absorbency, for example in relation to bail-in debt and risk weights.

Especially in light of the wider geographic scope of the Liikanen review, it has a remarkable amount in common with the UK reforms. Both envisage a move to structured rather than unstructured universal banking. (Separating trading from deposit banking is essentially the same as ring-fencing retail/commercial banking, just as building a fence to separate lions from deer is the same as building one around a deer park to keep out the lions.[9]) Neither favors adding a Volcker rule, still less adopting that instead of ring-fencing. And like the ICB, the Liikanen report stresses loss absorbency and its interrelation with structural reform.

There are differences, some of which reflect the different geographic scope. Thus, for example, a common European approach to trading-book risk weights makes sense, whereas a single-country approach could have detrimental consequences for geographic arbitrage. A more surprising difference concerns securities underwriting, which the Liikanen report would allow with deposit banking. Besides the historical observation that this is the opposite of the provisions of the Glass-Steagall Act, economic logic suggests that securities underwriting belongs with trading, as it involves writing large put options. Corporate customers could still obtain a comprehensive array of banking services, including underwriting, from a single bank, but with the risk lying outside the deposit bank entity.

Whereas the Liikanen and UK approaches are largely in harmony, legislation before the French and German parliaments takes a minimalist approach to structural reform. In essence, it requires that major banks conduct speculative proprietary trading in a separate subsidiary. Very little of the balance sheet of the affected banks—perhaps 1 percent or so—seems likely to be affected, yet if the US experience with the Volcker rule is a guide, the definitional and implementation difficulties are likely to be considerable. Still, these are steps in the direction of structural reform. It remains to be seen whether the farther-reaching reforms recommended in the Liikanen report will be adopted across Europe. The report is currently being considered by the European Commission in Brussels.

Its importance is heightened by the wider question of a banking union for the euro area, which is widely seen as crucial for future euro area macroeconomic performance. Whether or not a banking union—of a form that entails a degree of mutualization of the contingent liabilities of euro area banks by common deposit insurance or otherwise—is a good idea depends very much on the future resilience of the banks in question. A banking union has large potential advantages if they are well capitalized and sensibly structured, but could be a mistaken enterprise if not. Indeed, a union among unstructured and thinly capitalized banks could make the too-important-to-fail conundrum worse, and put more euro area taxpayers more on the hook for more banking risks.

Conclusion

The financial crisis began more than five years ago. The prolonged macroeconomic and fiscal costs of financial crises are manifest to all. Yet the progress of banking reform has been mixed, and much unfinished business remains. With regard to loss absorbency there are concerns that the Basel III capital requirements are unambitious and liable to be watered down in application. On the other hand, there are voices, including some in the United States, calling for substantial stiffening beyond Basel III. There has been surprisingly little public discussion, outside the UK and Switzerland, of the complementary issue of how much bail-in debt major banks should be required to have.

An international debate on structural reform nearly didn't happen at all but is now under way. Structural reform initiatives in the United States (the Volcker rule) and the UK (ring-fencing) might appear to contrast, but the deeper truth is that both are converging, though coming from different directions historically, on structured universal banking. The EU's adoption of the Liikanen report's recommendations would further promote international convergence, as well as being wise for Europe, especially with a banking union on the horizon. More resilient banks—with greater loss absorbency, safer structures, and lower contingent taxpayer dependence—are, moreover, a global public good.

Notes

I am grateful to my former colleagues at the UK's Independent Commission on Banking for many helpful discussions on the topics in this chapter, which provided background to my remarks at the IMF's "Rethinking Macro Policy II" conference in Washington, D.C., on April 16–17, 2013. A fuller discussion of the economic issues presented in the chapter is in Vickers (2012).

1. The definition of capital for this leverage cap is wider than equity capital, so this allows closer to 40 times leverage in relation to equity capital.

2. An economic case for very much higher capital requirements than Basel III is made by Admati and Hellwig (2013).

3. This is so whether the resolution strategy involves a "single point of entry" (i.e., typically into the parent company by the home regulator) or "multiple points of entry" (e.g., by several regulators on a geographic or functional basis).

4. Duffie (2012) provides a critical analysis of the issues.

5. I chaired the commission, which worked from June 2010 to September 2011. The other members were Clare Spottiswoode, Martin Taylor, Bill Winters, and Martin Wolf.

6. See HM Treasury (2012, 2013).

7. The Financial Services (Banking Reform) Act was passed in December 2013.

8. In Europe beyond the EU, reform in Switzerland is noteworthy. Like the UK, Switzerland has (two) very large banks in relation to GDP, and established a commission on banking reform. The Swiss Commission recommended much higher capital requirements than that for the Basel III baseline.

9. A metaphor by Martin Taylor.

References

Admati, A., and M. Hellwig. 2013. *The Bankers' New Clothes*. Princeton, NJ: Princeton University Press.

Duffie, D. 2012. "Market Making under the Proposed Volcker Rule." Faculty paper, Rock Center for Corporate Governance and Graduate School of Business, Stanford University, Palo Alto, CA. http://www.gsb.stanford.edu/news/packages/PDF/Volcker_duffie_011712.pdf.

HM Treasury. 2012. *Sound Banking: Delivering Reform*. Cm 8453. London: HMSO, October.

HM Treasury. 2013. *Banking Reform: A New Structure for Stability and Growth*. Cm 8545. London: HMSO, February.

Independent Commission on Banking (ICB). 2011. "Final Report: Recommendations." European Corporate Governance Institute, London, September. http://www.ecgi.org/documents/icb_final_report_12sep2011.pdf.

Liikanen, E., and the High-Level Expert Group on Reforming the Structure of the EU Banking Sector. 2012. "Final Report of the High-Level Expert Group on Reforming the Structure of the EU Banking Sector." European Commission, Brussels, October 2. http://ec.europa.eu/internal_market/bank/docs/high-level_expert_group/report_en.pdf.

Vickers, J. 2012. "Some Economics of Banking Reform." *Rivista di Politica Economica* 4:11–35.

13

Leverage, Financial Stability, and Deflation

Adair Turner

In 2009, Queen Elizabeth visited the Economics Department of the London School of Economics, discussed the financial crisis, and asked a simple question: "Why did no one see it coming?" It was a good question, but one that could now be expanded, because there were two failures.

First, there was a failure to foresee the crisis coming at all—a failure in, say, 2005 or 2006 or 2007 to understand that we were heading toward a major financial crash. There were some notable exceptions. To different degrees, Nouriel Roubini, Raghu Rajan, and Bill White issued some warnings. But on the whole, the world's central banks and regulators, finance ministries, and the IMF not only did not warn of impending disaster but in general propagated a thesis that financial innovation and increasing financial intensity had made crises less likely.

And then a second failure occurred in spring 2009, once the severe crisis of 2008 was behind us: a failure to foresee how difficult and slow the recovery would be. No official forecast anticipated anything like the scale and length of the subsequent recession, and almost no one anticipated the scale of the policy stimulus we would deploy in an attempt to offset recessionary forces. There were, to my knowledge, no official sector or market forecasts that policy rates, having fallen to the zero lower bound, would stay there for four years (so far) and probably for several years more.

How did this double failure occur? There were many specific reasons. In particular, the flawed structure of the euro area played a key role in explaining why the initial crash produced a subsequent major aftershock. But in this chapter I present the argument—not original but I think so fundamental that it is worth stressing—that central to our poor foresight was a sustained failure over several decades to appreciate and focus on the central importance to both financial stability and macroeconomic stability of the scale of debt contracts—the level of leverage both within the financial sector and within the real economy, and in the private sector quite as much as the public sector.

I also argue that once we do focus on the fundamental importance of debt and leverage, we may need to consider more radical policies, both macroprudential and monetary, than we have done so far.

Mervyn King pointed out in a lecture last autumn that the dominant new Keynesian model of monetary economics "lacks an account of financial intermediation, so that money, credit and banks play no meaningful role" (King 2012).

In retrospect, that was a very odd omission. After all, since monetary policy works through an interest rate, it must presumably work through the financial intermediation system, debt contracts, and banks. But it was not only an odd omission, it was also very dangerous, because debt contracts have very specific features that have major implications for financial stability and macroeconomic stability.

Those features were obvious to and a major focus for several mid-twentieth-century economists writing amid the wreckage of the 1929–1933 financial crash and the subsequent Great Depression, writers such as Irving Fisher and Henry Simons (Fisher 1933, 1936; Simons 1936). And if one reads those economists again, what is striking is the central role they ascribe to debt creation and debt destruction in the origins and development of the Great Depression, and how radical the policy prescriptions were that they proposed in response.

Henry Simons is typically thought of as a foundational figure of Chicago school economics and laissez-faire policy prescriptions. But he argued that "private initiative has been allowed too much freedom in determining the character of our financial system and in directing changes in the quantity of money and money substitutes." He wanted not only to make fractional reserve banking illegal but to severely restrain the role that even nonbank debt contracts, as opposed to equity contracts, could play in the economy.

Simons and Fisher believed that the more debt contracts there were in the economy, the more fragile it would become and the more vulnerable to harmful financial cycles of the sort that Claudio Borio describes in chapter 6 of this volume. There are at least five interlocking reasons why that could be so—why debt contracts are different from equity.

First is the phenomenon Gennaioli, Shleifer, and Vishny (2010) have labeled "local thinking": the tendency to ignore in the good times the downside tail of the distribution of possible debt returns. When we hold an equity contract, the observed movement of equity prices reminds us each day that returns can go up or down, that we hold a risky investment. But if we hold debt contracts, in the good times we observe only the non-default, full-payout result. There is therefore a danger that investors will come to believe that inherently risky debt contracts are risk-free investments, and therefore a danger that the aggregate value of apparently low-risk debt instruments created will exceed the value that could actually be risk-free, given the underlying real economic risks facing companies and households. As a result, as Gennaioli, Shleifer, and Vishny (2010) put it, a free financial system can manufacture large volumes of debt securities "that owe their very existence to neglected risk."

A second reason is the rigidities and fragilities created by default and bankruptcy processes. As Ben Bernanke noted, "In a complete markets world, bankruptcy would never be observed." Instead, we would see smooth, nonjumpy, continual redefinition of debt terms—steadily converting to equity—as creditworthiness declined (Bernanke 2004). And as Charles Goodhart and Demetrius Tsomocos explored in the 2011 Mayekawa Lecture, one of the main deficiencies of modern macroeconomic theory, with its representative agent fiction, is the absence of the possibility of default—of companies, households, or banks themselves (Goodhart and Tsomocos 2011). But in the real world, we do see defaults, and as both Bernanke and Irving Fisher described, their operation can play a major role in the propagation of recessions and depressions.

Third, debt is quite different from equity because it has to be continually rolled over. One could imagine a working market economy in which the new equity issue market closed entirely for, say, five years. There would obviously be disadvantages, but such closure would not in itself tip the economy into a recession because the preexisting equity investments would still exist—they are not continually repaid. But debt contracts continually mature, so that macroeconomic stability depends crucially on the smooth continuity of new credit supply, a vulnerability that made Simons so wary of short-term debt contracts that he hankered after an economy in which only long-term debt contracts (he suggested 50 years or more) would be allowed.

Fourth, a key focus of Simons and Fisher is the fact that banks do not just, as too many economics textbooks wrongly imply, intermediate existing money into credit. Rather, they create new credit and money de novo, and introduce maturity transformation risks.

And fifth, the potential exists for credit extension against assets—in particular, real estate—to itself influence the value of those assets, a process that can unleash Minsky-type cycles in which more bank credit creation can beget yet more, with both lender and borrower incentives and economics creating strong procyclical effects. In other words, a credit and asset-price cycle comes into being that, as Claudio Borio mentioned in chapter 6, is not just a part but the central feature of the financial cycle.

These distinctive features of debt contracts have, I believe, two implications:

• First, we cannot assume that the free market, left to itself, will arrive at an optimal balance of debt and equity contracts. Indeed, it will have a systematic long-term tendency to create too much debt, too much leverage.

• Second, the more leverage—probably best measured as the debt-to-GDP ratio—beyond some point, the more potentially fragile become both the financial system and the macroeconomy. That is what theory should, I believe, tell us, and what some empirical research is beginning tentatively to confirm.

In an important paper from the Bank for International Settlements, Steve Cecchetti and Enisse Kharroubi (2012) suggest that the debt-to-GDP ratio and long-term growth rates may be related in an inverse U function, with growth first increasing over some range of increasing financial intensity but then declining above some turning point.

Those findings would not have surprised the mid-twentieth-century economists who wrote in the wake of the 1929–1930 crash. But we somehow forgot the importance of debt stock levels or wrongly dismissed them as unimportant, and as a result ignored or assumed benign the huge increases in real economy and financial system leverage, in both the formal banking system and the shadow banking system, that occurred over several decades ahead of the crisis.

And in our regulatory response to the crisis, I still fear that we have not recognized the scale of the financial fragility risks that debt contracts can create. And I fear that we have not yet been adequately radical in our policy response.

We have significantly increased bank capital requirements. But there are, I believe, persuasive arguments—as, for instance, set out in Anat Admati and Martin Hellwig's (2013) new book—that optimal bank capital ratios (the ratios we would set if we were benevolent dictators of a greenfield economy) would be much higher, more like 25 percent to 30 percent.

Even more fundamentally, our regulatory response still does not overtly recognize that the level of real economy leverage is a potentially vital variable.

Take, for instance, the indicative measure proposed for the operation of the Basel III countercyclical buffer. It is that the buffer should be raised if credit growth is running significantly above past trend and reduced if it is below that trend. That implies that as long as credit growth is in line with trend—as long as it is smooth growth—that is fine, even if the trend growth is more rapid than nominal GDP growth. And even, therefore, if the debt-to-GDP ratio is relentlessly rising.

I believe that measure is inadequate and that we have to start treating aggregate leverage levels (private as much as public) as a crucial indicator and seek policy measures to contain that level through, for instance, limits on maximum allowed loan-to-income ratios.

Deflation in the Downswing of the Cycle

We failed to see the crisis coming, then, because we treated relentless financial deepening as either neutral or benign rather than dangerous. But what about the failure in early 2009, once the crisis had already occurred, to see how difficult recovery would be?

Here again I think our crucial blindness was related to debt: a failure to anticipate the strength of the deflationary impetus created by attempted private sector deleveraging in the aftermath of an excess debt crisis—a failure of foresight even though Japan had, over the previous 20 years, provided a strong illustration of that effect, well described in Richard Koo's account of a balance sheet recession (Koo 2009).

• Left by the upswing with debt stock levels they now believe excessive, constrained companies or households become determined to deleverage. They seek to generate financial surpluses with which to pay down debt. And their investment and consumption decisions become highly inelastic to reductions in interest rates.

• Policy rates at the zero lower bound, therefore, have little stimulative effect, and private demand falls. Public deficits rise, usefully providing an offset to low private demand but at the expense of rising public debt levels.

• At the aggregate level, leverage doesn't actually fall but simply shifts from the private to the public sector—the pattern clearly seen in Japan over the last 20 years and in the United Kingdom, Ireland, Spain, and the United States over the last four.

That description is, I think, persuasive. Eggertsson and Krugman's 2012 paper provides a formal mathematical explanation of the processes at work, integrating into a new Keynesian framework the assumption that some agents are constrained by debt stock concerns and, as a result, make different marginal decisions than nonconstrained agents do.

Again, what is surprising in retrospect is how novel that integration is and how absent debt stock levels were from previous models. After all, in the arena of international monetary policy we have discussed for decades the potentially deflationary impact of an asymmetry of response between debtor and creditor nations, the former constrained to cut back demand, the latter not constrained to stimulate. What Eggertsson and Krugman do is simply explore the same potential asymmetry as between constrained net debtors and unconstrained net creditors within an economy. That asymmetry, deleveraging, and balance sheet recession process is, I believe, a crucial factor in explaining the slow recovery since 2009.

So the question is, what policies will best help navigate this inherently challenging deleveraging environment? Again, I suggest that we need to be open to more radical policies than have been deployed so far. Let's suppose that we want to stimulate aggregate nominal demand, to produce a more rapid path of nominal GDP growth, as Michael Woodford proposes in chapter 4 of this volume Of course, we might not want to. Mervyn King warns in chapter 3 against assuming that deficient aggregate demand is the only problem, and I certainly agree with that, particularly in the UK.

But let's suppose it is at least part of the problem: how best to stimulate? The predominant current approach is by using unconventional monetary tools.

Policy rates have been at the zero lower bound for four years, but unconventional policies—quantitative easing, twists, credit easing, credit subsidy, central bank liquidity support, forward guidance—are available and have been deployed. All these tools work via one of two related transmission mechanisms: either (1) they seek to influence a wider set of interest rates than the current policy rate alone: long as well as short, expectations of forward rates as well as current rates, interest rates actually paid by end borrowers in the real economy as well as the policy rate in wholesale markets, or (2) they work by asset price and portfolio balance effects: higher bond or equity prices producing wealth effects and search for yield.

The best evidence seems to be that these policies, working via these channels, have had some positive impacts on both price levels and real output. But there must be two concerns about these policies.

• First, such policies, working through these indirect and expectational channels, must be potentially subject to declining marginal effectiveness in the specific circumstances of debt overhang in a balance sheet recession. Because if we really do have debt-constrained companies or households focused on deleveraging, they may be relatively inelastic to reduction in long-term rates or to the rates they actually pay, as well as to the current policy rate.

• Second, a long, sustained period of low interest rates must have adverse consequences of the sort Jeremy Stein highlights in chapter 10 and which the latest Global Financial Stability Report describes—with financial stability risk growing as financial market agents seek to take on leverage, to write put options, and to engage in leveraged carry trades. The elasticity to lower current and expected interest rates of responses focused on asset speculation and search for yield via financial innovation may turn out to be greater than the elasticity of response of real economy investment and consumption. A sole reliance on monetary policy stimulus, working via these indirect and expectational channels, may therefore carry dangers.

An alternative, or a complement, is fiscal stimulus—directly injecting purchasing power into the economy rather than operating via indirect channels. The classic argument against this is that the first-round effects of the stimulus are offset by crowding out, by the central bank response, and by Ricardian equivalence effects, making fiscal multipliers low.

But Brad DeLong and Lawrence Summers's (2012) recent paper provides persuasive arguments for believing that in the current conditions of debt overhang and private-sector deleveraging, and with central banks committed to maintain interest rates at the zero lower bound for several years ahead, fiscal multipliers are bound to be far higher. And that—together with the potential limitations and dangers of monetary policy working entirely via indirect channels—suggests the need for caution about a policy prescription that combines rapid fiscal consolidation offset, it is supposed, by unconventional monetary stimulus.

But equally, we cannot be unconcerned by dramatic increases in public debt levels. Richard Koo may be right that without the large Japanese fiscal deficits over the last 20 years, the Japanese economy would have suffered a great depression. But Japanese government debt levels over 200 percent of GDP and rising cannot simply be ignored. And to the extent that Japanese consumers and companies are aware of that debt burden—which, beyond some level, they must surely be—such debt levels may indeed generate Ricardian equivalence offsets to confidence and thus to demand.

As a result, it seems possible that balance sheet recessions can place us in a position where the authorities run out of ammunition—the pure monetary bullets ineffective or endangering adverse side effects, the fiscal magazine empty. But fiscal and monetary authorities combined never run out of ammunition. They can always do what Ben Bernanke proposed for Japan in 2003.

• He proposed "a tax cut for households and businesses that is explicitly coupled with incremental Bank of Japan purchases of government debt, so that the tax cut is in effect financed by money creation."

• He stressed that it would be important to be clear that "much or all of the increase in the money stock is viewed as permanent."

• He suggested that businesses and companies would willingly spend the money received since "no current or future debt service burden has been created" (i.e., no Ricardian equivalence offset would logically arise).

• He argued that the debt-to-GDP ratio would fall, since there would be no increase in nominal debt but a rise in nominal GDP.

This is helicopter money or, as I labeled it in a recent lecture, "overt money finance of an increased fiscal deficit" (Turner 2013). It is an available policy option and, in technical terms, there are no reasons for believing that it would be more inflationary (i.e., would produce a less favorable balance between price and output effects) than any other policy that would be successful in stimulating nominal GDP.

But there could certainly be powerful political economy reasons for excluding this option, for treating it as taboo. Because if the taboo were broken, politicians might want to use the option in excess and all the time, rather than in small amounts and in the specific extreme conditions of balance sheet recessions. And that may argue for not being explicit about debt monetization. As Michael Woodford commented in conversation at the London Business School (Reichlin, Turner, and Woodford 2013):

• If you inject a fiscal stimulus against the background of a central bank committed to maintaining low interest rates for several years,

• and that commitment is made credible by a price level or money GDP level target,

• and if you accept the possibility—indeed, the likelihood—that some of the increase in the monetary base will turn out post facto to be permanent,

• then you have a strategy substantially very close to Bernanke's helicopter money but without breaking the potentially valuable political economy taboo.

However, that strategy still does require a degree of coordination of fiscal and monetary policy, and an acceptance by the central bank that it is facilitating a fiscal policy stimulus rather than offsetting fiscal austerity via monetary policy stimulus working entirely via interest rate, expectational, and portfolio balance channels.

That coordination is made essential by the specific conditions of the postcrisis balance sheet recession. It would have been better if we had never gotten into this situation in the first place, never allowed excessive leverage to develop. But we did, and we need to design policy today in the specific conditions created by those past policy mistakes.

The crisis occurred and was not foreseen because we failed to appreciate the fundamental importance of aggregate leverage. And our failure to foresee the slow and difficult recovery reflected the fact that our macroeconomic models, while incorporating sticky prices and wages, largely failed to reflect the perhaps still more important rigidities introduced by debt contracts, debt stock levels, and default processes.

Integrating financial structure, debt contracts, default, and the banking system into macroeconomic models is therefore critical but still at an early stage.

Which makes the subtitle of the conference, "First Steps and Early Lessons," very well chosen.

References

Admati, Anat, and Martin Hellwig. 2013. *The Bankers' New Clothes: What's Wrong with Banking and What to Do about It*. Princeton, NJ: Princeton University Press.

Bernanke, Ben S. 2003. "Some Thoughts on Monetary Policy in Japan." Speech before the Japan Society of Monetary Economists, Tokyo, May. http://www.federalreserve.gov/boarddocs/speeches/2003/20030531.

Bernanke, Ben S. 2004. "Non-Monetary Effects of the Financial Crisis." In *Essays on the Great Depression*. Princeton, NJ: Princeton University Press.

Cecchetti, Stephen G., and Enisse Kharroubi. 2012. "Reassessing the Impact of Finance on Growth." BIS Working Paper 381, Monetary and Economic Department, Bank for International Settlements, Basel, July. http://www.bis.org/publ/work381.pdf.

DeLong, Brad, and Lawrence Summers. 2012. "Fiscal Policy in a Depressed Economy." Brookings Papers on Economic Activity, Brookings Institution, Washington, DC, Spring. http://www.brookings.edu/~/media/Projects/BPEA/Spring%20 2012/2012a_DeLong.pdf.

Eggertsson, Gauti B., and Paul Krugman. 2012. "Debt, Deleveraging, and the Liquidity Trap: A Fisher-Minsky-Koo Approach." *Quarterly Journal of Economics* 127 (3): 1469–1513.

Fisher, Irving. 1933. "The Debt-Deflation Theory of Great Depressions." *Econometrica* 1 (4): 337–357.

Fisher, Irving. 1936. "100% Money and the Public Debt." *Economic Forum*, Spring, 406–420.

Gennaioli, Nicola, Andrei Shleifer, and Robert Vishny. 2010. "Neglected Risks, Financial Innovation, and Financial Fragility." NBER Working Paper 16068, National Bureau of Economic Research, Cambridge, MA. June. http://www.nber.org/papers/w16068.

Goodhart, Charles, and Dimitrios Tsomocos. 2011. "The Role of Default in Macroeconomics." Mayekawa Lecture, Institute for Monetary and Economic Studies, Bank of Japan, Tokyo, November. *Monetary and Economic Studies*, vol. 29. http://www.imes.boj.or.jp/research/abstracts/english/me29-4.html.

King, Mervyn. 2012. "Twenty Years of Inflation Targeting." Stamp Memorial Lecture, London School of Economics, London, October.

Koo, Richard. 2009. *The Holy Grail of Microeconomics: Lessons from Japan's Great Recession*. New York: John Wiley & Sons.

Reichlin, Lucrezia, Adair Turner, and Michael Woodford. 2013. "Helicopter Money as a Policy Option." VoxEu, May 20. http://www.voxeu.org/article/helicopter-money-policy-option.

Simons, Henry. 1936. "Rules versus Authorities in Monetary Policy." *Journal of Political Economy* 44 (1): 1–30.

Turner, Adair. 2013. "Debt, Money, and Mephistopheles: How Do We Get Out of This Mess?" Lecture at Cass Business School, February. http://www.fsa.gov.uk/library/communication/speeches/2013/0206-at.

IV
Fiscal Policy

14

Defining the Reemerging Role of Fiscal Policy

Janice Eberly

Whereas much of the policy innovation during the financial crisis of 2008–2009 focused on monetary policy—and especially unconventional monetary policy—there has since been renewed attention to fiscal policy. The monetary focus manifested in part because monetary authorities were able to move quickly and decisively during the crisis, whereas fiscal policy tends to be slower, both in decision making and in implementation. But the renewed attention to the potential power of fiscal policy came as the severity of the crisis demanded that all available tools be brought to bear and also as the limits of monetary effectiveness may have been reached. The nature of the financial crisis and the use of unconventional monetary tools brought about a conceptual rethinking in monetary economics, particularly to incorporate financial markets into monetary models. There has not been such a ground-up rethinking so far in fiscal policy, although recent work suggests we might consider fiscal policy differently in a world where monetary policy is at the zero lower bound.

I will break out the questions addressed in this and the next few chapters into the phases of the business cycle, which implicitly focuses our thinking on the cyclical role of fiscal policy. However, I will return to the potential role of fiscal policy in economic trends at the conclusion of this introduction.

Starting with the pre-recession or boom period in an economy, how much headroom should a country maintain in its debt-to-GDP ratio? This question is the counterpart to the corporate finance concept of debt capacity and the question of how much spare debt capacity should be held in abeyance. The crisis taught us that while policymakers cut taxes, increased spending, and ran deficits during cyclical booms—either out of political expedience or as a strategy to put downward pressure on the size of government—they used up borrowing capacity that was needed later when the crisis eventually hit. Downturns are naturally associated with larger deficits, at the least from automatic stabilizers and even more from active fiscal policy, and with the need to tap debt markets. This task is typically easier and cheaper when the debt-to-GDP ratio inherited from boom times is relatively low. Such a precautionary approach to debt capacity is less controversial than the thorny quantitative question that follows: *how much* borrowing capacity should a country build up outside downturns, and if it depends on state-specific factors, what determines how large this capacity should be?

Second, coming to the downturn, how large are the fiscal policy multipliers, and if they are state-contingent, what do they depend on? Research so far emphasizes that fiscal multipliers can be much larger when monetary policy reaches the zero lower bound. Other work has shown that excess capacity or output gaps in the economy increase fiscal multipliers. This analysis is crucial to policymakers' approaching fiscal consolidation when an economy is still weak, either in the aftermath of a crisis or worse, during a crisis itself associated with structural fiscal imbalances. Policymakers face the essential conundrum that financial markets are looking for credible improvements in the structural fiscal stance at the same time that the economy will suffer most from fiscal tightening.

One approach to these questions is to put in place fiscal rules, just as central banks have proposed monetary rules to develop credible policy. In principle, such rules can allow for deficit spending when the economy is weakest and the multipliers are largest, with a credible commitment to fiscal sustainability as the economy improves. Rules can also help impose discipline during "good times" to rebuild debt capacity and bring down the debt-to-GDP ratio after a cyclical downturn. Similarly, such rules can allow for cyclical deficits during downturns, along the lines of automatic stabilizers, which naturally roll off as the economy strengthens. Rules can also ease the decision-making lags that limit the effectiveness of fiscal policy at typical business cycle frequencies. The effects of these stabilizers can be large: The Congressional Budget Office (CBO 2013) estimates that spending and forgone revenue associated with automatic stabilizers averaged over $350 billion per year in the United States from 2009 to the present (FY 2013), totaling more than 2.5 times the total stimulus included in the American Recovery and Reinvestment Act. Although the use of automatic stabilizers is well established, strengthening and broadening fiscal rules can be problematic. More general fiscal rules have well-known problems because they are rigid by design and difficult to customize to particular economic conditions; indeed, allowing judgment or "escape hatches" to accommodate unforeseen circumstances can undermine the credibility that a rule is designed to develop.

Finally, once the downturn has eased, how rapid should fiscal consolidation be during a recovery? Policymakers often undertake rapid fiscal consolidation under pressure from financial markets to reduce sovereign debt, or at least their borrowing. Countries not under immediate pressure argue that a reduction in borrowing is needed to forestall such pressure eventually. When should policymakers start to take this concern into account? Should policymakers react before reaching an upper bound on the debt-to-GDP ratio that they should not breach, or similarly, that financial markets will not tolerate? Concern about investors' appetite for sovereign risk can lead policymakers to tighten too early or too much, because the costs are perceived to be asymmetric: Waiting too long and risking a withdrawal of lending can be very costly.

These questions are almost entirely focused on cyclical management of debt and deficits. Yet the severity and persistence of the recent recession and the slow pace of subsequent recovery raise the concern that the crisis will have a lasting effect on the macroeconomy, perhaps by reducing potential output. The possibility that output may be permanently affected profoundly raises the stakes of a downturn, yet the mechanism through which a financial crisis or a severe downturn affects the productive capacity of the economy is not yet well understood. There is evidence that long-term unemployment causes deterioration of a worker's skills and reduces the probability of re-employment. Other potential mechanisms are less clear-cut. Is there a reduction in innovation or in technological change embodied in investment in physical capital? Does reduced labor mobility or reallocation hurt productivity? Some of these mechanisms would benefit from fiscal intervention, either broadly to increase economic activity, or specifically, for example, to promote skill development and job matching. Yet without understanding what causes the long-term damage to the economy, any policy intervention is largely speculative.

Finally, I began by emphasizing the ground-up rethinking in monetary economics to explicitly incorporate financial markets. Monetary policy has embraced credit markets as a mechanism for monetary stimulus, and the same may be true for fiscal policy. Fiscal use of credit policy has been employed primarily for microeconomic reasons: to remedy market failures and support social benefits where they exceed private benefits. In practice, however, credit policy was widely used in the crisis by fiscal authorities, particularly in the housing market and to support small business. As we rethink fiscal economics, policymakers could likely benefit from a better conceptual and empirical understanding of the potential role of credit and macroprudential policy in countercyclical fiscal policy.

Reference

Congressional Budget Office (CBO). 2013. "The Effects of Automatic Stabilizers on the Federal Budget as of 2013." CBO, Washington, DC, March. http://www .cbo.gov/sites/default/files/cbofiles/attachments/43977_AutomaticStablilizers3 -2013.pdf.

15

Fiscal Policy in the Shadow of Debt: Surplus Keynesianism Still Works

Anders Borg

The theme of this conference is rethinking macro policy, and I would like to outline some important lessons from the global economic crisis since 2008 for the design of fiscal policy, drawing on my experience as Sweden's minister for finance and as a member of the Ecofin Council (Economic and Financial Affairs Council of the European Union) over the past six years. In this chapter I focus on the current role of fiscal policy and on a number of important lessons the crisis has taught us, and conclude with a discussion of the problems Europe has to tackle. This chapter has three basic messages:

• First, fiscal policy should be used as a stabilization tool. It is very important to realize that institutions have to be reformed so that fiscal policy can play an active role in stabilizing the economy.

• Second, debt is important. High debt is a constraint on rational economic policy.

• Third, the main difference between fiscal policy views in the United States and in Europe has to do with the fact that the European problems are fundamentally structural. This does not mean there is no demand shortage in Europe, but the problems are to a larger extent structural than are those in the United States.

The Current Situation

If we take a longer view of this crisis, one stylized fact is that Europe has actually grown slowly—less than half a percentage point over the last six or seven years. Even in a 10-year perspective, Europe has growth of close to one percentage point. Fundamentally, then, there is a long-term, not

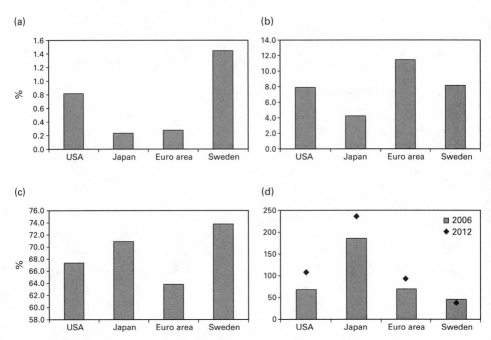

Figure 15.1
Key Indicators for the United States, Japan, the Euro area, and Sweden
a. GDP growth. Average growth rate, 2007–2012 (in %). b. Unemployment rate as of Q4 2012 (in %). Euro area data represent 17 countries. c. Employment rate, all persons ages 15 to 64, as of Q4 2012 (in %). Euro area data represent 17 countries and are as of Q3 2012. d. General government gross debt as a percent of GDP. *Sources:* a–c. OECD. d. *European Economic Forecast*, spring 2013.

a short-term, problem in Europe. This has also fed into unemployment. Unemployment in the euro area is now close to 12 percent. The employment rates in the United States and Europe are at least 5 to 10 percent lower than they should be in a well-functioning economy. And on top of that we have a very heavy increase in the debt level (see figures 15.1a–d). What might be the appropriate fiscal stance in these circumstances?

Fiscal Stance

We should be very cautious about assuming that the crisis is over. There is still a need for both fiscal and monetary policy to remain expansionary. At present, fiscal policy considerations involve striking a difficult balance among the need for consolidation of public finances, supporting growth, and tackling persistently high unemployment. In striking this balance, it is imperative that governments not lose the confidence of market actors, businesses, and citizens. This policy balance will obviously vary from country to country. Let me illustrate what I mean.

Italy and Spain and other countries under considerable pressure from the markets must meet their fiscal policy commitments at a sufficient pace to restore market confidence. There is a clear risk that backtracking on measures already decided on could lead to a return of market uncertainty. But it could be argued that weaker growth than expected should not be met with additional consolidation measures.

Countries in a somewhat stronger position but still facing considerable challenges, such as France and the UK, should let automatic stabilizers work fully. It is clear that the French government will need more time to reach the 3 percent deficit level. This is a reasonable position on the part of the French government and the European Commission. Letting the automatic stabilizers work fully at this time is a sound approach. It is also important to implement structural reforms to increase competitiveness and improve the functionality of the labor market to boost growth.

For countries with sufficient margins in public finances, an active fiscal policy to support recovery is desirable. I would argue that the situation in my own country, Sweden, calls for an expansionary fiscal policy. In Sweden the debt level is about 40 percent of GDP, public finances are in structural balance, and there is a high degree of long-run sustainability. But at the same time, Sweden has a high unemployment rate as a result of the crisis. In these circumstances it seems reasonable to continue to take measures on both the expenditure and the revenue sides to stimulate the economy.

The situation is different in Germany. Germany has an 80 percent debt level, and unemployment is around 5 percent. On top of this, there are some long-term issues concerning public finances. If there is fiscal space in Germany, I would argue that a substantial part of this space should be kept as a buffer—a safety margin—for two reasons. One is that there might be other countries in the euro area that will need new programs in the short or medium term; therefore, the anchor of the whole euro system must be on the safe side and on dry ground. There might also be a need to build a fuller banking union, which could have fiscal implications. A major part of the fiscal space in Germany should be used as a safety buffer, either for use in future programs for countries in difficulty or as part of a backstop arrangement, rather than to support a short-term stabilization policy in Germany. However, there are also arguments to consider as to whether Germany and others can do more to increase growth. From a general perspective, lower taxes for low-income earners and increased spending on growth-friendly expenditures, such as education and infrastructure, could be considered.

What Has This Crisis Taught Us about Fiscal Policy?

Fiscal Policy Is Important for Stabilizing the Economy

The crisis has shown the importance of fiscal policy supporting monetary policy in counteracting significant downturns, particularly when there are large gaps and the policy interest rate approaches zero. This is especially true for European economies with deep structural problems and ongoing private sector deleveraging. However, the ability to use fiscal policy effectively is dependent on whether fiscal policy is deemed credible by the public and the financial markets. The long-term sustainability of public finances is therefore crucial if fiscal policy is to play a larger role in stabilizing the economy.

It is a somewhat ironic conclusion that while we are now convinced that fiscal policy should be used actively, many countries have debt levels that do not permit such actions. If you believe that fiscal policy has a role to play, it should be very clear that in the long run, we need to bring down debts to a level that enables an active role for fiscal policy.

When it comes to the traditional view of stabilization through fiscal policy, the general conception has been that measures should be temporary, targeted, and timely. I see fiscal policy somewhat differently. Fiscal policy has three main targets: distribution, stabilization, and growth. Fiscal policy should deal with all three of these targets at the same time. Particularly in European countries with structural problems, it is very important that short-term measures aimed at stabilizing the economy also support increased long-term growth. When it comes to discretionary measures, temporary measures are preferable in theory; in practice, however, there are substantial risks that temporary measures will become permanent, so they should be used with caution.

Fiscal Policy Has Its Own Problems

If we are going to use fiscal policy, we need to realize that fiscal policy is a difficult animal to live with. One of the key difficulties of fiscal policy is that it is preceded by long decision lags, particularly regarding structural reforms. Structural reforms are often complex and demand long preparation. We can take the Swedish budget for 2013 as an example. In light of the weaker growth in the euro area and clear downside risks, together with increased international competition for the large Swedish export sector, there was a strong case for including structural measures to support growth. After the budget for 2012 was presented to the Riksdag (the Swedish parliament) in September 2011, the Ministry of Finance started to consider appropriate measures to strengthen the economy. In November, the basic elements of the reform agenda were chosen. The three main components were increased spending on infrastructure, increased spending on research and development, and cutting corporate taxation and broadening the tax base by reducing interest rate deductions. The tax proposal then had to be prepared by a government commission and was subsequently assessed by our legal counsel before it could be presented to the Riksdag. It took until April before there was a clear view on how this proposal would work and what it would cost. In August we decided how large the tax cut would be.

If you want to combine fiscal policy with structural measures, you need to set up an adequate planning framework. You need to decide a year ahead what the basic proposals in the budget will be, and you need to work with scalable measures that can be adapted to changes in the amount of room for reform.

In contrast, changes in monetary policy are decided and implemented almost instantly. This is a fundamental difference between fiscal and monetary policy. It is therefore important to think through how to deal with the long decision lags. Many of the political economy issues that you normally encounter with fiscal policy can be circumvented and solved by setting up institutions that are well equipped to handle long-term decision making. One important feature is to avoid automatic indexing of expenditures; for example, transfers that are fully indexed to wages. In Sweden, we have reduced the automatic adjustment of expenditures over the past 20 years. This reduction has served us well. Fully indexed expenditures tend to lead to uncontrolled expenditure growth and ultimately to budget problems. Such a feature also reduces the pressure for change in the public sector and ties the hands of democratically elected politicians to set priorities in the annual budget. A prudent trend for expenditures also makes sense in terms of stabilization policy. If expenditures are reduced semi-automatically, it is more credible that fiscal policy will return to a sustainable path when the economy recovers.

There is something deeply democratic about fiscal policy. Fiscal policy is about negotiations and reconciling conflicts between different principles. It has to deal with different interest groups. Interest groups represent ways of channeling different points of view in the debate and are a part of a well-functioning democracy. Economists have to accept that there is a need to see fiscal policymaking as a negotiation process in which democratic forces play a central role. However, it is also clear that when setting the framework for those negotiations, you are affecting the end results. With a well-organized negotiation process and a well-organized budget process, conflicts between principles and interests are much easier to solve. This leads me to my lesson about credibility.

Credibility Is Key

My final lesson is that credibility is key to a successful economic policy. I will make a different argument than is normally made about credibility. Modern societies are built on trust. Citizens must be able to rely on the social contract between individuals and the state. The social contract is based on every individual in society being able to rely on the fact that his or her contribution to society will yield a return when needed. This must apply in both the short and the long term. This is particularly the case in Sweden, where fiscal policy has a profound influence on citizens' life situations, given the substantial public provision of welfare services. Take, for example, health care or education. Regardless of the business cycle, you as a citizen must be confident that if you have a heart attack, you will get good health care, and that your children will get a good education when they go to school.

If there is uncertainty about the ability to handle fiscal policy in a welfare state, citizens will have trust problems. Countries that increase deficits and debt will create credibility problems that risk breaking down this trust. If we believe that a welfare state is more successful in creating good living conditions for people, it is more important to deal prudently with deficit and debt issues. In this way, European countries differ significantly from countries with substantially lower levels of publicly financed welfare provision, such as the United States.

Europe's Problems Run Deep

Where does this leave us in terms of the euro crisis? As I see it, how countries emerge from the crisis is not primarily about short-term stabilization but rather about the long-term prospects for growth and social cohesion. It is important to acknowledge the structural differences between the US and European economies. These differences are probably one of the main reasons for the polarized views on stabilization policy, both within academia and among policymakers.

If you take stock of the US economy, it is very hard to see any fundamental labor market problems. The US unemployment rate will probably go down to 5 or 6 percent again without any major structural reforms. There might be some problems with hysteresis in the labor market, but the fundamental factors—product market regulation, employment protection, unemployment benefits, marginal taxes, wage setting—all point in the direction of a low structural unemployment level. This is not true of many countries in Europe. The structural unemployment level in the euro area is probably slightly below 10 percent, and there are strong fundamental arguments for this high level. In Europe, markets generally are much more regulated. Also, the tax rates and unemployment benefits are higher (figures 15.2a–d).

My argument is not that we should transform the European economies to be like that of the United States in every respect. I tend to like the social market economy and the welfare state. Europe needs to reform, but the reforms should be in line with the European social model. However, it is important to realize that under these circumstances there is a much higher risk of high structural unemployment. If you evaluate structural public finances, it is also much more likely that the United States will lower its deficit level, and therefore deal with its debt problem automatically when the economy is reinvigorated. This is not the case in Europe.

Given the problems of high indebtedness, low long-run growth, and high structural unemployment, the bulk of fiscal measures in Europe, especially in the euro area, need to address these problems. We need to

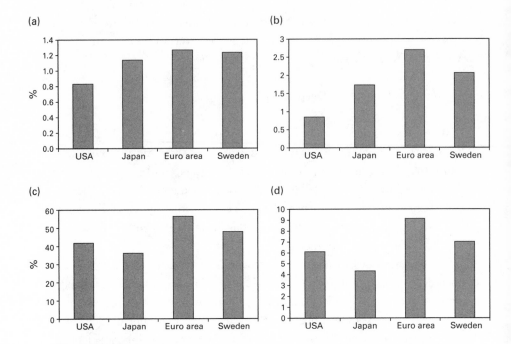

Figure 15.2
Differences between the US, Japanese, and European Economies
a. Product market regulation. Shown is the OECD overall product market regulation indicator for 2008 on an index scale of 0 to 6, where 6 is the most restrictive.
b. Strictness of employment protection. Shown is the OECD strictness of employment protection indicator for 2008 on an index scale of 0 to 6, where 6 is the most restrictive. c. Marginal tax rate. Marginal tax wedge as figured for principal earner (in %). d. Structural unemployment rate, percent of labor force, 2012.
Note: Euro area refers to a weighted average of GDP weights (2011) and represents 15 OECD countries.
Sources: a and b. OECD and own calculations. c. OECD. d. OECD *Economic Outlook* 2012.

confront the fundamental structural problems in the euro area, first and foremost the functioning of the labor market. If we are going to use fiscal policy, it's important to keep in mind that fiscal policy has goals for distribution, growth, and stabilization. When dealing with stabilization issues, we should also try to do things that stimulate growth in the long term. Rather than being temporary and timely, measures should be directed toward confronting more fundamental issues that will truly determine long-term growth prospects and the scope of our European social model. So, we should use fiscal policy, but it must be a constrained activism that inspires credibility not only among markets but also in terms of the trust of society.

Conclusion

• Fiscal policy should support monetary policy, particularly in dealing with specific structural and distributional problems. But fiscal policy has its own set of problems, particularly long decision lags inherent in structural reforms.

• Long-term sustainable public finances are a fundamental condition for conducting fiscal policy and maintaining confidence, especially for countries with high welfare ambitions and less effective labor and product markets.

• Europe must maintain its focus on structural reforms and tackle the fundamental issues that affect long-term conditions for growth, increased social cohesion, and increased confidence.

Note

I thank Philip Löf for his help in drafting the speech on which this chapter is based.

16

Fiscal Policies in Recessions

Roberto Perotti

Ideally, a government would like to use fiscal policy as a countercyclical tool while at the same time convincing the markets that it remains solvent and/or its government debt remains sustainable.[1] What it *can* do depends on the initial situation. In this chapter I consider a policymaker that has some "fiscal space." In other words, there is room for some, perhaps temporary, increase in the deficit. In more mundane terms, the "debt vigilantes" are not active. Admittedly, these are loose terms; I will not try to define them formally, and even less to determine a threshold for when "fiscal space" is available.

I will explore three popular options; the emphasis will be on policy issues, but I will also deal with the ensuing challenges to macroeconomic thinking.

Option 1: Ignore the availability of fiscal space, cut government spending and taxes. Then GDP, private consumption, and private investment will start growing, and this will take care of any issues with sustainability and solvency.

This is the notion of the "expansionary effects of fiscal consolidations." Obviously, its proponents have rarely argued that spending cuts by themselves will spur growth; accompanying structural reforms of labor, goods, and credit markets are also necessary.

What are the empirical foundations of this view? A first method to investigate the effects of a fiscal consolidation is simply to extrapolate from current estimates of tax and spending multipliers, from time-series vector autoregression studies. There are several recent surveys of existing results, mostly based on U.S. data, and estimates of fiscal multipliers were extensively debated in the first conference on rethinking macro policy. Therefore, I will concentrate on studies that focus explicitly on episodes of fiscal consolidation.

A method that has been widely used to study the effects of fiscal consolidations consists of a simple comparison of means of variables over time. Specifically: (1) define a "fiscal consolidation," for instance, as a country-year when the discretionary[2] decline in the primary deficit is more than, say, 1.5 percent of GDP, or as two consecutive country-years when it is at least 1 percent each year; then (2) take a macroeconomic variable of interest, such as private consumption, and compare the average of that variable in the two years after (or during) the consolidation with the average in the two years before the consolidation. This "mean comparison" approach would provide unbiased estimates of the average effects of consolidations if the latter were completely random events (in which case it is essentially a difference-in-difference estimator).

This is the methodology applied by Alesina and Perotti (1995) and Alesina and Ardagna (2010) with cyclically adjusted data, and by Alesina and Ardagna (2012) with the narrative IMF data of Devries and others (2011).[3]

The typical result is that spending-based consolidations (where the discretionary decline in the deficit consists of at least 50 percent spending cuts) tend to be longer-lasting and are associated with an increase in GDP growth or a small recession, while tax-based consolidations are short-lived and are associated with a slowdown in growth or even a recession. With some variations, all of private consumption, investment, and exports display this pattern. Also, in general, these variables are particularly responsive to cuts in social spending or spending on public wages and salaries—the two largest government spending items in all Organisation for Economic Co-operation and Development (OECD) countries.

Fiscal consolidations are typically multiyear events. In this method, a fiscal consolidation lasting four years would appear as three consecutive two-year consolidations; moreover, a given year can appear in all of the "pre," "during," and "post" groups at different dates. It is not clear what the mean comparison method delivers in these cases.

A second problem with this approach is that it is difficult to control for concomitant effects. For instance, one typical result is that spending-based consolidations are associated with real depreciation of the exchange rate and improvement in relative unit labor costs. Is this a consequence of spending-based consolidations or the result of policies typically implemented together with spending-based consolidations? As always, causality is difficult to ascertain.

The accompanying policies might take several forms that might be difficult to capture with one or two variables: consider, for instance, labor market reforms, or changes in exchange rate or monetary policy regimes. Finally, the government budgets and accompanying technical documents need to be studied in depth in order to determine the discretionary measures with a minimum of confidence.

For all these reasons, it is useful to complement the existing evidence with a different approach. Perotti (2013a) presents a detailed discussion of the four largest spending-based consolidations—Denmark in 1983 to 1987, Ireland in 1987 to 1989, Finland in 1992 to 1996, and Sweden in 1993 to 1997—based on the original budget documents and on contemporary discussion, such as OECD or IMF annual reports, and country-specific sources.[4] I focus on two questions. First, is there evidence that large budget consolidations can have expansionary effects in the short run? Second, how useful is the experience of the past as a guide to today's euro area countries?

The main conclusions of the case studies I present are the following:

1. Actual consolidations were smaller than previously thought, and not spending-based.

All these consolidations have long been considered quintessential cases of large, "spending-based consolidations." Two of these were truly enormous: As shown in table 16.1 in the column labeled "IMF," in Finland the discretionary primary deficit fell by 11.5 percent of GDP over 5 years (all of them spending cuts), according to the IMF narrative measure of Devries and others (2011), and in Sweden by 10.6 percent of GDP over 5 years (of which almost 7 percentage points were GDP spending cuts).

But a closer look at the budget documents shows that in many cases the announced spending cuts were not implemented, or else they were undone by supplementary budgets during the fiscal years. As a result, the decline in the budget deficit in Finland was only about 5 percentage points of GDP; moreover, nearly all of it consisted of revenue increases

Table 16.1
Large Fiscal Consolidations in Europe

Denmark, 1983–1987	Actual	IMF
Spending	–4.0	–4.3
Revenues	4.9	2.4
Surplus	8.9	6.7
Ireland, 1987–1989		
Spending	–3.0	–2.5
Revenues	–0.1	0.4
Surplus	2.9	2.9
Finland, 1992–1996		
Spending	–0.9	–12.1
Revenues	3.8	–0.6
Surplus	4.9	11.5
Sweden, 1993–1997		
Spending	–4.2	–6.8
Revenues	4.6	3.8
Surplus	8.8	10.6

Source: Perotti (2013a).

(see table 16.1, column labeled "Actual"). My estimate of spending cuts in Sweden is about half the IMF estimate. Only in Ireland were spending cuts larger than revenue increases.[5] These conclusions are corroborated by contemporary policy documents and discussions, which do not show any consciousness of living through a "budget bloodbath."[6]

2. Depreciation and the role of the exchange rate and monetary regimes.

Tables 16.2 and 16.3 display the behavior of the multilateral nominal exchange rate and of multilateral unit labor costs in manufacturing, respectively. During the consolidations, Denmark and Ireland used the exchange rate as a nominal anchor, by committing to a hard peg within the European Exchange Rate Mechanism (ERM). Denmark had repeatedly devalued its currency before the consolidation, thus entering the consolidation with a depreciated exchange rate, but at the cost of very high interest rates (up to 23 percent). During the consolidation phase, Ireland

Table 16.2
Nominal Effective Exchange Rate

	$t-1$	t	$t+1$	$t+2$	$t+3$	$t+4$	$t+5$
Denmark	−3.4	0.9	−2.3	2.2	5.7	3.6	−1.1
Ireland	8.0	−.4	−1.9	−.7	8.6		
Finland	−2.9	−12.2	−10.0	13.4	15.0	−2.4	−2.1
Sweden	2.4	−17.7	1.2	0.4	10.1	−3.3	−0.2

Note: Shaded area corresponds to years of consolidation.
Source: Perotti (2013a).

Table 16.3
Relative Unit Labor Costs in Manufacturing

	$t-2$	$t-1$	t	$t+1$	$t+2$	$t+3$	$t+4$	$t+5$
Denmark	−4.9	−1.2	1.6	0.9	4.1	8.8	11.5	−0.2
Ireland	1.5	9.3	−6.2	−7.3	−6.8	0.3		
Finland	5.3	−0.9	−20.7	−24.2	5.2	16.0	−5.5	−5.9
Sweden	2.9	−2.7	−26.8	−6.4	−4.1	12.8	−7.2	−6.4

Note: Shaded area corresponds to years of consolidation.
Source: Perotti (2013a).

also benefited from the large appreciation of the currency of its main trading partner, the UK, which was not part of the ERM.

Finland and Sweden also devalued repeatedly, but then floated their currencies just before the consolidation, experiencing a further depreciation. Overall, their currencies depreciated by between 15 and 25 percent in multilateral terms in the first two years of the consolidation. As a nominal anchor, Finland and Sweden introduced instead inflation targeting. There is some evidence that, while almost completely new at the time, this approach was regarded as credible from the start: According to insiders' accounts at the time, it "had a profound impact on the behavior of labor market participants" (Jonung, Kiander, and Vartia 2008, 37).

3. Income policies were key.

Fiscal consolidations were accompanied by explicit income policies, whereby the government, trade unions, and industrialists' organizations reached an agreement to exchange wage moderation for lower income taxes and social security contributions. Ireland returned to a tripartite wage settlement in 1987 (see table 16.3), which set a maximum increase in wages of 2.5 percent in 1988, 1989, and 1990. Finland and Sweden signed tripartite wage agreements at the start of the consolidations, and then, after some wage slippage three years into the consolidation (see table 16.3), the government summoned the unions and industrialists' associations again to sign other wage agreements. These developments were regarded as very significant by contemporaries: As Jonung, Kiander, and Vartia (2008, 35) write, based on contemporary accounts, "Perhaps the biggest change in the 1990s in Finland was the adoption and wide acceptance of a policy of long term wage moderation."

Income policies were particularly explicit in Denmark. Here the government renounced any depreciation of the exchange rate and relied instead on an internal devaluation: It suspended wage indexation, capped contractual wage increases, and froze unemployment subsidies and transfers, all in exchange for lower income taxes and social security contributions.

Wage moderation, which was made possible by income policies, was instrumental in maintaining the benefits of the nominal depreciations and in reducing inflation expectations and interest rates.

4. Recoveries were mostly export-driven.

All stabilizations were associated with large increases in GDP growth, typically at about 4 percent for a few years (table 16.4).

The source of the recovery is crucial in trying to shed light on the mechanism. Most models posit that a fiscal consolidation raises consumers' and investors' confidence via a wealth effect or other channels, and therefore should cause a quick increase in private consumption and investment. However, except in Denmark (where the recovery was already under way at the time of the consolidation), private consumption typically started recovering six to eight quarters after the beginning of the consolidation; in Sweden, in the first year, domestic demand collapsed, with investment falling by 15 percent (tables 16.5 and 16.6). Initially, and again with the exception of Denmark, the recovery was export-driven (table 16.7): In Finland, Ireland, and Sweden, exports increased at rates about 10 percent per annum for several years after the consolidation.

Table 16.4
GDP Growth

	$t-2$	$t-1$	t	$t+1$	$t+2$	$t+3$	$t+4$	$t+5$
Denmark	−0.9	3.7	2.7	4.2	4.0	4.9	0.3	−0.1
Ireland	1.9	0.4	3.6	3.0	5.6	7.7		
Finland	0.5	−6.0	−3.5	−0.8	3.6	4.0	3.6	6.2
Sweden	−1.1	−1.2	−2.1	4.0	3.9	1.6	2.7	4.2

Note: Shaded area corresponds to years of consolidation.
Source: Perotti (2013a).

Table 16.5
Private Consumption Growth

	$t-2$	$t-1$	t	$t+1$	$t+2$	$t+3$	$t+4$	$t+5$
Denmark	−1.7	1.4	2.0	3.8	4.3	7.5	−1.9	−1.7
Ireland	2.7	2.8	2.1	3.6	3.3	3.2		
Finland	−1.1	−3.7	−3.8	−3.5	2.4	4.5	3.8	3.3
Sweden	0.9	−1.3	−3.6	2.1	1.1	1.8	2.8	3.3

Note: Shaded area corresponds to years of consolidation.
Source: Perotti (2013a).

Table 16.6
Private Investment Growth

	$t-2$	$t-1$	t	$t+1$	$t+2$	$t+3$	$t+4$	$t+5$
Denmark	−17.6	10.3	4.3	11.2	15.3	19.3	2.3	−6.4
Ireland	−7.9	−0.5	−2.3	−0.2	13.5	13.9		
Finland	−5.7	−20.6	−17.9	−13.0	−1.6	18.5	9.3	9.2
Sweden	−8.5	−11.3	−14.6	7.0	9.9	4.7	0.6	8.8

Note: Shaded area corresponds to years of consolidation.
Source: Perotti (2013a).

Table 16.7
Export Growth

	$t-2$	$t-1$	t	$t+1$	$t+2$	$t+3$	$t+4$	$t+5$
Denmark	8.5	3.2	4.6	3.5	6.0	1.3	4.9	8.8
Ireland	6.6	2.7	13.9	8.1	11.4	9.2		
Finland	1.7	−7.2	10	16.3	13.5	8.5	5.9	13.9
Sweden	−1.9	2.0	8.3	13.5	11.3	4.4	13.8	9.0

Note: Shaded area corresponds to years of consolidation.
Source: Perotti (2013a).

Table 16.8
Long-Term Interest Rates

	$t-1$	t	$t+1$	$t+2$	$t+3$	$t+4$	$t+5$
Denmark	21.2	15.0	14.4	11.6	10.1	11.3	9.9
Ireland	11.2	11.3	9.4	9.2	10.3		
Finland	11.7	12.0	8.8	9.0	8.8	7.1	6.0
Sweden	10.0	8.6	9.7	10.3	8.1	6.7	5.0

Note: Shaded area corresponds to years of consolidation.
Source: Perotti (2013a).

This was made possible by the combination of nominal depreciation and wage moderation: Between 1992 and 1995, multilateral unit labor costs in Sweden fell by almost 40 percent (see table 16.3).

Denmark, which alone pursued a hard peg policy, experienced all the hallmarks of the "exchange rate based stabilizations" studied in a large literature in the eighties and nineties (see, e.g., Ades, Kiguel, and Liviatan 1993): domestic demand initially boomed as inflation and interest rates fell fast, but as income policies by themselves proved untenable after about two years, competitiveness and the current account worsened; eventually, growth ground to a halt and consumption declined for three years. The slump lasted for several years (see table 16.4).

5. High and declining interest rates.

In all countries the consolidations were accompanied by large and fast declines in nominal interest rates from very high levels. In Denmark the 10-year interest rate fell from 21 percent in 1982 to 11 percent in 1987, in Finland it fell from 12 percent in 1992 to 7 percent in 1996, and the rate fell by similar amounts in the other two countries (table 16.8). This was made possible by wage moderation, which in turn made the nominal anchors credible.

In Denmark and Ireland, the declines in interest rates led to large increases in house prices and possibly a large wealth effect on households. According to Giavazzi and Pagano (1990), this was largely responsible for the spur in private consumption.

What are the key policy conclusions we can derive from these episodes? Causality is difficult to establish in economics, all the more so from a few case studies. But a few patterns can be detected that could provide useful insights—and caveats—for the current situation, particularly of euro area countries.

1. The oft-cited expansionary consolidations of Europe in the 1980s and 1990s were smaller and less spending-based than previously thought.

2. All started at very high levels of nominal and real interest rates, which then declined quickly. Interest rates are at historical lows today except in those countries on the periphery, where they include a default risk premium.

3. Wage moderation was the key to a credible peg in Denmark and Ireland, and to maintaining the benefits of devaluations in Finland and Sweden. But wage inflation is hardly a problem in today's low-inflation scenario. In addition, income policies were in turn instrumental in achieving wage moderation. But for political and perhaps cultural reasons, income policies are not on the agenda today.

4. Except in Denmark, exports were the prime factor of the recovery for several quarters, and thereafter kept growing at a sustained pace for several years; domestic demand initially stalled or even fell. All countries (including Denmark and Ireland, which pegged the exchange rate during the consolidation—the more relevant case for today's euro area members) devalued repeatedly before the consolidations. This option is obviously not available to euro area members except vis-à-vis non-euro-area members. Ireland also benefited from the appreciation of the currency of its main trading partner, the UK. On the other hand, the Danish expansion was short-lived, as it quickly ran into a loss of competitiveness that hampered growth for several years.

The observations above suggest that the notion of "expansionary fiscal austerity" *in the short run* is probably an illusion: A trade-off does seem to exist between fiscal austerity and short-run growth.

How does this evidence compare with the econometric evidence from time-series studies? Contrary to widespread opinion, there is very little disagreement on the fact that a positive shock to government spending causes total GDP to rise. The disagreement concerns the effect on private consumption and private investment, and on private GDP. I do not want to revisit this debate here but would like to point out that the evidence that government spending crowds out private GDP comes from shocks to defense spending or to total government spending when defense spending shocks dominate (e.g., during World War II). The response of private GDP and its components to civilian spending shocks is positive and large (figure 16.1).

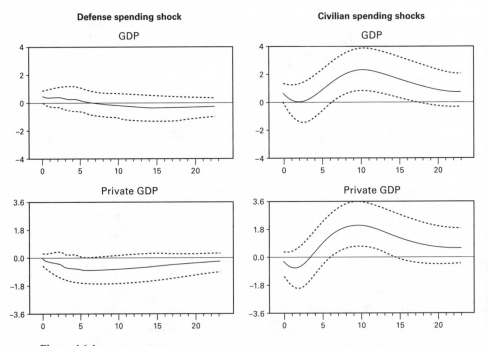

Figure 16.1
Effects of Different Government Spending Shocks, Government Spending versus Private GDP
Source: Perotti (2013b).

There is one important caveat to all this, however: We know very little, indeed next to nothing, about multipliers on government transfers, as opposed to government spending on goods and services.

Option 2: Expand government spending temporarily.

The second option for a government with some fiscal space wishing to use fiscal policy as an antirecessionary tool is to increase government spending, and convince markets that it will cut back on spending later. The advantages of this policy are clear. It reconciles solvency and sustainability with the use of countercyclical fiscal policy; and it takes advantage of the higher spending multipliers at the zero lower bound (ZLB) or, more generally, in a recession (more on this later).

This option has often been proposed as particularly suited for the current situation. But one has to be careful. Multiyear budget plans are dangerous objects: For politicians, there is an obvious incentive to announce spending cuts for the future, and when the future comes, to postpone them. This can be seen clearly in the Clinton budgets (eventually the problem was solved by the economic recovery); and also in the experience of Finland and especially Sweden in the early 1990s, described above, when, at the beginning, a new government would announce plans for large spending cuts in the following five years, which cuts, however, materialized only in a very small part.[7]

Two important stipulations often accompany this proposal: budget targets and commitments should be set in cyclically adjusted terms, and a "fiscal council" should be set up to monitor the implementation of the plans. In theory, both make a lot of sense. In practice, however, we should not forget that cyclical adjustment is an art more than a science; the dispersion of cyclically adjusted numbers on the same aggregate by different institutions at a given point in time and by the same institution at different points in time should be an important warning. Because of this uncertainty, cyclically adjusted figures will be prone to political manipulation and to endless bickering, and in the end may be more confusing to markets than the raw figures.

Fiscal councils, too, make a lot of sense in theory. The parallel is often drawn with the move to make central banks independent in the past three decades. But there is one fundamental difference. Central banks control very few instruments (and just one until a few years ago, the policy interest rate), with limited distributional effects—or at least with distributional effects that are not immediately apparent. Fiscal policy consists of a myriad of instruments, with enormous distributional implications. No government and no parliament will ever relinquish it completely. This is not to say that fiscal councils might not have a role, but it is hard to escape the conclusion that they will work in countries where the cultural and political environment is already well disposed to a responsible fiscal policy.

The policy of increasing government spending to take advantage of the extra kick from the ZLB is gaining momentum in Europe, as a backlash against "German austerity" also gains strength everywhere. Academically, it is supported by some empirical evidence to the effect that government spending might have a higher multiplier during recessions (see, e.g., Eggertsson 2010). However, this is only indirect evidence concerning the ZLB itself, as not all recessions coincided with interest rates close to zero. In addition, the mechanism at work is not clear. Theoretically, fiscal policy is more powerful at the ZLB because, in a sticky price model, a persistent increase in government spending causes a rise in expected inflation and therefore a decline in the real interest rate if the nominal interest rate is fixed at zero; from the Euler equation, this causes private consumption to increase today. However, at first sight, the experience of those countries that did increase government spending with very low interest rates at the beginning of the crisis, or of Japan in the 1990s, seems hard to square with this mechanism.

In addition, a higher multiplier does not mean necessarily higher welfare. In a representative agent model, it is easy to see that welfare could decline even if the multiplier at the ZLB is large, and in a nonrepresentative agent model in general savers will be harmed by this policy (see Bilbiie, Monacelli, and Perotti 2013).

Option 3: Cut taxes temporarily.

The results based on tax data from Romer and Romer suggest that the tax multiplier can be very large (Romer and Romer 2010; Mertens and Ravn 2013), although probably not as large as in the original Romer and Romer study (Perotti 2012). Another advantage is that this policy might be Pareto improving, whereas a policy of increasing government spending is not. Although savers are hurt by an increase in government spending, even at the ZLB, they might still benefit from a temporary tax cut. When there are liquidity constrained individuals, a tax cut is like a transfer from savers to borrowers today, offset by a transfer in the opposite direction tomorrow. Both borrowers and savers can benefit from this operation (see Bilbiie, Monacelli, and Perotti 2013).

However, in the real world, a tax cut has one disadvantage: it might have bad distributional effects, as it does not benefit the low end of the distribution of income. This suggests two areas that we need to learn more about. The first is the general equilibrium effect of alternative types of tax changes, with different distributional effects. The empirical evidence we have from the Romer and Romer data concerns aggregate changes in taxes (Mertens and Ravn [2013] do study the different effects of personal and corporate income taxes). More generally, we need to understand better how to design economically and politically feasible policies to protect the low end of the distribution during periods of fiscal adjustments.

Notes

1. A government is solvent when future taxes are enough to cover future spending plus the existing debt. A government that is not currently perceived as solvent must therefore reduce deficits now or later (or use inflation to reduce the current value of debt). The current level of debt is sustainable if, at the current primary deficit, GDP growth is sufficient to keep the current debt/GDP ratio constant. A government whose debt is not perceived as sustainable must engineer higher growth or a lower interest rate if it does not want to reduce the primary deficit.

2. The "discretionary" change in the deficit is the part of the change in the deficit that is not due to the automatic response of the deficit to the economic cycle. In this sense, it can be interpreted as the part of the change in the deficit due to intentional actions by policymakers, such as changes in tax rates, in replacement rate for unemployment benefits, in defense spending, etc. The same definition applies to each individual budget component.

3. There are two methods to obtain "discretionary" measures of a change in a budget variable. First, the "cyclical adjustment" method: Estimate the elasticities of that budget variable to, say, output and inflation, and subtract from the actual change in the budget variable the change in output multiplied by the output elasticity and the change in inflation multiplied by the inflation elasticity. Second, the "narrative" method, pioneered by Romer and Romer (2010) for revenue changes: Use budget documents to infer the discretionary change in tax revenues or spending enacted by any law that has consequences for the budget. Devries and others

(2011) compute yearly discretionary changes in government spending and revenues during periods of deficit reductions in 15 countries.

4. The pros and cons of case studies vs. an econometric approach are well-known. Hence, I will not revisit this debate here.

5. All this still excludes bank support measures. For instance, in Finland the government spent about 10 percent of GDP to support the banking sector.

6. For instance, an official in the Irish administration at the time later wrote:

Briefly, there was no significant reduction in the real volume of current spending as a result of [the expenditure review set up by the new government in 1987]. There was a further squeeze on capital spending, a mistake in retrospect, but most of the adjustment came on the revenue side. The "slash and burn" stories about 1987, references to the finance minister as "Mac the Knife," decimation of public services and so forth are just journalistic invention. It never happened. (McCarthy 2010, 45)

7. Mauro (2011) attributes this undoing of the original plans mostly to shocks. I believe that in many cases, it is just a simple issue of time inconsistency.

References

Ades, A., M. Kiguel, and N. Liviatan. 1993. "Exchange-Rate-Based Stabilization: Tales from Europe and Latin America." Policy Research Working Paper 1087, World Bank, Washington, DC.

Alesina, A., and S. Ardagna. 2010. Large Changes in Fiscal Policy: Taxes versus Spending. In *Tax Policy and the Economy*, vol. 24, ed. Jeffrey R. Brown. Cambridge, MA: National Bureau of Economic Research.

Alesina, A., and S. Ardagna. 2012. "The Design of Fiscal Adjustments." Faculty paper, Bocconi University, Milan.

Alesina, A., and R. Perotti. 1995. "Fiscal Expansions and Adjustments in OECD Economies." *Economic Policy* 21:207–247.

Bilbiie, F., T. Monacelli, and R. Perotti. 2013. "Tax Cuts vs. Government Spending: Welfare at the Zero Lower Bound." Faculty paper, Bocconi University, Milan.

Devries, P., J. Guajardo, D. Leigh, and A. Pescatori. 2011. "A New Action-Based Dataset of Fiscal Consolidation." IMF Working Paper 11/128, International Monetary Fund, Washington, DC. Data set available at www.imf.org/external/pubs/cat/longres.aspx?sk=24892.0.

Eggertsson, G. 2010. "What Fiscal Policy Is Effective at Zero Interest Rates?" In *NBER Macroeconomics Annual 2010*, vol. 25, 59–112. Cambridge, MA: MIT Press.

Giavazzi, F., and M. Pagano. 1990. "Can Severe Fiscal Contractions Be Expansionary? Tales of Two Small European Countries." In *NBER Macroeconomics Annual 1990*, vol. 5, 75–122. Cambridge, MA: MIT Press.

Jonung, L., J. Kiander, and P. Vartia. 2008. "The Great Financial Crisis in Finland and Sweden: The Dynamics of Boom, Bust, and Recovery, 1985–2000." Economic Papers 350, Directorate-General, Economic and Financial Affairs, European Commission, Brussels, December. http://ec.europa.eu/economy_finance/publications/publication13551_en.pdf.

Mauro, P., ed. 2011. *Chipping Away at Public Debt*. New York: Wiley.

McCarthy, C. 2010. "Ireland's Second Round of Cuts: A Comparison with the Last Time." In *Dealing with Debt: Lessons from Abroad*, ed. J. Springford, 41–54. CentreForum (Centre for Reform) Canada, Ernst & Young.

Mertens, K., and M. Ravn. 2013. "The Dynamic Effects of Personal and Corporate Income Tax changes in the United States." *American Economic Review* 103 (4): 1212–1247.

Perotti, R. 2012. "The Effects of Tax Shocks on Output: Not So Large, but Not Small Either." *American Economic Journal: Economic Policy* 42:214–237.

Perotti, R. 2013a. "The Austerity Myth: Growth without Pain?" In *Fiscal Policy after the Great Recession*, ed. A. Alesina and F. Giavazzi. Chicago: University of Chicago Press.

Perotti, R. 2013b. "Defense Government Spending Is Contractionary; Civilian Government Spending Is Expansionary." Faculty paper, Bocconi University, Milan.

Romer, C., and D. Romer. 2010. "The Macroeconomic Effects of Tax Changes: Estimates Based on a New Measure of Fiscal Shocks." *American Economic Review* 100 (3): 763–801.

17

Fiscal Policy

Nouriel Roubini

The recent global financial crisis has brought the attention of analysts and policymakers back to the role of fiscal policy during the crisis and its aftermath. Several important questions need to be addressed: What is the relationship between levels of public debt and economic growth? What are the causes of high debt and deficits—loose fiscal policy or weak economic growth? What is the size of fiscal multipliers, and how do they depend on business cycle conditions? Is there a risk of fiscal dominance? How can we reduce a debt overhang and achieve a smoother deleveraging from high debt ratios? What is the optimal pace of fiscal consolidation? The question of fiscal policy is a critical one, so I will to try to answer these questions.

The first question one needs to address concerns the relationship between high public debt and economic growth, and the costs of that high debt. Economic theory suggests that at some point, high public debt can have a negative effect on economic growth. It can lead to high real interest rates and crowd out investment and consumption. It can increase the risk of a debt crisis with all the collateral damage of a debt default occurring. It can force policymakers to increase taxes to avoid a debt crisis, but high taxes cause distortions that negatively affect economic growth.

So those are the factors that can lead to lower growth in the presence of high and rising public debt levels. Recent research work by a number of scholars, especially Carmen Reinhart and Kenneth Rogoff, (Reinhart and Rogoff 2010) suggests that there could be a significant empirical relationship between high public debt and lower economic growth. According to them, the critical threshold in advanced economies occurred when debt was greater than 90 percent of GDP (lower in emerging markets).

This is when the negative effects on economic growth become significant. Indeed, the median debt ratio for advanced economies has gone from about 60 percent of GDP before the crisis to a level closer to 100 percent today.

When one considers Reinhart and Rogoff's empirical results, there are two important things to keep in mind. One is, of course, the causality issue. Is it the high debt ratios that cause lower economic growth, or shocks that lead to significant recessions, or financial crises that cause economic weakness and thus lead to an increasing debt ratio? So the first question is the causality one.

Recent academic work (Herndon, Ash, and Pollin 2013) has shown some serious methodological problems with Reinhart and Rogoff's results: The relationship between high debt and economic growth might not be as robust as they thought it was. Thus, the recent conventional wisdom that high debt leads to lower growth rates has been seriously challenged empirically.

As Olivier Blanchard, Giovanni Dell'Ariccia, and Paolo Mauro suggest in the introduction to this book, another big risk and potential effect of high debt is the risk of multiple equilibria. If you have a lot of public debt and it has to be rolled over, there is a risk that you may end up in a situation in which there is a self-fulfilling run on public debt. This will make the spreads higher and unsustainable, and you may end up in a situation in which a liquidity problem leads to insolvency. An illiquid but solvent sovereign might end up in default if such a run does occur; this is a bad equilibrium that you cannot rule out. All else equal, having a lower debt ratio and less of a liquidity risk with a longer-maturity debt can reduce the risk of such a bad equilibrium.

Of course, there is a solution to a liquidity crisis. We know it in the case of bank runs, but the same thing occurs in the case of a run on government debt. If you have a lender of last resort—a central bank that can provide liquidity to a sovereign by monetizing its debt—you can avoid that bad run equilibrium. This was certainly the situation with the euro area in the summer of 2012, when interest rates on Italian debt rose to almost 7 percent and those on Spain's debt were closer to 8 percent. When Mario Draghi gave his "whatever it takes" speech and the European Central Bank (ECB) announced its Outright Monetary Transactions (OMT) program, a significant reduction in those yields and spreads occurred as both the currency redenomination risk of a euro area breakup and the risk of a run on public debt were sharply reduced. This suggests an element of self-fulfilling bad equilibrium in the case of Spain and Italy in the summer of 2012, when the spread kept on rising to unsustainable levels. The existence of a lender of last resort can help avoid those bad equilibria.

Similarly, are rates in the United States and Japan low because these markets are safe havens during periods when tail risks are high and risk is off? Or are those low rates the result of large-scale quantitative easing that is effectively a form of debt monetization that reduces the risk of runs on public debt and keeps long rates lower than they otherwise would be?

Of course, one needs then to address the moral hazard problems that such intervention/insurance against liquidity runs on public debt may induce.

The second question that is worth discussing concerns the causes of high debt problems. The policy answer on what we should do about high debt ratios depends in part on what led debt to increase and reach such a high level. When one looks at the experience of the last few years, of course one finds examples of countries in which fiscal policy was loose and reckless. The obvious example might be Greece, which was running very large and unsustainable budget deficits until the onset of its debt crisis in 2010. Policymakers there effectively cheated and lied about the true size of the deficit, which turned out to be 15 percent of GDP, much higher than previously announced.

Of course, if you run very large budget deficits for reasons that have to do with political distortions that lead to an increase of debt that becomes unsustainable, you are in a typical situation where you're going to have a debt crisis owing to reckless fiscal policy. And those high debt ratios will have sharply negative effects on economic growth.

However, the experience of the past decade suggests that many of the financial crises led to a large increase in public debt and deficits that started with private-sector, not public-sector, financial excesses. These were credit, housing, and asset bubbles of one sort or another that eventually burst, and once they burst they caused a significant increase in budget deficits and public debt. These increases were first driven by the ensuing recession that triggered automatic stabilizers. Thus, revenues fell sharply over time while spending rose.

Second, whenever a financial crisis does occur—such as the one in 2008–2009—there's also the risk that a great recession might turn into another Great Depression. Therefore, the optimal policy response to avoid such a depression was a fiscal stimulus—most necessary in a situation in which private demand is collapsing. If private consumption and investment are in free fall and you don't have a large fiscal stimulus (an increase in spending or a reduction in taxes or a combination of the two), an economy could fall into a depression. In fact, one of the lessons of the Great Depression was that you need a fiscal stimulus when private demand is collapsing.

Third, the fiscal cost of cleaning up, bailing out, and backstopping the financial system, or even corporations (the GM and Chrysler bailouts) or households, implies there will be large costs. In these financial crises, lots of contingent liabilities will emerge, and that will be the source of additional increases in public debt.

Again, the experiences over the last few years, perhaps especially the examples of Ireland, Iceland, Spain, the United Kingdom, and the United States—and even emerging markets such as Dubai—were all essentially private-sector-induced excesses that led to bubbles. Those excesses eventually led to a bust, and the resulting increase in public debt and deficit was the result of that severe financial crisis. This implies that perhaps the policy response to a balance sheet crisis might be different from the response to a situation in which there was reckless fiscal behavior in the first place. In balance sheet crises—where the bust leads the private sector to sharply deleverage by cutting spending on consumption and investment——a large fiscal stimulus is necessary to prevent the collapse of private demand from causing an even more severe recession. Thus, fiscal stimulus (along with aggressive monetary easing) rather than fiscal contraction is the appropriate policy response to a private-sector-induced balance sheet crisis. This is the policy that economists such as Richard Koo have correctly identified as appropriate following balance sheet crises.

The third question to discuss has to do with the size of fiscal multipliers. Does a fiscal expansion increase GDP? How large are those fiscal multipliers? Are they greater than 1 or not? The related question is whether fiscal consolidation is expansionary. There is a popular hypothesis that a fiscal consolidation will have a positive confidence effect (a "confidence fairy") on economic growth; that is, that reducing the fiscal deficit will increase economic activity even in the short run. Is that view correct?

If one looks at the empirical evidence, four results emerge. First, as Roberto Perotti shows in chapter 16, there is no real evidence that fiscal consolidation is expansionary in the short run; rather, it tends to have negative effects on economic activity. This is the case even in the euro area, where fiscal consolidation may be needed over time to avoid a debt crisis. In fact, the front-loading of fiscal austerity in the euro area periphery is one of the reasons this region fell into a double-dip recession in 2011–2012.

Second, the work that the IMF has done is consistent with the view that fiscal austerity is contractionary, at least in the short run. If you raise taxes and thus reduce disposable income, or if you cut government spending, even unproductive government spending, you are reducing aggregate demand. Therefore, reducing disposable income and aggregate demand will have a negative effect on economic activity in the short run. Also, when you have synchronized fiscal austerity in many parts of the world, the fiscal multipliers will be larger. Indeed, until 2012, fiscal austerity was limited to the periphery of the euro area and the UK. But in 2013 even the United States will have a significant fiscal drag and, given the European Fiscal Compact, even the core of the euro area (Germany and others) will implement fiscal austerity. Then, in a situation in which many countries are practicing austerity at the same time, those fiscal multipliers could end up being actually larger than when fiscal austerity is less synchronized globally.

Third, there are about a dozen econometric/statistical studies about the 2009 US fiscal stimulus. Most of these studies report that it was expansionary on GDP and that the results were large and significant.

Fourth, there is increasing evidence that the fiscal multipliers are larger when you are bound by a zero interest rate policy and when there is a meaningful slack in the economy, that is, when you are in recession or you are growing very slowly.

So, a fair reading of the empirical evidence suggests that fiscal stimulus is effective in stimulating growth, especially after a financial crisis, when the economy has a large slack and is in a liquidity trap; conversely, excessively front-loaded fiscal consolidation has a negative effect on growth.

The empirical evidence and the conceptual arguments about how to appropriately respond to a balance sheet crisis with a fiscal stimulus explain some of the severe economic contraction that the euro area economies experienced. For example, in Spain and Ireland, there was clear evidence of a balance sheet crisis driven by private-sector behavior. But how much of the severity of the crisis in Spain, with an unemployment rate of 27 percent and rising (55 percent and rising among the young) was due to the fact that there was initially very limited fiscal expansion and then, when spreads rose, there was significant front-loaded fiscal austerity?

Roberto Perotti in chapter 16 argues that the optimal response to high deficit and debt depends in part on whether a country has "fiscal space" or not, meaning whether active bond market vigilantes have increased the country's sovereign spreads and led to a loss of market access or not. The argument has also been made that in the case of the euro area periphery there was no fiscal stimulus option: If the markets are punishing a country and spreads are high and rising, or if the country has lost market access, the only option is fiscal adjustment.

This argument is only partially valid and includes at least three important caveats. First, whether a country has fiscal space or not depends in part on whether it has a central bank that is willing to do quantitative easing and monetize public debt. In the case of the euro area, if the behavior of the ECB had been more dovish, the implication for fiscal space would have been different.

The second point is the existence of a central bank that is willing to avoid a self-fulfilling bad equilibrium. This implies that a run against the public debt or the widening of the sovereign spread can be avoided even if actual debt monetization doesn't occur but is only available as an option. Think about the ECB's OMT program: In a sense, this has been the most successful monetary policy tool ever, because not a single euro has been spent yet to backstop Italy, Spain, or any other country. But the spreads in Italy and Spain have fallen by 250 to 300 basis points in 2013, compared to what they were in the summer of 2012.

So, the mere existence of a potential lender of last resort can lead to a better equilibrium, even if the lender doesn't act. That's an important factor in determining whether a country has market access or not.

Third, even if a country (its sovereign) doesn't have market access, either because it has lost it or because the private sector is imposing market discipline, the existence of official creditors (e.g., the IMF, the EU, the European Financial Stabilization Mechanism [EFSM], the European Stability Mechanism [ESM]) can provide a sovereign with some fiscal pace. Given the existence of official external creditors that can substitute for the private ones, the question is, what is their optimal use? There has always been a debate about a country—say, an emerging market country that gets in trouble—and the existence of an organization that provides it with financial support conditional on austerity and reforms. The IMF allows a country under financial stress to have a better path of fiscal consolidation than it would have if that official financing didn't exist.

In the case of the euro area, of course, the existence of official creditors (a euro-area-wide lending and liquidity mechanism) also gives sovereigns under pressure some degree of flexibility. Therefore, in evaluating whether a country has fiscal space or not, the considerations above matter. Countries such as the United States, the UK, and Japan still have very low interest rates despite a large fiscal deficit and debt in part because central banks have been willing to do quantitative easing and effective debt monetization. Meanwhile, in countries in the euro area where debt ratios are no higher than those of the United States, the UK, or Japan (and in some cases are lower), spreads were high and widening when the ECB was essentially refusing to provide that type of monetary easing.

The next issue worth discussing is fiscal dominance and how much one should be concerned about it. In a situation in which budget deficits are large and there is a political bias toward deficits, there is always the risk of fiscal dominance. The risk is that a central bank is going to be forced essentially to monetize these deficits to prevent a debt crisis. In a game of chicken between a fiscal authority and a monetary authority, it is the latter that blinks if fiscal dominance rules.

On the issue of fiscal dominance, there is a difference between the views of the ECB and the Bank of Japan (BOJ) under Masaaki Shirakawa (who both worried about the fiscal dominance effect) and the views of the Fed and the BOJ under Haruhiko Kuroda (who don't seem to be worrying about such risk).

One can interpret the Fed views as follows. First, the central bank cannot really bully fiscal authorities into fiscal discipline. A central bank can't threaten the fiscal authority and force it to make fiscal adjustments by denying a necessary monetary easing.

Second, if the central bank tries to bully the fiscal authorities, it might end up in a political clash with them, and the ensuing backlash could lead to a formal loss of central bank independence.

Third, if the central bank withholds a necessary monetary policy stimulus because it wants to force the fiscal authority to adjust, it might not succeed and might actually cause a severe recession. So, monetary policy should do what's necessary for the economy regardless of what's happening on the fiscal side.

Thus, the best that a central bank can do—as the Fed chairman has done—is to jawbone fiscal policymakers to make the necessary fiscal adjustment. Using the threat of withholding necessary monetary stimulus to induce fiscal adjustment has negative and perverse effects.

However, the ECB's and the German view of the issue of fiscal dominance has been very different. For example, in the case of the euro area, the OMT has been made conditional on strict and effective fiscal and structural conditionality as a way of actively limiting fiscal dominance.

Second, by reducing spread, the existence of the OMT has led to concerns in Germany and even in the Bundesbank that there is policy delay and slack in the euro area periphery. According to this view, complacency and moral hazard exist in the euro area periphery; austerity and reforms are not occurring at the pace desired by the ECB and the core of the euro area. Therefore, the German view and the Bundesbank's view is that market discipline is sometimes good and necessary to force governments to implement without delay the necessary policy actions. On the other hand, excessive market discipline—in the form of higher spreads—is destabilizing attempts to reduce deficits and make debts sustainable. Thus, market discipline is a double-edged sword.

Certainly there are risks of fiscal dominance in the presence of the liquidity support of the central bank. And there is also a risk of moral hazard whenever you have other official resources—such as the ESM, EFSM, and IMF loans—to support sovereigns under pressure. But the argument about moral hazard is a bit excessive. Assume you are a government and you have to do painful fiscal austerity, but suppose that the confidence fairy does not come along (i.e., spreads don't fall despite austerity and reforms) because there is uncertainty about the credibility of the government actions and about how long the government is going to stick with the policies. There is a serious risk that fiscal adjustment and reform may fail in a situation in which markets do not yet find the country's policies fully credible. In this case, if you don't have official support (whether from the central bank or from official creditors), the incentive to practice painful austerity and make reforms might be low, because even if you attempt them you might fail and end up in a debt crisis. Therefore, moral hazard is reduced rather than increased with the presence of official money because you have a carrot inducing the government to implement painful policies that are likely to fail in the absence of official financing. Here, the carrot is that if the government implements the necessary and painful efforts, liquidity will be provided that reduces the risk of a bad equilibrium. Therefore, in the presence of official financing, a self-fulfilling crisis is avoided and moral hazard is reduced rather than increased.

A few years ago, I wrote a paper with Giancarlo Corsetti and Bernardo Guimarães (Corsetti, Guimarães, and Roubini 2004) in which we showed, using the analytical framework of global games, that the existence of official financing can reduce moral hazard rather than increase it. Official financing provides a carrot that gives an incentive to a government that might otherwise reason, "If I am likely to fail, why should I make the policy effort in the first place?" The presence of official financing reduces the probability of a bad equilibrium, so the argument that official support causes moral hazard and fiscal dominance might be incorrect.

The next question to address is how to reduce a debt overhang; that is, what is the optimal approach to deleveraging from high levels of public and private debt? There are several options. The first one is fiscal austerity: a government can cut spending, raise taxes, and thus increase public savings. But that option, if too front-loaded, leads to the Keynesian paradox of thrift: if the fiscal adjustment is too fast, the economy may contract again, and the goal of reducing deficits and debt may fail. This is partly what has been happening in the euro area and the UK. The second option is a coercive debt restructuring/reduction. That option might become necessary and unavoidable if a country has an issue of solvency rather than liquidity.

Another option is very aggressive monetary policy (zero policy rates and quantitative easing); this is effectively a form of debt monetization that leads to a low nominal interest rate and possibly negative real interest rates. This option might not be inflationary if the country is in a liquidity trap and there is a large amount of slack in the goods and labor markets. A variant of this option is financing from official creditors (the IMF, the EU), which provides a breathing space for a slower adjustment of spending and savings.

Another option is to cause expected or unexpected inflation to wipe out the real value of nominal public debt. Yet another option might be to use capital levies on wealth or on creditors as a way of resolving the debt overhang. A variant of that is to use financial repression and capital controls to keep government bond yields lower than they otherwise would be.

All except the first option, adjustment and higher savings, imply some redistribution of wealth from creditors and savers to debtors and borrowers (e.g., an indebted government). But the adjustment from a debt overhang that depresses the spending of debtors necessarily implies that such a transfer of wealth should occur over time. The political question is, who should be making such redistribution policy decisions? Should the decision be made by fiscal authorities through a capital levy on wealth or debt restructuring, or should the central bank have the power to accomplish the same result via debt monetization?

Some argue that such power should not be given to the central bank, as these are eminently fiscal and thus political decisions. But if low nominal rates and negative real ones from debt monetization allow a smoother deleveraging process that reduces the risks of a recession deriving from excessive austerity and prevents a more disruptive debt restructuring or the distortionary costs of financial repression, capital controls, and capital levy, debt monetization could be the least costly option.

The final issue worth addressing concerns the optimal pace of fiscal consolidation following a financial crisis that has led to a large increase in public debt.

In most cases in which market access has not been lost or in which official financing (from the central bank or from official external creditors) is available, the optimal pace of fiscal consolidation would entail a fiscal stimulus in the short run, while the economy is weak and the private sector is deleveraging its indebted balance sheets, plus a credible plan for medium- to long-term fiscal consolidation, to be implemented when the economy has recovered enough and private balance sheets are mostly mended. This short-/medium-/long-term adjustment can be helped by effective debt monetization by a central bank, which makes the dele-veraging process smoother and avoids the risk of runs on banks and governments. Delaying fiscal adjustment forever can cause a "zombification" of governments and private agents and eventually a debt crisis, even if the initial surge in the public deficit was due to a private-sector balance sheet crisis. Conversely, excessively front-loading the fiscal consolidation risks pushing a fragile economy into a double-dip recession that will only make the deficit and debt problems worse.

Compared to this optimal path of fiscal consolidation, the major advanced economies—the euro area, the UK, and the United States—have followed a suboptimal path. In the euro area and the UK, fiscal austerity has been front-loaded in the short run. This is one of the reasons—along with a monetary policy that wasn't loose enough and zombie banks that were not appropriately recapitalized, thus driving a credit crunch—why both regions have fallen into a double-dip recession.

In the United States, gridlock and lack of bipartisanship in Congress make it look as though the country has no credible path for medium- and long-term fiscal consolidation, as Republicans block further tax increases while Democrats block spending and entitlement reforms. Meanwhile, in the short run (thanks to the same gridlock), the fiscal drag will be excessive in 2013 because of a front load of fiscal consolidation engendered by the sequestration deadlock. So the United States is taking the opposite of the optimal path: too much short-run fiscal drag in 2013 and 2014, with no credible plan for consolidation in the medium term. Still, compared to the euro area and the UK, which have front-loaded their fiscal austerity since 2011, the United States successfully postponed its central government austerity until 2013, which explains why the country is growing, however anemically, while the euro area and the UK have been contracting.

The fiscal adjustment in the euro area has been an example of poor policy planning; it explains why the periphery of the region is still stuck in a recession that is becoming a near depression in some countries (Greece and Spain) and why the recession is even spreading to some parts of the core (France and Belgium). A few remarks are important concerning the euro area fiscal adjustment.

First, the austerity has been excessively front-loaded in the euro area periphery, with seriously damaging effects. It should be significantly back-loaded.

Second, the flexibility that the EU Commission allows in achieving cyclical adjusted targets and the fiscal relief it offers to countries in recession are palliatives that occur after the patient has nearly been killed. Setting very aggressive structural fiscal targets for a country, then allowing some cyclical slack on those targets once the austerity measures have caused a recession that worsened the deficit is no rational solution. Structural fiscal targets should be realistic in the first place to avoid such austerity-induced recession.

Third, the adjustment in the euro area is asymmetric between periphery and core, and thus recessionary and deflationary. If countries and governments that overspend and undersave should spend less and save more, countries (like Germany) that oversave and underspend should spend more and save less (in part, through fiscal policies of tax reduction and spending increase). Otherwise, the adjustment is asymmetric and recessionary, as it leads to a shortage of aggregate demand for the whole region.

Fourth, there is fiscal space in the core of the euro area, especially in countries such as Germany, where interest rates are low and market access is ample. It is true that the public debt in Germany is 80 percent of GDP and that implicit liabilities from aging are additional fiscal burdens. But sovereign spreads are so low in Germany that if the country were to implement for a couple of years a fiscal stimulus in the form of a reduction in taxes and increases in government spending as a way of boosting its own economic growth and that of the overall euro area, this policy action would not lead to any loss of fiscal credibility as long as the country had a plan for medium- to long-term fiscal consolidation. What we are speaking about is a short-term program to try to jump-start economic growth in a euro area that is in a deep recession.

Fifth, while the growth problems of the euro area are more structural than cyclical compared with those of the United States, in 2012–2013 the euro area didn't grow even at its low potential growth rate, as it was in a recession. The fact that the region was stuck in a recession suggests that the lack of aggregate demand, not just supply-side constraints, explains this persistent economic downturn.

Moreover, some of the necessary structural reforms are, like fiscal austerity, contractionary in the short run. Suppose, for example, that a country makes its labor market more flexible and reduces hiring and firing costs. The first impact of such reform will be a rise in the unemployment rate, as the firms that could not fire redundant workers will now be able to do so. That surge in the unemployment rate is exactly what happened in Germany when it implemented its structural reforms in the early 2000s. The implication is that there has to be a trade-off between structural reforms and fiscal austerity, rather than a damaging recessionary front load of both. For example, if a country implements rapid structural reforms that are recessionary in the short run, it should be given greater fiscal flexibility, as the reforms might make the recession worse in the short run. That is exactly what Germany was claiming when it implemented its Agenda 2010 and its unemployment rate was rising; the Germans asked the EU for a fiscal break because their reforms were causing a rise in unemployment that was leading to a larger fiscal deficit. They argued, correctly, that the reforms would eventually increase growth. In the short run they were causing an increase in the deficit, but that deficit would go away once the effects of the reforms on growth materialized in the medium term.

So, there has to be a trade-off between austerity and reforms. You cannot just front-load both the austerity and the structural reforms. If you do more on the structural side, you have to provide for greater fiscal flexibility in the short run; otherwise, the recession is likely to become more severe.

A final observation about the euro area: There is absolutely no talk about a growth agenda. There is talk about a banking union, a fiscal union, a political union. But if you're not going to have economic growth, and if the austerity makes the recession worse, you will eventually have a social and political backlash against the austerity. Also, sovereigns are trying to stabilize their public debt, domestic and foreign, as a share of GDP. But one can work as much as one wants on the numerator of the debt ratio, but if the denominator (GDP) keeps falling, debt ratios will keep rising and will become unsustainable. That is what is happening right now in the euro area: Despite draconian fiscal adjustment, public debt ratios are still rising, and they may eventually become unsustainable.

Excessively front-loaded fiscal consolidation in both the periphery and the core of the euro area has been counterproductive. It is an important factor in explaining why the region has been stuck in a deep double-dip recession in 2012–2013.

References

Corsetti, Giancarlo, Bernardo Guimarães, and Nouriel Roubini. 2004. "International Lending of Last Resort and Moral Hazard: A Model of IMF's Catalytic Finance." CEPR Discussion Papers 4383. London: CEPR.

Herndon, Thomas, Michael Ash, and Robert Pollin. 2013. "Does High Public Debt Consistently Stifle Economic Growth? A Critique of Reinhart and Rogoff." University of Massachusetts Amherst, Working Paper #322, April http://www.peri.umass.edu/fileadmin/pdf/working_papers/working_papers_301-350/WP322.pdf.

Reinhart, Carmen, and Kenneth Rogoff. 2010. "Growth in a Time of Debt." *American Economic Review* (May):573–578.

V

Exchange Rate Arrangements

18

How to Choose an Exchange Rate Arrangement

Agustín Carstens

The choice of the appropriate exchange rate regime for any country is an issue that has been extremely important in the past and still is today. It is a policy decision that, to a large extent, conditions the macroeconomic framework of a country. This chapter discusses a number of issues related to this important decision. First it discusses the importance of choosing the exchange rate regime. It then analyzes the implications of the degree of exchange rate rigidity or flexibility for the domestic economy, particularly for other macroeconomic policies. Then it discusses the specific case of the euro area. Finally, it explores the side effects associated with the choice of an exchange rate regime.

There is hardly a more important economic decision that a country has to make than choosing its exchange rate regime. There are at least two reasons for that:

• First, such a decision conditions the scope and flexibility of the rest of the macro policies that the country can implement. Certainly this consideration alone makes choosing the exchange rate regime an extremely relevant decision.

• Second, such a choice affects the country's economic relationship with the rest of the world.

The conditioning effects of the choice of an exchange rate regime imply very difficult trade-offs that policymakers have to evaluate with utmost determination and care when deciding on the exchange rate regime that best suits their country's economy.

In particular, the decision boils down to establishing the degree of flexibility that the exchange rate should have, that is, how much the relative value of the domestic currency can vary with respect to other national currency or currencies. Usually when defining an exchange rate regime, authorities refer to the relative price of the domestic currency with respect to the currency of its main trading partner and/or the currency that dominates in the region.

In principle, it can be said that the less flexibility that is allowed for the exchange rate, the more rigidity the country imposes on the rest of its policies. For instance, when a country fixes its exchange rate, it sacrifices monetary policy as an independent policy instrument, because to a large extent, the country imports the monetary policy of the country that it fixes the value of its own currency against. Under these circumstances, the ability of the national central bank to perform its duty as lender of last resort to the banking system or the sovereign is severely compromised. Furthermore, the sustainability of the regime also imposes restrictions on fiscal policy and makes it essential to preserve a healthy financial system.

In fact, insofar as fixing the exchange rate imposes very strong conditions on the rest of the macro framework, choosing such a regime usually has been used as a commitment device. That is, for a country to make a specific exchange rate sustainable, it has to observe all the constraints such a regime entails. Put differently, the stronger the policy commitment, the more credible the exchange rate regime will be.

Nevertheless, for decades the real challenge for most countries has been to acquire and preserve the ability and political will to remain true to such commitments and keep the exchange rate regime credible. Time after time it has been seen that eventually, after some years, sometimes even after months, these commitments tend to be ignored, and the exchange rate regime collapses. The way that authorities handle a regime switch is also very important since if the switch is mishandled, it has the potential to generate negative consequences for growth and development for years to come.

It should be noted that establishing a flexible exchange rate regime imposes other types of restrictions and exposes the country to other types of risks. Under such a regime, the main challenge is to construct an effective nominal anchor for the economy. There is a broad range of options in this regard, ranging from the adoption of monetary aggregate objectives to inflation targeting. Recent events have shown the limitations of inflation targeting, in particular the fact that central banks should not ignore asset-price inflation so that they can preserve financial stability.

Regarding fixing the exchange rate, there are many different ways to implement it. The simplest alternative is to fix the value of a given currency with respect to another currency. The "ultimate" fix would entail establishing a currency union in a region, allowing national currencies to disappear altogether in favor of adopting a single currency such as the euro. The sustainability of such a complex regime imposes very strict and demanding conditions on all the member countries. With respect to the euro area, the real question is how effective it has been as a whole in fulfilling those conditions in a credible way. In this setting, a lot has been left to be desired; therefore, important efforts through policy adjustments have to be made not only to preserve the credibility of the regime but also to enhance it, so that the possibility of the breakdown of the euro is taken out of the picture for good.

There is another very important dimension to to exchange rate regimes, related to the fact that an exchange rate is the relative price of two currencies. Therefore, from a national perspective, such a relative price can be affected by the actions (monetary expansion, capital controls, etc.) that other countries may undertake, such actions often having negative unintended (or intended) consequences on the exchange rate. Thus, the domestic currency can appreciate or depreciate in response to actions taken by another country, giving rise to debates encapsulated by phrases such as "currency wars" or "beggar thy neighbor policies."

With respect to this point, it has recently been argued that monetary policies in some advanced countries have generated huge capital inflows to other economies, particularly emerging and developing ones, consequently generating substantial real exchange rate adjustments. Some of these adjustments are nonequilibrium appreciations, affecting the tradables sector and the growth potential of emerging economies. This is a typical example of a spillover effect of an advanced economy's monetary policy action. Furthermore, such an effect can trigger or lead to different types of reactions, including some form of retaliation, leading to net deadweight losses for the world as a whole.

To deal with these issues, international coordination might be attempted around a set of exchange rate objectives. This has been done with the help of the IMF in the past. A valid question is whether the international community should try to do this again.

In sum, the choice of an exchange rate regime is a fundamental decision that a country has to make. Such a decision has important implications for the economy as a whole, as it affects the degrees of freedom of other policies, as well as the relationship of the domestic economy to that of the rest of the world. Therefore, the huge political economy implications that the election of the exchange rate arrangement entails makes it a highly relevant topic. To illustrate this, I will finish on a lighter note, with an anecdote: At the beginning of the 1990s, Mexico was facing a major crisis, and for practical purposes its only option was to go from a fixed to a flexible exchange rate regime. Society was not supportive at all. The then central bank governor was summoned by the senate to explain the rationale for Mexico going from a very unsuccessful fix with recurrent adjustments, with often tragic consequences, to a flexible exchange rate. And he couldn't get the point across that for Mexico, the best decision was to go to a flexible exchange rate regime.

Finally, the governor had a brilliant idea to explain such a move by using an analogy. He said to the senators, Imagine that you have the task of painting a house. Now, you can do it in two ways. One way would be to place the paintbrush in a fixed position and move the house, which would be the equivalent to fixing the exchange rate. The alternative is to keep the house in its position and move the paintbrush. With a steady hand, it is very likely that the task could be completed in a cheaper, more beneficial, more efficient way with a flexible brush.

This simple analogy convinced the senate, and since then we have had in Mexico a flexible exchange rate, and it has worked very well.

19

Rethinking Exchange Rate Regimes after the Crisis

Jay C. Shambaugh

The exchange rate regime decision is one of the most important ones a country can make in terms of macroeconomic policy. It has important implications for how a country will manage its financial account and its monetary policy options. This brief chapter cannot run through all aspects of the decision but will instead focus on one thing: what have we learned from the 2008–2009 crisis about the experience of fixed versus floating exchange rates, as well as the institutional design of currency unions.

My thesis is that we have relearned many things we should already have known before the crisis. In many areas, such as fiscal policy at the zero lower bound, monetary policy at the zero lower bound, or macroprudential policy, this crisis surprised many and, at the very least, provided evidence for issues about which we did not have a clear understanding. Conversely, regarding exchange rate regimes, an undergraduate who had taken a basic international macroeconomics class could probably have described ahead of time most of the key events that took place. That student would have known that in general, floating can serve as a shock absorber, external adjustment may be easier if you float, and entering a currency union at the wrong price can be very painful. These are things we already knew, but they are also things we saw time and again throughout the crisis.

One surprise was that when pegs broke during the crisis, they did not spiral wildly out of control. This time around, when a fixed exchange rate broke, countries tended to loosen the bands they kept the exchange rate in, as opposed to having a sharp depreciation. That was a new experience, but the other core stylized facts are things that academics and policymakers should have understood.

These same lessons can serve as reminders for what the institutional structure should be for currency unions, and they highlight the cost of inadequate shock absorbers within a currency union.

Floating as a Shock Absorber

A popular if rather dark joke of early 2009 asked "What's the difference between Ireland and Iceland?" The answer: "One letter and six months." As it turned out, there was another very stark difference (among many others): one had a floating exchange rate and the other did not. Coming into the crisis, Iceland was likely in much worse shape, with a current account deficit greater than 20 percent of GDP in one year, whereas the external deficit peaked at close to 5 percent in Ireland. Both, though, had large credit booms and somewhat spectacular financial busts. And yet the two countries had very different experiences.

In figures 19.1a–f, the solid line is Ireland and the dotted line is Iceland. Iceland experienced a sharp depreciation when the crisis hit (figure 19.1a). It had a higher inflation rate coming out of the crisis (figure 19.1b). But the inflation did not offset all of the depreciation, so there was a substantial real effective exchange rate depreciation (figure 19.1c). In the real economy, real exports grew faster (figure 19.1d). The figure for real GDP (figure 19.1e) shows a modest difference, although, depending on the base year used, this picture could look different. The last figure (figure 19.1f), though, shows the starkest difference: the sharp jump in the unemployment rate in Ireland relative to that in Iceland.

There are many other differences between these two countries, and Iceland has not necessarily been a paragon of financial policy management, but the contrast is a reminder that when there are severe shocks, it is useful to have the pressure release valve of the exchange rate.

If one looks more broadly, there were a number of countries, whether Israel, Poland, Sweden, or the UK, that when the crisis hit benefited from the ability to have their exchange rate change. Even more broadly, in the two decades before the crisis, pegged and nonpegged countries tended to grow at around the same rate. But during the crisis the pegged countries grew about a percentage point more slowly. There may have been different shocks, as well as many other policies all mixed together in that result. So the point is in no way conclusive. And some countries that maintained

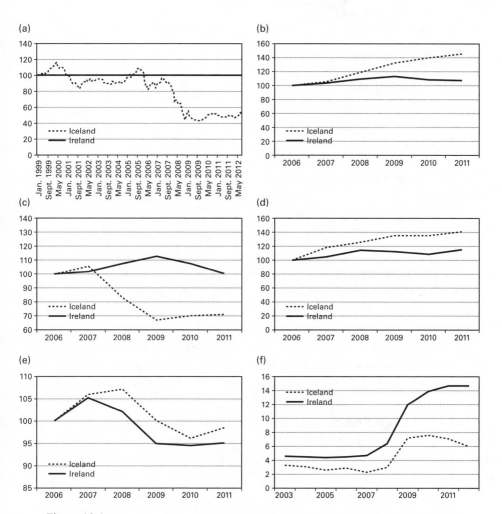

Figure 19.1
a. Exchange rate versus the euro (Jan. 1999 = 100). b. Consumer Price Index (2006 = 100). c. Real effective exchange rate index (2006 = 100). d. Real export index (2006 = 100). e. Real GDP index (2006 = 100). f. Unemployment rate.

a floating exchange rate in the past five years felt they were appreciating too much, and they likely would have preferred to have been pegged rather than to experience the appreciation. But a floating exchange rate, both in theory and from casual observations made during the crisis, can serve as a shock absorber.

Exchange Rate Changes and External Adjustment

The bigger question is what happens when adjustment is needed. Pegging versus floating should not make a country grow faster or slower over time, but exchange rate flexibility should help in making an external adjustment if one is needed.

Looking now at external adjustment with fixed rates, one thing economists have known for a long time is that it should be more difficult for a country to manage a substantial change in its current account if the exchange rate is fixed. Prices are sticky. They are especially downward sticky. Thus, it is hard for substantial real depreciation to occur if the nominal exchange rate cannot change.[1] This should make it more difficult to have a substantial external adjustment.

Table 19.1 looks at 10 countries that had very large current account deficits going into the crisis and very large external adjustments during this crisis. They entered the crisis with a current-account-deficit-to-GDP ratio of at least 10 percent, and they cut the ratio by at least 10 percentage points. There is a roughly even split between pegged and nonpegged economies. This is quite important, as it highlights the fact that a fixed exchange rate does not mean a country cannot have external adjustment.

Table 19.1
Experience of Countries Making Major External Adjustment in the Crisis

	Number	Number That Grew	Average ΔGDP	ΔE vs. Base	ΔREER
Pegged	6	0	−10%	0%	3% appr.
Nonpegged	4	3	7%	15% depr.	4% depr.

Note: E is the nominal exchange rate measured against a relevant base country. REER is the real effective exchange rate index.

On the other hand, of the six countries that were pegged, none of them experienced real GDP growth over the period from 2008 to 2011, whereas three of the four nonpegged countries did. On average, the pegged countries contracted by about 10 percent, as opposed to an expansion in the nonpegged countries. The nonpegged countries experienced a relatively mild average change in the exchange rate against the base country; they were not all large depreciations, but there was a substantial difference in the real economy experiences of the countries. These are small countries, and it is a small sample. This is not rigorous econometric evidence, but the experience we would have predicted going into the crisis did broadly happen. When financial flows seized up and it was more difficult to finance externally, the pegged countries that made large adjustments had a harder time than did the floating rate countries.

Relative Prices on Entry into a Currency Union

Economists have also known for a long time, certainly since 1925, when Keynes was writing critical things about Churchill (Keynes 1925), that if you enter a currency union at the wrong price, it can be painful. Keynes pointed out that rejoining the gold standard at the wrong price was very painful for Britain, and this is something that both theory and the experience of countries after World War I demonstrate.

When one looks at the lead-in to the euro, the convergence criteria were inflation, debt and deficits, and a stable exchange rate. In a recent discussion about the euro area with my students, I asked, "What were the convergence criteria?" A student raised her hand and said, "The balance of payments deficit couldn't be too big." Someone tapped her on the shoulder and said, "No, you mean 'fiscal.'" She said, "Right, right, fiscal deficit can't be too big." And I thought to myself, that is somewhat telling. While it may seem intuitive that they would, the rules were not putting limits on the balance of payments deficit. There was no rule that purchasing power parity had to hold. Policymakers were about to fix the nominal exchange rate forever. But, confirming that relative prices were at the right level was not part of the entry criteria.

Over the period from entry until 2007, current account deficits and surpluses were quite persistent in the euro area. Figure 19.2a shows the current-account-to-GDP ratio at entry (x-axis) and the current-account-to-GDP ratio in 2007 (y-axis).

The relationship is quite strong and the slope is nearly 1. This persistence has been documented before (see, e.g., Lane and Pels 2012 or Kang and Shambaugh 2013 for discussion). The next two figures look across other groups of countries to see if the pattern is any different.

Figure 19.2b looks at the more recent entrants to the euro area and/or countries pegged to the euro.

The line also has a slope close to 1, but the fit around the line is not quite as tight (the R^2 is lower). Figure 19.2c takes the remaining countries from the Eurostat database that are neither the original 12 entrants into the euro (those that entered prior to 2003) nor later entrants and pegs.

There are roughly 15 countries floating in that data set. Relative prices can move fluidly for these countries, as the nominal exchange rate is floating. Yet there is almost a perfectly straight line for this group, too. In the buildup to the crisis, current accounts, no matter the exchange rate regime, were very persistent. Countries that were running deficits kept running deficits. Countries that were running surpluses kept running surpluses. There did not appear to be pressure to push countries back toward a balanced current account. It does not seem that floating exchange rates helped these countries back to balance.

However, the question becomes, once adjustment had to happen, was there a difference? Here the answer appears to be yes. Figures 19.3a–c show the current account in 1999 (or entry into the euro currency union) on the x-axis and the change in the unemployment rate during the crisis on the y-axis.

The relationship appears to be steeper for the early euro members. Countries that had a big current account deficit at entry into the euro wound up having a much higher spike in the unemployment rate once adjustment had to happen. For pegged countries or late entrants, the relationship is not as steep, meaning that a given current account deficit correlates with a smaller increase in the unemployment rate. For countries with a floating exchange rate, the relationship is essentially flat. The current account in 1999 had almost no bearing on the unemployment response during the crisis. The current account deficit is a country's net borrowing from the world—the country's borrowing, not the government's. Those countries that were borrowing extensively when the euro

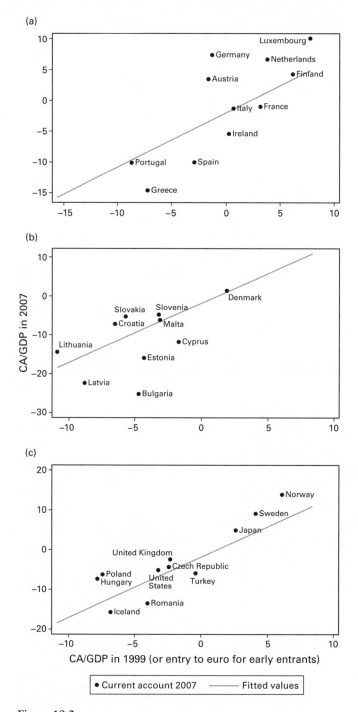

Figure 19.2
a. Early entrants, current-account-to-GDP ratio. b. Pegs and late entrants. c. Floats.

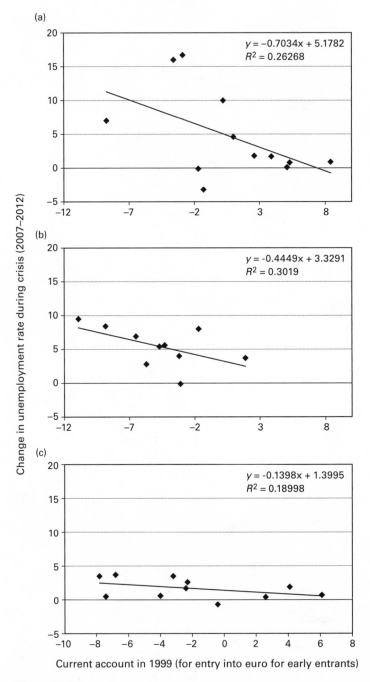

Figure 19.3
a. Euro. b. Late entrants and pegs. c. Floats.

began appear to have paid a price once adjustment had to happen. That is less true for floating exchange rate countries. They had more flexibility in how they approached the crisis.

It may be worth noting that many of the more recent entrants into the euro area have had fairly substantial current account deficits on entry. The most notable case is that of Cyprus, which had a current account deficit of 16 percent of GDP in its first year as a member of the euro area. Slovenia (5 percent deficit) and the Slovak Republic (3 percent deficit) did not have extremely high deficits, but were certainly not in external balance. Estonia, which had a 2 percent surplus in 2011, is the only recent entrant with a surplus. These recent entries raise the question of whether exchange rates are being fixed permanently at the right price.

The Non-Exchange Rate Crisis of Breaking Pegs

One experience in the crisis that is somewhat new is the way in which exchange rate pegs broke. It is well established that exchange rate pegs are fragile.[2] Figure 19.4 shows the percentage of countries that were pegged in any given year between 1973 and 2011 that broke their peg.[3] There is a small spike right around 2008, so more countries than usual broke their pegs during this crisis, which is not surprising, given the nature of the crisis.

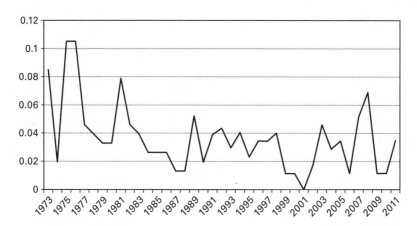

Figure 19.4
Percentage of countries with pegged exchange rate that broke their pegs, by year, 1973–2011.

(a)

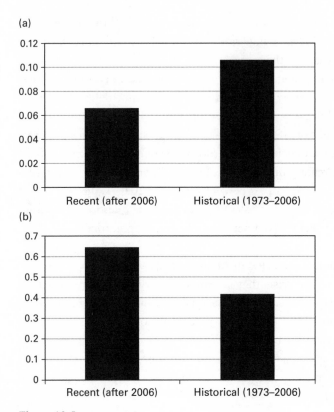

(b)

Figure 19.5
a. Median annual range of exchange rate change across countries in year that they broke a peg, post-2006 versus 1973–2006. b. Fraction that held tight to range after breaking peg, post-2006 versus 1973–2006.

What was more surprising is what is seen in figures 19.5a and b. Figure 19.5a shows that of those countries that broke their peg after 2006, the range of their exchange rate against the country they were pegging to was not particularly large after they broke the peg.

The median range is just over 6 percent, relative to a median range of over 10 percent in the post-1973 era. In a sense, many of these pegs did not really break. The countries simply loosened the band somewhat. Figure 19.5b makes this clearer. It shows the percentage of the countries that broke their peg, but merely went from a 2 percent band to a 5 percent band, a broader range, but not high exchange rate volatility.

Almost two-thirds of the countries in the crisis that broke their previously tight peg simply loosened the bands and stayed somewhat pegged to the base. This contrasts to roughly 40 percent in the 1973–2006 time period.

The above findings suggest a strong preference in some countries for exchange rate fixity. Even though the crisis highlighted some of the challenges that come with having a fixed exchange rate—specifically, that adjustment can be difficult with a fixed exchange rate—plenty of countries want to stay close to pegged, even if they cannot maintain a tight peg. In any given year, around half the countries in the world have a fixed exchange rate. If we drop a number of very small countries from the sample, it is close to 40 percent pegging. Also, though, which countries peg changes from year to year. The debate over exchange rate regimes does not have a corner solution that economists often like. Not every country is going to float, and not every country is going to peg. This reminds us of the importance of figuring out the costs and benefits of pegging.

Implications for Currency Unions

A number of these stylized facts have implications for currency unions. Again, many of the things we have observed in currency unions—particularly in the euro area—are things that were well understood in the literature more than a decade ago.

Certainly from a macroeconomic perspective, the euro area has not done well. GDP growth has been slower than that of a typical country and even a typical advanced country. The unemployment rate is much higher than in other advanced economies as well. These facts, though, should not necessarily be a reflection on the wisdom of currency unions. The euro area floats against the world, so the average performance of the euro area is not a reflection of the fact that it has a currency union internally. Weak economic performance could simply be a reflection of worse shocks. Alternatively, it could be a reflection of worse macroeconomic policy management, of monetary policy that has been too tight or fiscal policy that has been too tight.

What tells us more about the wisdom of the euro as a currency and the institutional structure that supports it is what happens when the need for

(a)

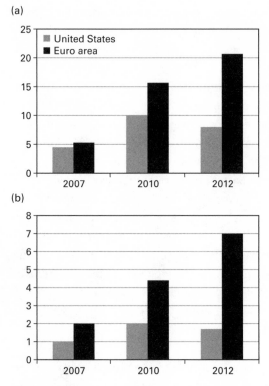

(b)

Figure 19.6
a. Range of unemployment rates, United States versus euro area. b. Standard deviation of unemployment rate, United States versus euro area.

adjustment differs across countries within a currency union. In that sense, this crisis has revealed some of the true problems within the euro area. Figures 19.6a and b show the range and standard deviation of unemployment rates across US states and across the euro area (the gray bars are the United States, the black are the euro area).

In both areas, there is a stark jump when the crisis hits from 2007 to 2010. The range and standard deviation of unemployment rates are higher. From 2010 to 2012, though, the dispersion starts coming down in the United States. The states with high unemployment rates are having their unemployment rate fall faster. In the euro area, the dispersion has kept going up as unemployment rates have fallen in some countries that were already doing well but have continued to rise in the worst-hit countries.

This sequence of events suggests a lack of adequate shock absorbers within the euro area. Differential monetary policy within the currency union and exchange rate adjustments are no longer possible, and labor mobility and fiscal federalism are not sufficient to offset shocks in one region and smooth them in relation to another. Again, this is not a surprise or a new observation. The entire optimal currency area theory was founded by a paper noting the importance of a shock absorber (labor mobility) for a currency union to be an optimal currency area (Mundell 1961). It was well known at the founding of the euro that forming a currency union without these shock absorbers was likely going to be painful if a substantial asymmetric shock took place.[4]

Summary

A number of important observations seem to have come out of this crisis. Countries with fixed exchange rates need to recognize that external adjustment is going to be very challenging. This suggests two things: one, it is important to avoid excessive borrowing if there is a fixed exchange rate, again, not necessarily by the government or the state but for the economy overall, because if the country needs to rebalance the external account rapidly, the adjustment will likely be very painful. And two, it suggests that if exchange rates are fixed, there needs to be some other way to cushion big shocks.

The contributions to this volume emphasize the way fiscal policy and monetary policy operate at the zero lower bound, and this work suggests that it is important to have fiscal stabilizers within a currency union, because if the monetary policy is going to run into the zero lower bound, not having any agency that is acting to stabilize the economy with fiscal policy is going to be a problem. In addition, states or countries within a currency union should not radically cut back on their fiscal policy in a recession, because we know they're going to be doing so in an environment with very high multipliers. Therefore, currency unions also need to have some way to avoid that situation.

Also, economists and policymakers have learned more about the macro and finance linkages and what some have referred to as "doom loops" between the banks and the sovereigns, highlighting the fact that it is crucial that weaknesses in banks do not become an asymmetric shock within a currency union. If when Washington Mutual got into trouble the state of Washington had been responsible as a fiscal backstop, the state of Washington would have been in a very challenging fiscal position. Instead it was an FDIC problem, not a problem for the state of Washington. This highlights the need for deposit insurance, bank supervision, a lender of last resort, and bank resolution, all at the currency union level, because if they do not exist, it suggests that the financial system could be the originator of asymmetric shocks.

Euro area institutions are changing, in some cases far more rapidly than anyone could have imagined five years ago. On the other hand, one of the things the crisis seems to highlight is that we cannot ignore what we know. The implications of exchange rate regimes are an area of economics in which the standard literature could have predicted most of what took place. It was well known prior to the launch of the euro that labor mobility was weak and fiscal federalism nonexistent. The fact that this lack of shock absorbers would make the euro a risky bet was well established. Likewise, the lack of an official lender of last resort and the lack of a prudential supervisory role for the ECB were widely discussed.[5] As a profession, we have learned more about macrofinancial linkages, but the risks of a currency union with fragmented backing supervision were understood.

When one steps back and considers the exchange rate regime decision, it is clear that very small countries are going to peg, especially if they are tied to one economy. Also, it seems that very large economies with open financial markets are not willing to subjugate monetary policy to the exchange rate. The question is what countries in between should do. The countries of the euro area clearly have decided to sacrifice other policy options for exchange rate stability. Doing so, though, without the necessary institutional structure was a gamble. The gamble was that the needed change in the institutional structure and in the economy would happen before a big crisis. The question now is, now that the costs are apparent, can policymakers fill in the needed institutional structure fast enough?

Notes

1. See Shambaugh (2012) for discussion.

2. See Obstfeld and Rogoff (1995) and Klein and Marion (1997) for earlier discussions. Klein and Shambaugh (2008) explore the duration as well as the propensity of broken pegs to reform.

3. A peg is defined here as a country that stays within a 2 percentage point up or down range over the course of a year (excluding single-year pegs, which may be due to a lack of volatility) or those that are perfectly flat, with the exception of a one-time realignment. See Klein and Shambaugh (2010) for an extensive discussion of exchange rate regime classifications.

4. See Obstfeld (1997) and Obstfeld and Peri (1998) for discussion.

5. See Obstfeld (1997) for discussion.

References

Kang, Joong Shik, and Jay C. Shambaugh. 2013. "The Evolution of Current Account Deficits in the GIPS and the Baltics: Many Paths to the Same Endpoint." IMF Working Paper, International Monetary Fund, Washington, DC.

Keynes, John M. 1925. *The Economic Consequences of Mr. Churchill*. London: Hogarth Press.

Klein, Michael, and Nancy P. Marion. 1997. "Explaining the Duration of Exchange-Rate Pegs." *Journal of Development Economics* 54 (2): 387–404.

Klein, Michael W., and Jay C. Shambaugh. 2008. "The Dynamics of Exchange Rate Regimes: Fixes, Floats, and Flips." *Journal of International Economics* 75 (1): 70–92.

Klein, Michael W., and Jay C. Shambaugh. 2010. *Exchange Rate Regimes in the Modern Era*. Cambridge, MA: MIT Press.

Lane, Philip, and Barbara Pels. 2012. "Current Account Imbalances in Europe." Centre for Economic Policy Research Discussion Paper DP8958, Centre for Economic Policy Research, London. http://papers.ssrn.com/sol3/papers.cfm?abstract_id=2066331.

Mundell, Robert A. 1961. "A Theory of Optimum Currency Areas." *American Economic Review* 51 (4): 657–665.

Obstfeld, Maurice. 1997. "Europe's Gamble." *Brookings Papers on Economic Activity* 2:241–317.

Obstfeld, Maurice, and Giovanni Peri. 1998. "Regional Non-adjustment and Fiscal Policy." *Economic Policy* 13 (26): 205–248.

Obstfeld, Maurice, and Kenneth Rogoff. 1995. "The Mirage of Fixed Exchange Rates." *Journal of Economic Perspectives* 9 (Fall): 73–96.

Shambaugh, Jay. 2012. "The Euro's Three Crises." *Brookings Papers on Economic Activity*, Spring, 157–211.

20

Exchange Rate Arrangements: Spain and the United Kingdom

Martin Wolf

The effort to bind states together may lead, instead, to a huge increase in frictions among them. If so, the event would meet the classical definition of tragedy: hubris (arrogance); ate (folly); nemesis (destruction).
—Martin Wolf, *Financial Times*, December 1991

The creation of the euro was among the most revolutionary developments in monetary history. Advanced European economies agreed to replace their national monies with a shared fiat currency, managed by a jointly owned institution, the European Central Bank (ECB). They did this, moreover, without agreeing to any of the other features of contemporary monetary areas, notably mechanisms for fiscal transfers or for common regulation and support of the banking system. In all these respects, the governments of member states remained sovereign, if notionally constrained by a set of rules governing fiscal deficits and debt.

A possible justification for this extremely limited institutional infrastructure was that the rules concerning fiscal policy and the central bank's ability to act as lender of last resort in a crisis would together be enough to ensure adequate stability. They would either prevent crises or, if they failed to do so, make them at least reasonably manageable. Another possible justification was the belief that it was essential at least to start. Once the euro area was launched, any failure to prevent or manage severe crises would motivate policymakers to create missing institutions or improve existing ones.

By early 2013, after at least three years of crisis, the institutional framework of the euro area had been shown to be inadequate. The fact that the crisis forced rapid institutional and policy innovations proves that. What had existed before the crisis proved inadequate, but whether a severe crisis would produce the reforms needed to make the euro area better able to cope remains unclear.

To work out what reforms are needed, we must start by asking what went wrong. This is a topic on which Paul De Grauwe, formerly at the University of Leuven and now at the London School of Economics, has shed much light in a number of important and illuminating notes and papers.[1] His conclusion is that the euro area simply needs a great deal of reform, particularly in the policies of the central bank. My conclusion is that the euro was a bad idea. Both conclusions might be correct.

Certainly, the loss of sovereignty for the governments of member states has imposed large costs on them and their citizens. An excellent way to show this is via the contrasting experiences of Spain and the United Kingdom in the crisis. Spain lacks the tools to handle such a big financial crisis with any ease. The UK does not lack those tools, though it has failed to use them as fully as it might have.

The Contrasting Cases of Spain and the United Kingdom

Spain and the UK are both crisis-hit countries. Since the crisis, both have been in poor fiscal positions. They also have big problems in their banking industries, though they are not quite the same problem: Spain's is largely debt created by a huge domestic property boom; the UK banks have that problem, but they have also been damaged by their global operations. Surprisingly, perhaps, the fiscal consequences of their distinct crises are remarkably similar, as shown in figure 20.1. The expected path of the ratio of net public debt to GDP in these two countries is almost identical.

For those who think the main determinant of the interest rate on government debt is the public debt burden, the implication is clear: the interest rates on Spanish and UK public debt should be quite similar. But they are not. The yield on 10-year UK public debt is far more like that on German 10-year public debt than like that on Spanish debt, as figure 20.2 shows, even though Germany's debt is expected to be under far better control than the UK's. The divergence between the yields on Spanish and UK debt has been very large indeed. This has made it far more difficult for the Spanish government to manage its debt and has

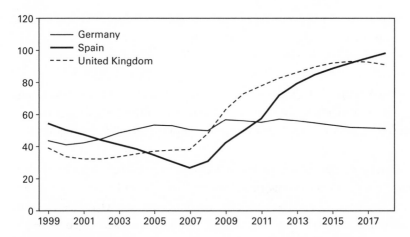

Figure 20.1
Ratio of Net Public Debt to GDP, Spain, UK, and Germany.
Source: International Monetary Fund, World Economic Outlook database, April 2013.

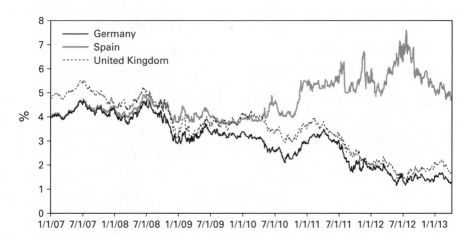

Figure 20.2
Yields on 10-Year Government Bonds, Spain, UK, and Germany.
Source: Thomson Reuters Datastream.

adversely affected broader credit and monetary conditions in Spain relative to those in the UK.

Why should the interest rate difference between the two countries have been so very large? The answer lies mainly in the fact that the UK is a sovereign country, with its own finance ministry, central bank, and floating currency, while Spain is a subordinate government inside a currency union that has no shared treasury and a supranational central bank (the ECB).

Suppose holders of a government's debt believe that it might be unable to roll the debt over on reasonable terms. They would rationally fear an outright—possibly sudden—default. Creditors cannot seize the assets of bankrupt governments as they can take hold of the assets of companies. This is because national governments are sovereign in their own jurisdictions. So lenders will demand an interest rate that protects them against default risk. But at such an elevated interest rate, the government may be driven into the default that lenders fear, making their prophecy of doom self-fulfilling.

This is the danger of multiple equilibria. Olivier Blanchard, IMF economic counselor, puts it this way:

At high levels of debt, there may well be two equilibria, a "good equilibrium" at which rates are low and debt is sustainable, and a "bad equilibrium" in which rates are high, and, as a result, the interest burden is higher, and, in turn, the probability of default is higher. When debt is very high, it may not take much of a change of heart by investors to move from the good to the bad equilibrium.[2]

Preventing such a shift is one of the jobs of central banks. Thus, a central bank guarantees liquidity in the market for sovereign debt. That hugely reduces the risk of a sudden default. This reduction of liquidity risk increases confidence in lenders. As usual, liquidity and solvency risks are closely related.

The principal reason why interest rates in Spain have been so much higher than those of the UK is that Spain had no such lender of last resort. Spanish debt was subject to liquidity risk, and so, when liquidity risk looked significant, markets priced the debt accordingly, pushing Spain into a bad equilibrium. The ECB was not believed to be willing or able to ensure liquidity in the markets for sovereign debt of the euro area. In a panic, then, everybody fled to the safest debt, Germany's, causing a big crisis in countries with worse debt positions.

Lessons from ECB Interventions

The plausibility of the view that the biggest problem facing Spain has been the lack of a central bank of its own is strengthened by what happened when the ECB did finally indicate its willingness to intervene in the market for public debt of countries in difficulty. The decline in yields on Spanish debt shown in figure 20.2 dates almost precisely to July 26, 2012. This is when the president of the ECB, Mario Draghi, said to an audience in London, "Within our mandate, the ECB is ready to do whatever it takes to preserve the euro. And believe me, it will be enough."[3] This statement in turn led to the announcement by the ECB on August 2 of its Outright Monetary Transactions (OMT) program aimed "at safeguarding an appropriate monetary policy transmission and the singleness of the monetary policy."[4] Rightly or wrongly, markets concluded that the risk of a sudden outright default on Spanish bonds had greatly diminished. This in turn pushed the price of bonds from a bad equilibrium to a better one. As yields fell, the government did indeed start to look more solvent, thereby justifying the markets' renewed optimism.

Not coincidentally, the decline from the previous interest rate peak, in late 2011, dates from the announcement by the ECB of its three-year Long-Term Refinancing Operation in early December 2011.[5] But that operation proved unsuccessful in keeping interest rates down. That is why the ECB was driven to adopt the OMT program in the teeth of opposition from Jens Weidmann, president of the Bundesbank.[6]

Moreover, the same declines occurred in Italy as in Spain, strongly supporting the argument that it is ECB policy rather than actions by governments that explains the sharp decline in interest rates on the long-term government bonds of vulnerable countries.[7] The ability of the ECB to trigger such a decline in yields is exactly what De Grauwe predicted. Now that it has become fact, he has analyzed this adjustment in another important article. The point he makes is that these were largely self-fulfilling panics that the ECB has, for the moment, ended.[8]

The crises, then, were in large part the result of allowing government bond markets to operate without grown-up supervision. Fortunately, the grown-ups are back. That is good news for the euro area and the world. A huge amount of unnecessary and ill-timed fiscal austerity has been imposed, just because the euro area did not have a proper central bank. It now has something that is at least a bit more like a proper central bank. It shows.

Why ECB Intervention Did Not Eliminate the Spanish Risk Premium

However, the intervention of the ECB, pleasingly effective though it has been in lowering rates, has not reduced Spanish interest rates to UK levels, at least at the time of this writing. Why should that be? One can see two possible sets of explanations.

First, the ECB's OMT program operates under important limitations. The most important one is that the program is not unconditional, though in principle it is potentially unlimited. Without conditionality, the ECB could not have obtained internal approval or external consent, above all from the German government, to intervene. Thus, the ECB stated on September 2, 2012:

A necessary condition for Outright Monetary Transactions is strict and effective conditionality attached to an appropriate European Financial Stability Facility/ European Stability Mechanism (EFSF/ESM) programme. Such programmes can take the form of a full EFSF/ESM macroeconomic adjustment programme or a precautionary programme (Enhanced Conditions Credit Line), provided that they include the possibility of EFSF/ESM primary market purchases. The involvement of the IMF shall also be sought for the design of the country-specific conditionality and the monitoring of such a programme.[9]

Another restriction is that the explicit rationale of the program is not to support government debt markets but rather to make monetary policy work effectively. This rationale is ingenious, since it allows the ECB to claim, imaginatively, that the aim of the program is monetary and so within its broad remit, rather than fiscal and so outside that remit. Thus, the ECB announced:

The Governing Council will consider Outright Monetary Transactions to the extent that they are warranted from a monetary policy perspective as long as programme conditionality is fully respected, and terminate them once their objectives are achieved or when there is non-compliance with the macroeconomic adjustment or precautionary programme.

As a result, the ECB stated, "Transactions will be focused on the shorter part of the yield curve, and in particular on sovereign bonds with a maturity of between one and three years." This makes sense for normal monetary policy, but the restriction limits the commitment of the ECB to support the market in sovereign debt.

A second set of explanations for the failure to achieve convergence of long-term interest rates between Spain and the UK is that the former suffers from a number of handicaps that the latter does not. These include the risk of exit from the euro area or of breakup of the euro area, deflation risk, and other economic differences.

It is impossible for the ECB, or any institution, to eliminate the risk that Spain might leave the euro area or that the euro area might itself break up. So long as that risk continues to exist, investors in Spanish bonds need to take out insurance against the possibility of a sudden and costly redenomination into bonds in a new currency that would then swiftly depreciate. Furthermore, in the event of such a redenomination, it is likely that exchange controls would also be imposed, which creates another risk for investors in Spanish government bonds.

Furthermore, if the euro area were not to break up or if Spain were not to exit, Spain would remain vulnerable to deflation risk. Indeed, outright deflation is the mechanism through which external competitiveness is restored inside the currency union. But deflation would raise the real value of Spanish debt, making its debt less sustainable. If the deflation were big enough, the time profile of debt might end up substantially worse than shown in figure 20.1. This would be particularly true if the deflationary process also inflicted a deeper than expected depression, depressing the denominator still further.

Finally, it seems that Spain's initial disequilibrium was rather larger than that of the UK. Its current account deficit was 10 percent of GDP in 2007, for example, against 2 percent in the UK. Consequently, the adjustment Spain needed would have seemed far bigger. Again, Spain's net international investment position was substantially more negative than that of the UK, making the country more dependent on foreign investors, who are usually, for good reason, more fearful of default than domestic ones are. Spain also had a larger boom in construction than the UK. For all these reasons, Spain was likely to suffer a longer and deeper recession than the UK, as indeed has happened. Investors might reasonably suppose that the government of a country undergoing such a deep and intractable slump might not make meeting its debt obligations a priority. In all, investors might reasonably reach the conclusion that Spain was not as good an investment risk as the UK.

The rating agencies seem to have reached that conclusion. As of this writing, in June 2013, Standard & Poor's rated the UK's sovereign bonds at AAA and Spain's at BBB–. Moody's rated them at Aa1 and Baa3, respectively. Fitch's rated them at AA+ and BBB. This huge gap between the two countries' bond ratings may partly reflect the additional and important fact that the UK has had a longer record of managing its debt well than has Spain. It may also reflect the normal behavior of the rating agencies: "I am your rating agency, therefore I follow you" seems to be their long-standing motto with regard to the market. But the big fact is that the rating agencies downgraded Spain's sovereign bonds massively compared with the UK's.

Meanwhile, the UK possessed fundamental countervailing advantages. First, adjustment to a shift in the desire to hold sterling-denominated liabilities has worked, at least in part, via the price of the currency rather than the price of bonds. Such price flexibility reduces the need for quantity adjustments in response to shifts in the desire to hold a country's liabilities. In Spain, instead, a larger quantitative adjustment has been required. This is shown in the scale of the recession, revealed in figure 20.3, and the size of the current account adjustment, shown in figure 20.4. From one point of view, Spain's adjustment is impressive. But it is also a powerful indicator of the collapse in Spain's domestic absorption compared with the UK's.

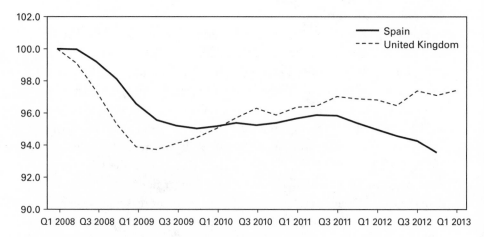

Figure 20.3
GDP in the Crisis, Spain and UK.
Source: International Monetary Fund, World Economic Outlook Database April 2013.

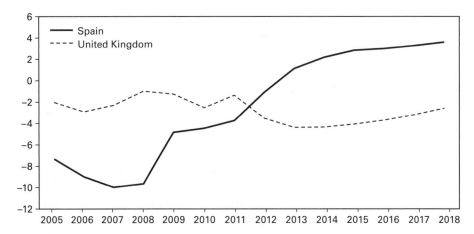

Figure 20.4
Current Account Balances (as a share of GDP).
Source: International Monetary Fund, World Economic Outlook Database April 2013.

In addition, the UK has captive savers who need to match the currency of their assets with those of their liabilities. Thus, in a crisis, the UK government's liabilities provide a safe haven to such investors, among which will be insurers and pension funds. In the euro area, however, the relevant safe haven is the debt of the German government in particular, and to a lesser extent that of other stable creditor countries, such as the Netherlands. Thus, in a crisis, fearful domestic savers will fly toward UK government debt and away from Spanish government debt.

Why the Disadvantages of a Currency Area Are Partly Unavoidable

Nearly all these differences between the UK and Spain, from the lack of a proper central bank to the scale of the economic disequilibria, derive from the fact that Spain is a member of the euro area while the UK is not. Membership in the currency area has proved to be a big disadvantage in handling a severe financial crisis. A crucial question is whether, with a different institutional structure, these disadvantages might have been or can be avoided.

To some extent, the answer must be no. The advantages possessed by a country with its own floating currency and central bank are large, at least when handling the contractionary consequences of a huge financial crisis.

Remember, too, that the aim of creating the euro area was to promote internal capital flows. Thus, the huge cross-border flows of private finance that preceded (and then triggered) the crisis were hardly some accidental bug in the system. They were a deliberate feature. Similarly, the euro area was designed, quite deliberately, around the idea of a goal-independent central bank required to focus on price stability and expected not to finance governments directly, whatever happened. Moreover, in a multicurrency union, the only alternative to such a highly independent central bank would have been subordination to a committee of finance ministers. While such an arrangement is conceivable, it would have been extraordinarily ponderous and, in any case, unacceptable to Germany and a number of other member countries. So we have to regard the independence of the central bank and the nature of its mandate as a feature at least of this currency union. As a result, the ECB cannot make an open-ended and unconditional commitment to purchase public debt. A limited or conditional commitment cannot be completely credible, and an incompletely credible commitment by the central bank will not shift adverse expectations durably or completely.

Of course, some of these features of the euro area were not logically necessary. Germany might, for example, have had a different philosophy of monetary policy and macroeconomic management. It might have been more like that of the United States. This would have made it easier for the ECB to intervene in sovereign debt markets, as De Grauwe wanted, on a large scale. The difficulties experienced in the currency union would then have been smaller. But the facts that creditor countries would like to restrict the support they offer to debtor countries and that countries in trouble face exceptionally difficult problems in managing the crisis and subsequent adjustment are inherent in almost any conceivable currency union.

Why the Euro Was a Bad Idea

What is the conclusion? It is that there were huge risks in the creation of the euro, some inescapable and some inherent in its design. The nature and extent of these risks have been revealed in the crisis.

Why were people unconcerned about these risks prior to the crisis? A big part of the reason is that many people believed that currency risk was the principal source of crises. This view was certainly consistent with experience in the 1960s, 1970s, 1980s, and 1990s. Consequently, proponents of the euro thought that the elimination of separate currencies would eliminate most of the risks of crises.

Events have proved this view false. Indeed, since 2010, euro area policymakers and economists have discovered that the opposite is true. First, currency risk cannot be eliminated, since there is always the possibility that currencies might be recreated. Second, currency risk will reemerge in other ways, particularly in the form of shocks to the supply of credit and financial and fiscal crises. Finally, when such risks become real, they will inflict huge financial, economic, social, and political pain.

The big lesson the crisis has taught us is that high-income countries embedded in a currency union are more vulnerable to balance-of-payments *cum* financial crises than similar countries with floating exchange rates and their own central banks. The currency union has, in fact, replaced the brief currency crises and exchange rate realignments of the old exchange rate mechanism with what now appear to be long-running solvency, employment, and political crises. A more active central bank, one willing to push sovereign debt toward good equilibria and away from bad ones, would be a big help. In the course of the crisis, the ECB has become more of such a bank. But for reasons largely inherent in the creation of any currency union and certainly inherent in the euro area, the ECB is not going to act like a national central bank. The question for members to decide is whether the stresses they suffer as a result are worth it.

Notes

1. See Paul De Grauwe, "The Governance of a Fragile Eurozone," University of Leuven, April 2011, http://www.econ.kuleuven.be/ew/academic/intecon/ Degrauwe/PDG-papers/Discussion_papers/Governance-fragile-eurozone_s.pdf; idem, "Managing a Fragile Eurozone," *Vox*, May 10, 2011, http://www.voxeu .org/article/managing-fragile-eurozone; Paul De Grauwe and Yuemei Ji, "Mispricing of Sovereign Risk and Multiple Equilibria in the Eurozone," CEPS Working Document, January 20, 2012, http://www.ceps.eu/book/mispricing-sovereign-risk-and-multiple-equilibria-eurozone; and idem, "Mispricing of Sovereign Risk and Multiple Equilibria in the Eurozone," *Vox*, January 23, 2012, http://www .voxeu.org/article/mispricing-sovereign-risk-and-multiple-equilibria-eurozone.

2. Olivier Blanchard, "Rethinking Macroeconomic Policy," blogpost, IMF Direct, April 29, 2013, http://blog-imfdirect.imf.org/2013/04/29/rethinking-macroeconomic-policy.

3. Mario Draghi, president of the European Central Bank, speech delivered at the Global Investment Conference, London, July 26, 2012, http://www.ecb.int/press/key/date/2012/html/sp120726.en.html.

4. European Central Bank, "Technical Features of Outright Monetary Transactions," press release, European Central Bank, Brussels, September 6, 2012, http://www.ecb.int/press/pr/date/2012/html/pr120906_1.en.html.

5. European Central Bank, "ECB Announces Measures to Support Bank Lending and Money Market Activity," press release, European Central Bank, Brussels, December 8, 2011, http://www.ecb.europa.eu/press/pr/date/2011/html/pr111208_1.en.html.

6. Michael Steen, "Weidmann Isolated as ECB Plan Approved," *Financial Times*, September 7, 2012.

7. See Joe Wiesenthal, "In One Chart, Here's Why Roger Altman Is Wrong about How the Markets Forced Austerity on Europe," BusinessInsider.com, May 2013, http://www.businessinsider.com/in-one-chart-heres-why-roger-altman-is-wrong-about-how-the-markets-forced-austerity-on-europe-2013-5; and Paul Krugman, "All about the ECB," blogpost, NewYorkTimes.com, May 10, 2013, http://krugman.blogs.nytimes.com/2013/05/10/all-about-the-ecb.

8. See Paul De Grauwe and Yuemei Ji, "More Evidence That Financial Markets Imposed Excessive Austerity in the Eurozone," CEPS Commentary, February 5, 2013, http://www.ceps.eu/book/more-evidence-financial-markets-imposed-excessive-austerity-eurozone; idem, "Panic-Driven Austerity in the Eurozone and Its Implications," *Vox*, February 21, 2013, http://www.voxeu.org/article/panic-driven-austerity-eurozone-and-its-implications.

9. European Central Bank, "Technical Features of Outright Monetary Transactions," press release, European Central Bank, Brussels, September 6, 2012; http://www.ecb.int/press/pr/date/2012/html/pr120906_1.en.html.

21

Exchange Rate Arrangements: The Flexible and Fixed Exchange Rate Debate Revisited

Gang Yi

China as an Optimal Currency Area

China is a large country with tremendous differences across its land. The diversities between eastern and western regions to some extent exceed those of the euro zone. For instance, in the eastern part of China (such as the Pearl River Delta), the per capita income is about five times that of the western part (such as Guizhou Province and Qinghai Province), whereas inside the euro area, Germany's per capita income is only about 1.5 times that of Greece. However, even with these differences, China is still better positioned as an optimal currency area than the euro area and can issue a common currency, for China satisfies several key elements that are required by an optimal currency area.

The first one concerns fiscal setting. China, as a sovereign country, possesses a centralized fiscal transfer payment system that enables the transfer of funds from the relatively rich regions in the coastal area to the poor regions in its less-developed middle and western regions every year. Second, China has a highly mobile labor market. Many people from the low-income regions seek better job opportunities in high-income regions; consequently, at least 160 million rural workers are now working in China's cities. Third, China has a very unified domestic market that shares an integrated system of trading and transportation. Domestic markets, such as the commodity market and the product market, are all homogeneous. Fourth, China's macroeconomic policies are very effective and coordinated. Those are some of the reasons why China can be viewed as an optimal currency area, even though the regional differences between the rich and the poor, in terms of per capita income, are still very large.

As long as fiscal transfer and macroeconomic policies work well and the labor market remains highly mobile, China as an optimal currency area will operate smoothly and stay sustainable, though the diversity within China will likely remain.

The other reason I'd like to mention is the ability of the Chinese government to address financial systemic risks. For example, I was involved in tackling financial crises as a key representative of the People's Bank of China. Local financial crises were breaking out in provinces or regions, including Guangdong Province and then in Hunan Province in the late 1990s, as well as Xinjiang Uygur Autonomous Region and Ningxia Hui Autonomous Region.

Guangdong is a developed area with many people who are very rich. But in the late 1990s, Guangdong experienced major fiscal insolvency and financial institution problems. Other regions, such as Ningxia and Xinjiang, although less developed, also experienced financial difficulties. When addressing these kinds of problems, we usually have to decide first whether the central bank should intervene by providing liquidity as the lender of last resort. We also need to figure out how to handle local government debt and deal with the relationship between local governments and the central government. We have to design a framework that not only can avoid moral hazard but also can calm the crisis situation. In this way, the capabilities of the People's Bank of China and other financial supervisors to identify problems and address potential systemic risks have been tested and proven, and they solidified the ground on which the common currency is established.

China's Policy Choices over Exchange Rate Regimes

There has been an ongoing theoretical debate in the history of exchange rate regimes since the beginning of the 1970s, when the Bretton Woods system collapsed and the exchange rate regimes of many countries kept evolving. In reality, exchange rate arrangements do not fall into a simple dichotomy of fixed or floating exchange rates.

According to the IMF, there are eight categories of exchange rate arrangements, and the IMF's view regarding exchange rate arrangements has also evolved over time. During the Bretton Woods era, the IMF was of the opinion that fixed exchange rate arrangements were better. Before the

Argentine crisis, it argued for the bipolar view (either fixed or floating), while after the crisis it called for floating exchange rates. After 2009 the IMF took the view that all exchange rate arrangements had merits and shortcomings.

The floating exchange rate arrangement has several merits. First, using a floating exchange rate makes it easy to adjust to economic shocks, and the arrangement itself is less vulnerable to speculative attacks. It also helps to avoid the resource misallocation caused by exchange rate distortions. But a floating exchange rate also has its problems. For example, it may cause uncertainty or excess fluctuation or overshooting, and it leads to a larger exchange rate risk. Fixed exchange rate arrangements are favorable because they give rise to lower inflation (for developing countries) and facilitate more investment and trade. However, they also result in exchange rate distortions and are vulnerable to currency crisis and speculative capital flows.

Here I will briefly discuss China's progress in exchange rate regime reforms. In 1994, China unified the dual-track exchange rate regime, which used to offer two different foreign exchange prices of the renminbi. Since then, China has been implementing a managed floating exchange rate regime, and reforms were pursued in a "minibang" approach rather than a "big bang," which perfectly suited China's specific circumstances. From 1994 through 2002, the real effective exchange rate (REER) of the renminbi, which is regularly compiled by the Bank of International Settlements, increased very rapidly together with the US dollar, to which the renminbi was pegged. Between 2002 and 2005, when the US dollar weakened in value, the renminbi started to depreciate along with the dollar, which caused some problems and disputes.

In 2005, the preconditions for foreign exchange mechanism reform were broadly in place. For example, the financial reforms were well under way, and major state-owned banks were overhauled and listed (or were to be listed). The foreign exchange market was developed to a better level, and China's capital account was gradually opened. Most importantly, China was experiencing stable growth and low inflation, which provided a relatively favorable background for reform. Therefore, when the opportune time arrived, China decided to depeg the renminbi against the US dollar, and the more flexible renminbi exchange rates followed shortly after. From the 2005 reform to the end of February 2013, the renminbi nominal exchange rate to the US dollar appreciated about 32 percent, and the REER of the renminbi appreciated by more than 36 percent. The trend of the renminbi exchange rate has changed from unilateral appreciation to two-way floating, and the price now falls into a broad equilibrium range.

However, the reform process was interrupted by the global financial crisis, when we had to narrow the daily floating band of the renminbi because of the situation in the post–Lehman Brothers period. That said, the renminbi did not depreciate as much as the currencies of other emerging market economies did. But the reform process was not suspended for long. On June 19, 2010, China decided to further promote the market-based exchange rate mechanism reform with reference to a currency basket, emphasizing the fundamental role of market supply and demand and the flexibility of the renminbi. On April 16, 2012, China widened the renminbi daily floating band to ±1 percent from ±0.5 percent. Also since 2012, the People's Bank of China has significantly reduced market intervention. To date, market forces are playing a dominant role in the formation of the renminbi exchange rate. China's exchange rate regime without a doubt is becoming more and more market-oriented.

Nevertheless, a floating exchange rate regime does not rule out foreign exchange market intervention. In some circumstances, intervention is still well justified. For example, when the exchange rate exceeds the predetermined band, or when the capital account experiences large imbalances and there are excessive trades in the foreign exchange market, or when the financial market falls into crisis-scale turmoil, market intervention can be restarted to the extent that the intervention is done in a two-way manner, with the intent of preventing or correcting a large, short-term fluctuation of the exchange rate.

As a result of more flexible exchange rates, in both nominal and real terms, China's current account surplus as a percentage of GDP experienced a significant downward adjustment. The ratio of China's current account surplus to GDP peaked in 2007 and 2008, but declined rapidly thereafter. By 2011 it had declined to 1.9 percent, and in 2012 the ratio was 2.3 percent.

The direction of renminbi exchange rate reform is irreversible. China will continue to enhance exchange rate flexibility, and in the near future, China will increase the floating band of the renminbi even further, letting market supply and demand play a fundamental role in exchange rate formation. China will also reduce central bank intervention, enhance the self-rebalancing capability of foreign exchange market, and improve the self-pricing and risk-management capabilities of the financial institutions.

Exchange Rate and Real Economy Adjustments

The exchange rate and the real economy are interlinked naturally. When the exchange rate adjusts, the real economy will be influenced by the exchange rate and reflect the exchange rate changes in its own adjustment. China has achieved good performance in the first three of four macroeconomic objectives, namely, growth, employment, and inflation. Regarding the fourth objective, balance of payments, China went through a period when its current account surplus was relatively large, but in recent years the surplus has started to converge to normal levels.

The question here is, how can we put this adjustment on a sustainable track? It is very important to emphasize that pursuing a more or less balanced balance of payments account is our goal. And this process of adjustment, which started years ago, will continue in the future. The adjustment first started in salary; therefore, we can find a steady increase in labor costs. Recently, especially in the past five years, labor costs have increased even more rapidly.

Since the 1990s, labor costs in China have increased more slowly than productivity increases. Over the past five years, labor costs have increased at a slightly greater rate than productivity, which implies that China's competitiveness has been decreasing. In my view, this is a healthy adjustment, for it helps bring up consumption. It can also be viewed as a catch-up effect. This process will continue as long as firms remain profitable, and I am of the opinion that they will.

The second adjustment also concerns labor costs, but not in terms of salary. I refer to the social security system: pensions, medical insurance, other insurance mechanisms, and so forth. In recent years the social security system for workers has been improved further, and we have paid special attention to designing a nationwide social security system that covers not only city workers but also rural workers, that is, migrant workers from the rural areas. At the moment, we are striving to further enhance the nationwide social security system and to ensure that migrant workers can enjoy their rights as citizens with regard to social security benefits. If we can make this system work, this portion of the costs will surely increase, leading to higher labor costs.

The third source of rapid cost increases is environmental costs, which refers to air pollution, soil pollution, and water pollution, all of which have been a serious problem in China recently. The Chinese government and the people realize that the current situation is not sustainable, and their investment in environmental protection (which, in other words, relates to cost) has been increasing tremendously. Improved environmental practices in industry and manufacturing are also expected to decrease the competitiveness of China's products. In the future, it is possible that China's energy prices and the prices of other resources (such as water and utilities) will continue to increase until they reach economically sustainable levels. All of these adjustments that I have mentioned are healthy, but they will undoubtedly affect China's competitiveness.

What is the bottom line? In my opinion, as long as we can maintain a more or less balanced balance of payments account, this adjustment process can continue, which is healthy for China and will also contribute to the rebalancing of the world economy. As far as I can see, this process will continue going forward, and through channels such as prices it will adjust the economy and achieve what we have been pursuing for years, that is, a relatively balanced balance of payments account. China has become a major importing country. Right now, the annual import volume of China is about US $2 trillion. If this trend continues, a modest estimate suggests that the lower bound of import growth rate for China will be about 6 percent annually. And by the year 2020, China's imports will be around US $3 trillion, which is helpful to balancing China's current account position.

VI

Capital Account Management

22

Capital Account Management: Toward a New Consensus?

Duvvuri Subbarao

Intellectual Shift on Capital Controls

The change in our worldview on capital account management is by far one of the most remarkable intellectual shifts brought on by the crisis. In her opening remarks at the conference, IMF Managing Director Christine Lagarde said that the crisis shattered the consensus on many macroeconomic issues and shibboleths. Nowhere is this more true than in the broad policy area of capital account management. In my view, the three big issues on which the precrisis consensus has dissolved are the following: first, movement toward a fully open capital account; second, the use of capital controls as short-run stabilization tools; and third, the desirability of foreign exchange intervention. I will comment briefly on each of these.

Movement toward a Fully Open Capital Account

The first issue on which consensus was broken is the need for a fully open capital account. Before the crisis, the consensus was that every country should eventually move toward a fully open capital account. The debate was only about the appropriate strategy—in particular, about sequencing and timing—for transitioning to full capital account convertibility.

China and India

Let me invoke the example of India. Moving toward full capital account convertibility has always been our policy goal. The only variable was the road map for getting there, which, it was agreed, should be redefined from time to time, consistent with the evolving situation. There was also general agreement that we should start by floating the exchange rate and decontrolling interest rates and finish with the capital account, with the rationale that this strategy would best preserve macro stability.

There has been a long and vigorous debate in China too on opening up the capital account, with a roughly similar consensus as in India about sequencing. Over the past few years, though, China has apparently changed its strategy, as is evident from the country's policy direction. If you accept that measures to internationalize the renminbi are a big step toward capital account convertibility, then this initiative by China has been much bolder than its actions on freeing up exchange and interest rates.

Controls and Financial Stability

The crisis has, however, changed all this. It shifted the debate from the strategy and timing for capital account convertibility to questioning the very imperative for capital account convertibility. In other words, the consensus that every country should eventually move toward a fully free capital account is now broken.

The main argument in support of the new view—that full capital account convertibility need not be an eventual goal—is that controls prevented emerging markets from adopting some of the financial products that proved toxic in advanced countries. So, there is merit, it is argued, in retaining capital controls. Against this is the old argument, which is still quite persuasive, that as countries become more integrated economically, they will need to become more integrated financially.

With that background, the questions concerning moving toward a fully open capital account are the following:

1. Although there is virtual consensus that free trade in goods is welfare enhancing, opinion is divided on the virtues of financial openness. What explains this difference? In what ways is financial liberalization different from trade liberalization?

2. Is full capital account convertibility still an appropriate objective for every country?

3. If so, what is the best strategy for achieving it? Should it be *festina lente*, or "make haste slowly"?

Capital Controls as a Stabilization Tool

The second issue on which the precrisis consensus has been broken is the use of capital controls as a stabilization tool. Before the crisis, the consensus was that capital controls are bad, always and everywhere. That consensus no longer holds. The received wisdom today is that capital controls are not only appropriate but even desirable in certain circumstances. Even so, there are many unsettled debates.

Effectiveness of Capital Controls

The first big debate is about the effectiveness of capital controls. People have questioned effectiveness on the basis of mainly two arguments: first, capital controls do not alter the volume of flows but alter only their tenor, and second, capital controls can easily be circumvented by disguising short-term flows as long-term flows.

Price versus Quantity Controls

Then there is the debate over what types of control are effective. Countries have used both price-based controls such as taxes, as well as quantity-based controls. However, evidence on which of them has been effective, and under what circumstances, is not conclusive. Two contributors to this volume address this issue from a Latin American perspective in chapters 23 and 24.

In India, for example, we deploy both price-based and quantity-based controls. Our experience has been that although quantity controls are more effective in the short term, they can also be distorting, inefficient, and inequitable.

Capital Controls versus Prudential Measures

There is also an argument about whether capital controls can be substituted by prudential measures. It is not clear that they are always exact substitutes. If capital inflows are intermediated through the banking system, then prudential measures can be applied directly to domestic banks, circumventing the need for controls. But what if the inflows are direct? That is to say, loans are channeled directly from foreign entities to domestic companies. In that case, the only mechanism to prevent excessive leverage, and foreign exchange exposure, may be by imposing controls.

Against that backdrop, the questions regarding capital controls as a short-run stabilization tool are the following:

1. Can we define the distortion that capital controls are meant to correct? For example, how do we determine whether capital flows are excessive or dangerous?

2. What have we learned about the effectiveness of capital controls as a stabilization tool?

3. When can prudential measures be substituted for capital controls?

4. What criteria should we adopt to choose between price-based and quantity-based controls?

5. Are capital controls symmetric as between inflows and outflows? In other words, should we use one type of controls to control inflows and another type to limit outflows?

Foreign Exchange Intervention

The third important issue on which the precrisis consensus has dissolved is foreign exchange intervention. The precrisis consensus, at least among advanced economies, was that intervention in the foreign exchange market is suboptimal. That consensus no longer holds, with even some advanced economies defending their currencies from the safe haven impact. Emerging markets, for their part, have had a long and varied experience struggling with foreign exchange intervention. The policy dilemma in the event of receiving capital flows beyond the country's absorptive capacity can be quite complex.

If you didn't intervene in the foreign exchange market, then you would have currency appreciation quite unrelated to fundamentals. If you intervened but did not sterilize the resultant liquidity, you become vulnerable to inflation pressures and asset-price bubbles. If you intervened in the foreign exchange market and sterilized the resultant liquidity, you may find interest rates firming up, which would attract even more flows—a classic case of Dutch disease. What all this says is that there is really no benign option for dealing with volatile capital flows.

There is one other important issue relating to foreign exchange intervention. Both currency appreciation and currency depreciation, quite unrelated to fundamentals, are complex problems. But there is a significant asymmetry between intervention for fighting appreciation and intervention for fighting depreciation.

When you are fighting currency appreciation, you are intervening in your own currency. Your capacity to do so is, at least in theory, unlimited, quite simply because you can print your own currency. But when you are fighting currency depreciation, you are intervening in a hard currency. Your capacity to intervene is therefore limited by the size of your foreign exchange reserves. What complicates the dilemma is that the market is aware of this.

So, there is the real danger that by intervening in the foreign exchange market, you could end up losing foreign exchange reserves and not gaining on the currency. The lower your reserves dip, the more vulnerable you become. And the vulnerability can become quite serious if your reserves go below the level that markets perceive as necessary to regain market access. It should also be clear that a failed defense of the exchange rate is worse than no defense at all. When you decide to intervene in the foreign exchange market, it is important to make sure that your intervention is successful.

In that context, the questions on this topic of foreign exchange intervention are the following:

1. Under what conditions is it appropriate for countries to intervene in the foreign exchange market?

2. Under what conditions is foreign exchange intervention preferable to capital controls?

3. In most cases, countries claim that they are intervening in the foreign exchange market not to target any particular rate but to manage the volatility in the exchange rate. Is it necessary, then, to define up front your measure of volatility that will trigger intervention?

I have raised very difficult questions for which I have no answers. The expert contributors of the upcoming chapters shed light on the situation in their own countries.

Note

I thank the IMF, Professor Olivier Blanchard, and Managing Director Christine Lagarde for inviting me to the conference at which I delivered this paper, and for the privilege of chairing the session on which this section of the book is based.

23

Capital Flows and Capital Account Management

José De Gregorio

International financial integration and capital account management have been central issues in the policy discussion in recent years. However, these issues are not new in emerging market economies. Some of these economies have had disastrous experiences with financial crisis, most of the time caused by mishandled financial integration and weak macroeconomic policies. The resilience of emerging market economies, in particular their financial systems, during the recent global financial crisis shows that some key lessons have been learned.

The external balance has usually been at the center of financial and currency crises. Periods of exuberance, capital account liberalization, rigidities in the exchange rate, and weak financial systems create periods of overheating, which are followed by costly adjustments. Domestically, these episodes have been induced either by fiscal profligacy or by unsustainable private sector booms. How to take advantage of foreign financing while making the economy resilient to changes in international conditions has become an important question for policymakers and researchers.

Before proceeding with the discussion, it is useful to clarify some ideas. Often, there is no clear distinction between net and gross capital inflows, and little understanding regarding how to tackle them and the potential consequences and risks.

Net capital inflows are the counterpart of current account deficits.[1] Excessive net inflows may be an indication that the economy is running an unsustainable current account deficit. Domestic expenditures could be at levels that cannot be permanently financed and thus will be followed by a sharp correction. At first glance, the current account—or net inflows—is what matters for exchange rates, in particular for the real exchange rate, which is the relative price between domestic and foreign goods that gives the signal for resource allocation and demand patterns consistent with savings and investment decisions.

Gross inflows, in turn, are the response to portfolio allocation. Gross flows are central to financial stability. The form and volume that gross flows take have a direct impact on the vulnerability of the financial system. It has long been argued, rightly, that foreign investment and equity flows are more stable, while banking flows are more likely to be subject to sharp reversals.

In this regard, a separation between net and gross inflows becomes relevant. Net inflows have to do with real exchange rates and competitiveness, while gross flows have to do with financial stability. There are interactions between net and gross flows as well as exchange rate developments and financial stability, but as a starting and organizing distinction it is a useful one.

In this chapter I discuss three relevant issues on financial integration, as well as the challenges capital flows impose on policymaking. First I review the evidence on capital flows, then I discuss the benefits of financial integration. Finally, I go over the issue of capital account management and policies to limit the vulnerabilities coming from financial openness.

Evidence on Capital Inflows into Emerging Markets

After running significant current account deficits before the debt crisis, Latin America had no access to voluntary international capital markets. Capital flows resumed in the early 1990s as result of low world interest rates and the resolution of the debt crisis. These developments raised several policy concerns (Calvo, Leiderman, and Reinhart 1994), and the expression "the problem of capital inflows" was coined. This preoccupation was intensified by the Mexican crisis of the mid-1990s and later by the Asian crisis.

Capital inflows were financing increasing current account deficits. These deficits could become unsustainable and force a severe adjustment. Unsustainability can be driven by the current account or the financial (capital) account. In the first case, mounting artificial appreciation of the currency as a result of exchange rate rigidities would be expected to be followed by massive depreciation and a currency crisis. In the second case, when the source is the capital account, even an apparently sustainable current account deficit could be reversed by a sudden halt in capital inflows as a result of changes in foreign investors' risk appetite, fear of insolvency, or simply contagion after a general withdrawal of investors from emerging markets. Of course, making the distinction between a capital- and a current-account-driven reversal is quite difficult, since they are ex post the same. It is surprising that the cross-references between current account reversals and sudden stops are rather scarce.

As figure 23.1 shows, in the mid-1990s there was indeed a deficit in the current account in emerging markets. It started earlier in Asia and lasted until the Asian crisis. In Latin America, it started in the early 1990s and lasted until 1998. On average, it was not massive, but there were disparities across countries. Mexico had an average deficit of 6.2 percent from 1992 to 1994. Something similar occurred in some Asian countries that were hit during the Asian crisis, such as Malaysia and Thailand. However, it was not the case in Korea and Indonesia. The reversal in Asia was

Figure 23.1
Current Account Balance (% of GDP).
Note: The graphs for Latin America and developing Asia represent simple averages across countries. Latin America includes Argentina, Brazil, Chile, Colombia, Mexico, Peru, and Venezuela. Developing Asia includes China, India, Indonesia, Korea, Malaysia, the Philippines, and Thailand. The emerging markets category corresponds to the IMF's weighted average definition.
Source: International Monetary Fund, *World Economic Outlook.*

sharp, whereas in Latin America it took place more gradually after the late 1990s and was followed by several years of low growth.

Things have been rather different recently. During the 2000s, emerging markets were net exporters of capital. Emerging market economies have been running, on average, current account surpluses; hence, in net terms, capital has been flowing out of these markets. Only recently, Latin America had a current account deficit.

In recent years, capital has been flowing "uphill" (Prasad, Rajan, and Subramanian 2007) from developing countries to advanced economies. This phenomenon has been dominated by the large deficits in the United States and the large surpluses in oil-exporting countries. China has also played a relevant role in financing the US current account deficit, as shown in figure 23.2. This pattern is evident since the mid-1990s, but it was much more pronounced in the years before the crisis. The line in the

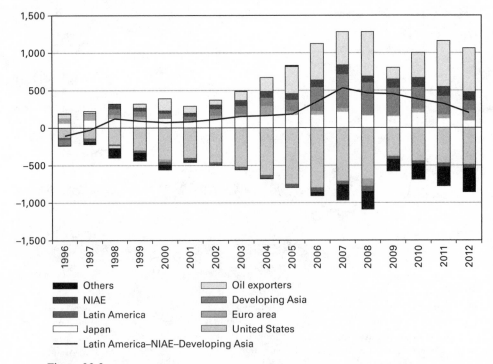

Figure 23.2
World Current Account (billions of US dollars).
Source: International Monetary Fund, *World Economic Outlook* (WEO); 2013 is the WEO forecast. NIAE, newly industrialized Asian economies.

figure shows the current account balance of Latin America, the newly industrialized Asian economies, and developing Asia.[2] They have clearly been net exporters of capital since the late 1990s.

What is the basis for concerns about capital inflows to emerging market economies? There are two reasons. The first is that gross inflows have increased over time, despite outward net flows. Figures 23.3a and b show gross inflows for the sample of Asian and Latin American countries.

The increase in gross flows is very significant. The figures show, consistent with the usual narrative, that the most important and stable component of inflows in Latin America is foreign direct investment (FDI). Banking debt flows, which make up the bulk of the "other investment" category, are much less important and also more volatile. In contrast, in Asia, the role of portfolio flows and banking flows is much more important; indeed, the retrenchment of debt flows during the global financial crisis was much more severe in Asia than in Latin America.[3] This suggests several policy issues regarding financial stability and the vulnerability of emerging markets to external financial turmoil.

However, despite a contained current account deficit, it is possible to observe net (unofficial) capital inflows if there is accumulation of international reserves. Under no foreign reserves accumulation, net capital flows equal the current account. Since emerging markets have been accumulating large amounts of international reserves, capital flows could be flowing into emerging markets despite a surplus in the current account. Figure 23.4 replicates figure 23.2, subtracting from the current account balance the accumulation of international reserves. The latter is a capital outflow, so the difference is total outflows including reserve accumulation, and so net inflows is a negative number.

It is clear that despite no demand to finance excess domestic expenditure, capital has been flowing to emerging markets because of the additional demand for reserves. Indeed, surges in capital inflows during recent years have come together with large accumulations of reserves and moderate current account deficits, even surpluses in some countries. This is very different from the experience of the 1990s, when the incidence of current account deficits was much more relevant (De Gregorio 2014).

In recent years, emerging market economies have not been flooded by capital flows, and net flows have come together with reserve accumulation. Causality among reserves, capital flows, and current account

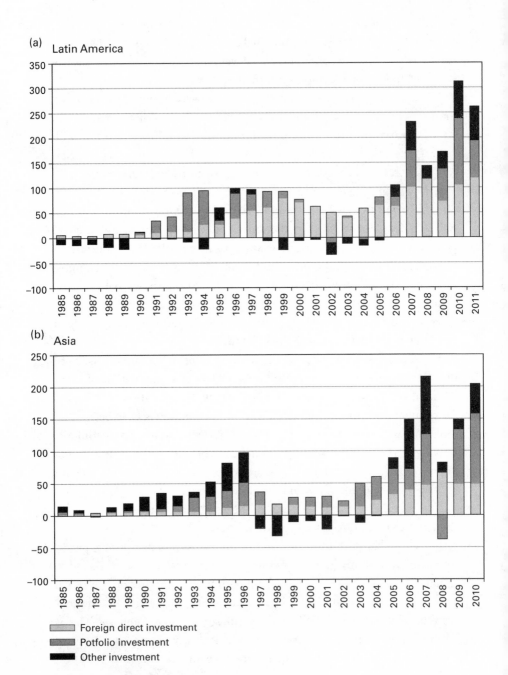

Figure 23.3
Gross Capital Inflows (billions of US dollars).
a. Latin America. b. Asia.
Source: International Monetary Fund, International Financial Statistics.

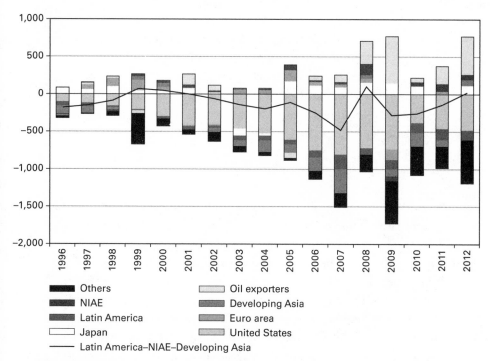

Figure 23.4
World Current Account Minus Reserves Accumulation (billions of US dollars).
Source: International Monetary Fund, *World Economic Outlook*.

balance is a difficult issue. In the accounting definitions, accumulation of reserves (ΔR) is equal to the balance in the current account (C) plus the balance in the financial account (F). If there is an increase in reserves, $\Delta R > 0$, $\alpha \Delta R$ will result in an improvement in the current account balance, while the remaining $(1 - \alpha)\Delta R$ will result in an increase in capital inflows.

If the accumulation of reserves results only in an increase in capital flows, α will be zero. In contrast, if all the accumulation of reserves absorbs capital that is flowing in, without further flows, the current account should be affected with a value of α equal to one. There is little evidence on this, and estimates are wide, ranging from 0.4 (IMF 2012) to 0.8 (Bergsten and Gagnon 2012).[4] Of course, the value of α depends on the characteristics of the countries, but in order for this parameter to be large, one needs to show that the effects of sterilized intervention on the exchange rate are sizable; otherwise, it is difficult to affect the current account through reserve accumulation. But evidence on the impact of intervention on exchange rate is elusive and the effects are at most are limited. Therefore, according to this indirect evidence, the value of α is likely to be low. However, much more research is needed, since this issue is at the core of other issues such as currency manipulation, capital flows absorption, and the impact of reserve accumulation in the global adjustment.

Financial Integration

The evidence for the positive effects of financial integration on economic performance is elusive. Most surveys and recent research have found small or no significant effects, and the policy conclusion is generally that in order to reap the benefits from financial integration, it must be done within a healthy regulatory and supervisory framework. Certainly, unfettered financial integration has proved to be risky and, most of the time, has had very negative consequences. However, the evidence does not support financial autarky. Indeed, the evidence also shows that as countries grow, their level of financial integration increases.

Several recent papers survey and provide additional evidence on financial integration and growth. For example, Obstfeld (2009) concludes that "despite an abundance of cross-section, panel, and event studies, there is strikingly little convincing documentation of direct positive impacts of financial opening on the economic welfare levels or growth rates of developing countries." And from a policy point of view, "This survey discusses the policy framework in which financial globalization is most likely to prove beneficial." Obstfeld also reports that high levels of income are correlated with high levels of financial integration. Of course, causality does not go from financial integration to development but from high levels of income to more financial integration.

Similarly, Kose and others (2009) find that "overall, our critical reading of the recent empirical literature is that it lends some qualified support to the view that developing countries can benefit from financial globalization, but with many nuances. On the other hand, there is little systematic evidence to support widely cited claims that financial globalization by itself leads to deeper and more costly developing country growth crises." They also find that financial integration might have collateral effects that may induce productivity growth, such as improved institutional quality and better macroeconomic policies.

In a recent meta-regression analysis, based on 2,340 regressions, Jeanne, Subramanian, and Williamson (2012) fail[ed] "to produce robust evidence of a positive relationship between financial globalization and growth, raising questions about the pursuit of all forms of international financial integration as an urgent policy goal."

However, the evidence shows that there are important differences according to the type of capital flows. Borensztein, De Gregorio, and Lee (1998) found that for countries with a minimum level of human capital, FDI spurs economic growth. This evidence is confirmed by Jeanne, Subramanian, and Williamson (2012), who found "somewhat reassuringly, portfolio equity and FDI flows are more likely to generate positive and significant effects on growth compared with banking or portfolio debt flows."

The evidence on the weak link between financial integration and economic growth does not come from the impact of financial integration on the incidence of financial crisis. As reported by Kose and others (2009), based on evidence from Edwards (2005), countries with higher capital mobility do not have more external crises, and the cost of crisis is no greater in countries that restrict capital inflows.

The most supportive evidence on the potential benefits of financial integration comes from looking at threshold effects. The conclusion from this literature is that economies need a minimum level of governance, institutional development, quality of macroeconomic policies, and other characteristics to be able to absorb capital flows without detrimental effects on growth. This point was first raised in Prasad and others (2003) and recently revisited by Chen and Quang (2012). These findings may be related to indirect effects of opening up on productivity growth. Still, the evidence is not strong enough to provide definite conclusions.

Two additional findings have raised doubts about the benefits of financial integration. First, countries that have grown the most are those that rely less, not more, on foreign savings (Prasad et al. 2007). However, this is probably because countries that have grown fast, especially in East Asia, have relied more on a very high savings rate and capital accumulation, so their need for net foreign capital are relatively small. We know there is a two-way relationship between savings and growth. High-savings economies, in part because of higher growth, have less need of foreign finance. A second and related finding is the "allocation puzzle" of Gourinchas and Jeanne (2011), in which capital flows to low, not high, total factor productivity growth countries. However, as the authors emphasize, this is also related to the links between savings and growth, rather than a direct consequence of financial integration. Therefore, these additional findings are not necessarily related to the effects of integration on economic growth, but they point toward more fundamental determinants of economic growth that also have an impact on the degree of financial integration.

Summing up, the evidence shows the following:

• There is not a clear link from financial integration to economic growth. Financial integration by itself is not an engine of growth. However, there is no evidence that it is harmful.

• The type of capital flows matters for economic growth. FDI and portfolio equities tend to be more supportive of economic growth, while this is not the case for banking flows. This could be because financial crises come mostly from distortions in the banking sector.

• High income is correlated with high financial integration. As economies develop, their financial integration with the global economy increases. Therefore, financial integration is a result of economic growth, and we do not know what would happen if economies avoided integration while they grew. Is it possible to keep growing with a closed capital account? The evidence indicates that this is unlikely.

• Some evidence shows that there are some threshold effects; that is, countries need to have some minimum institutional standards to benefit from financial globalization.

The main policy implication is that opening up requires a regulatory and supervisory framework that allows a country to reap benefits from integration while preserving financial stability and avoiding costly financial crisis. Economies must face the challenge of integration as growth proceeds.

The Latin American experience regarding financial integration and the incidence of crisis is quite informative. As figure 23.5 shows, Latin American countries have become more integrated but also more resilient.

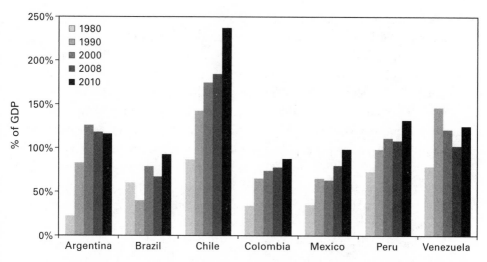

Figure 23.5
International Financial Integration in Latin America (% of GDP).
Note: The index corresponds to international assets plus liabilities over GDP.
Source: Lane and Milesi-Ferretti database.

During the debt crisis, there was less financial integration, and integration was more tilted to debt flows. Latin American countries financed rapid credit booms, and countries that increased credit the most suffered deeper crises (De Gregorio and Guidotti 1995). Being financially open, in a context of appropriate domestic regulation, does not necessarily result in greater vulnerability. The Achilles' heel has been the credit boom.

This discussion has some relevance to trade openness. A cursory look at the global evidence indicates that more open economies did not have worse cycles during the crisis than more closed economies. Economies more open to trade could have suffered much more at the beginning of the crisis, but their whole cycle was not necessarily worse. Being open to trade does not make an economy more vulnerable.

Management of the Capital Account

The first line of defense against massive capital flows is exchange rate flexibility. Unsustainable exchange rate management and one-sided bets are an incentive for capital flow volatility. In addition, an inflation-targeting regime and sound fiscal policies should help prevent excessive capital inflows, which is the same as excessive current account deficits.

However, this is not enough. First, the value of the currency needed to reduce incentives for capital inflows might be sufficiently high that policymakers find it inconvenient. There is a well-grounded bias to have relatively weak currencies in order to foster export-led growth. In this case, capital controls would be serving a competitiveness purpose. Second, the nature of flows might be such that authorities find it prudent to change the composition of flows or reduce some specific inflows, such as excessive reliance on short-term banking flows. In this case, the control would be serving a financial stability purpose and could be considered a macroprudential tool.

Before we discuss policies oriented toward the short-term management of capital flows, it is important to comment on long-term financial integration. Many years ago there was a lot of discussion of sequencing. What must come first, financial opening or financial liberalization? This is no longer an issue. The first task is to develop the domestic financial system. Setting a strong supervisory and regulatory framework is crucial to ensure that the capital account has a sound domestic financial system. Foreign financial institutions might help with the development of the domestic financial system, but they might also be a cause of concern if regulation is weak.

The form in which international banks operate in different countries is quite important to ring-fence the domestic financial system from problems originating in the home countries of the foreign banks. A first important step is to encourage foreign banks to have the same rules and regulations as domestic ones. This calls for the establishment of subsidiaries of foreign banks rather than branches. Subsidiaries have their own boards, which are responsible for bank operations in the host country, and they have strong limits on operations with the parent company. Branches can more easily transmit turbulence to the host country. Subsidiarization is not a panacea, but it has worked reasonably well in Latin America.

A highly debated issue is the use and effectiveness of capital controls. When capital controls are used for financial stability purposes, it is possible to relabel them macroprudential tools. When their purpose is to affect the exchange rate and the current account balance, they are capital controls, although some may call them macroprudential tools as a communication device.

The empirical evidence on effectiveness is varied, since capital controls are used for several goals and effectiveness is country-specific. They are used to control the volume of flows, to change their composition, to ensure monetary independence, and to depreciate the exchange rate. These objectives combine some financial stability concerns with macroeconomic stability concerns. The latter refer to limiting exchange rate pressures and reducing net flows, which is the same as reducing the current account balance.

Regarding purely financial stability concerns, the main risk of gross inflows stems from cross-border banking flows. A number of macroprudential tools can be used to preserve financial stability, and restrictions on cross-border flows can be one of them. In Korea, a tax levy on banks' noncore liabilities was implemented to curb the increasing importance (deemed to be a source of vulnerability) of cross-border flows (Bruno and Shin 2013).

Recent work (Magud, Reinhart, and Rogoff 2011; Ostry et al. 2011; Habermeier, Kokenyne, and Baba 2011) has reviewed the existing evidence on capital controls. Broadly, the evidence has not found significant effects on the exchange rate. Some small effects have been found on the volume of inflows. The most frequent finding is that capital controls affect the composition of inflows, increasing maturity.

Let me use the evidence from Chile, the poster child for market-based capital controls, to clarify some points.[5] Most of the claims about effectiveness look at the statistical significance without looking seriously at the economic significance. An effect could be significantly different from zero but of a very small, and therefore irrelevant, magnitude. In the case of Chile, the paper by Gallego, Hernández, and Schmidt-Hebbel (1999) is the only one that found significant effects on the volume of flows. They estimated that the total impact of capital controls in Chile was to reduce inflows by about 2 percent of GDP, while total capital inflows amounted to nearly 27 percent of GDP. Certainly it is a very small effect, and not robust across studies.

Only some small short-run effects on the real exchange rate have been identified. Only Edwards and Rigobon (2009) estimate statistically significant effects on the extent of the appreciation of the peso. However, the magnitude of such effect is economically small. According to their estimates, the elimination of the control, which consisted of an unremunerated reserve requirement, from its maximum would have appreciated the exchange rate between 2 percent and 2.5 percent.

The most frequent finding—and not only in Chile— has been a change in the composition of inflows. The evidence for Chile is that short-term debt would have declined by 0.5 percent to 1 percent of GDP as a result of capital controls (Cowan and De Gregorio 2007). Again, this is not an economically significant effect.

To be consistent with the discussion of the evidence on financial integration, one could argue that capital controls do no harm. However, there are two concerns, supported by some evidence, regarding negative effects of capital controls.

As long as capital controls are able to change the composition of debt flows by increasing the cost of short-term relative to long-term borrowing, firms that rely on short-term debt (mostly small and medium-size enterprises and firms with a short credit history) will be negatively affected. There is some evidence in the Chilean case of a change in the structure of financing, which could have induced distortions (Forbes 2007). However, this is a characteristic of most macroprudential tools aimed at tapering credit expansion: They have the unavoidable cost of making credit more expensive; otherwise they would be ineffective.

Although I do not think this effect could have been too significant— because the quantity effect is not so large—the main risk of capital controls is to create the false idea of insulation. Policymakers may think they have gained monetary independence to set the interest rate at any level without repercussions on the exchange rate. Indeed, the most famous Latin American cases of capital controls—Chile in the 1990s and Brazil in the late 2000s—took place in the context of very high interest rates, which could have been partly responsible for the large appreciations their currencies went through. Indeed, by late 1996, at the peak of the capital inflow surge in Chile, the monetary policy rate was about 15 percent,[6] while the federal funds rate was at 5.25 percent. Brazil had a similar experience: By mid-2008, when the real reached its maximum, the monetary policy rate was at 12 percent and rising to 13.75 percent, while the federal funds rate was at 2 percent.[7]

Because of concerns about potential costs, some countries might find it worthwhile to apply capital controls, as the effectiveness is country-specific. For controls to be effective and minimize costs and distortions, it is important that macroeconomics policies be well aligned with macroeconomic and financial stability. Controls could serve as a complement and not a substitute for sound macroeconomic and financial policies. But having strong macroeconomic policies and a strong financial system could make it unnecessary to consider capital controls, as was the experience in many emerging markets that made it successfully through the global financial crisis.

Notes

1. This ignores the accumulation of reserves here; that is discussed below.

2. The countries in each category are those defined by the IMF in the *World Economic Outlook*.

3. For further discussion on cross-border banking flows, see CIEPR (2012).

4. The elasticity computed in IMF (2012) is interacted with capital controls, and the value ranges from zero for no capital controls to 0.4 with the strongest capital controls in the sample.

5. For details, see Cowan and De Gregorio (2007). For a discussion of Latin America, see De Gregorio (2014).

6. By that time, monetary policy was set in UF (unidad de fomento), an indexed unit of account, so to have the nominal equivalent, which is the one used in the text, I use the yearly inflation rate at that time.

7. In the case of Brazil, Chamon and Garcia (2013) found no significant effects on the exchange rate, concluding that the IOF (Portuguese initialism for Tax on Financial Transactions) did not prevent appreciation. They argued that the "real game-changer" for the appreciating trend of the real (which has reverted in recent years) was the cut in the monetary policy interest rate.

References

Bergsten, C. Fred, and Joseph E. Gagnon. 2012. "Currency Manipulation, the US Economy, and the Global Economic Order." Policy Brief PB12-25, Peterson Institute of International Economics, Washington, DC.

Borensztein, Eduardo, José De Gregorio, and Jong-Wha Lee. 1998. "How Does Foreign Direct Investment Affect Economic Growth?" *Journal of International Economics* 45 (1): 115–135.

Bruno, Valentina, and Hyun Song Shin. 2013. "Assessing Macroprudential Policies: Case of Korea." Faculty paper, Princeton University, Princeton, NJ.

Calvo, Guillermo A., Leonardo Leiderman, and Carmen M. Reinhart. 1994. "The Capital Inflows Problem: Concepts and Issues." *Contemporary Economic Policy* 12:54–66.

Chamon, Marcos, and Marcio Garcia. 2013. "Capital Controls in Brazil: Effective? Efficient?" International Monetary Fund, Washington, DC.

Chen, Jinzhao, and Thérèse Quang. 2012. "International Financial integrations and Economic Growth: New Evidence on Threshold Effects." Working Paper 2012-06, Université Paris Ouest, Paris.

Committee on International Economic Policy Reform (CIEPR). 2012. *Banks and Cross-Border Capital Flows: Policy Challenges and Regulatory Responses.* Washington, DC: Brookings Institution.

Cowan, Kevin, and José De Gregorio. 2007. "International Borrowing, Capital Controls and the Exchange Rate: Lessons from Chile." In *Capital Controls and Capital Flows in Emerging Economies: Policies, Practices and Consequences*, ed. S. Edwards. Chicago: University of Chicago Press.

De Gregorio, José. 2014. *How Latin America Weathered the Global Financial Crisis.* Washington, DC: Peterson Institute of International Economics.

De Gregorio, José, and Pablo Guidotti. 1995. "Financial Development and Economic Growth." *World Development* 23 (3): 433–448.

Edwards, Sebastian. 2005. "Capital Controls, Sudden Stops, and Current Account Reversals." NBER Working Paper 11170, National Bureau of Economic Research, Cambridge, MA. http://www.nber.org/papers/w11170.

Edwards, Sebastian, and Roberto Rigobon. 2009. "Capital Controls, Exchange Rate Volatility and External Vulnerability." *Journal of International Economics* 78 (2): 257–267.

Forbes, Kristin J. 2007. "One Cost of the Chilean Capital Controls: Increased Financial Constraints for Smaller Traded Firms." *Journal of International Economics* 71 (2): 294–323.

Gallego, Francisco, Leonardo Hernández, and Klaus Schmidt-Hebbel. 1999. "Capital Controls in Chile: Effective, Efficient?" Working Paper 59, Central Bank of Chile, Santiago.

Gourinchas, Pierre-Olivier, and Olivier Jeanne. 2011. "Capital Flows to Developing Countries: The Allocation Puzzle." Faculty paper, University of California at Berkeley, Berkeley, CA.

Habermeier, Karl, Annamaria Kokenyne, and Chikako Baba. 2011. "The Effectiveness of Capital Controls and Prudential Policies in Managing Large Inflows." IMF Staff Discussion Note 11/14, Monetary and Capital Markets Department, International Monetary Fund, Washington, DC, August 5. http://www.imf.org/external/pubs/ft/sdn/2011/sdn1114.pdf.

International Monetary Fund (IMF). 2012. "External Balance Assessment (EBA): Technical Background of the Pilot Methodology." International Monetary Fund,

Washington, DC, August 3. http://www.imf.org/external/np/res/eba/pdf/080312 .pdf.

Jeanne, Olivier, Arvind Subramanian, and John Williamson. 2012. *Who Needs to Open the Capital Account?* Washington, DC: Peterson Institute of International Economics.

Kose, M. Ayhan, Eswar S. Prasad, Kenneth Rogoff, and Shang-Jin Wei. 2009. "Financial Globalization: A Reappraisal." *IMF Staff Papers* 56 (1): 8–62.

Magud, Nicolas E., Carmen Reinhart, and Kenneth S. Rogoff. 2011. "Capital Controls: Myth and Reality—A Portfolio Balance Approach." NBER Working Paper 16805, National Bureau of Economic Research, Cambridge, MA. http://www.nber.org/papers/w16805.

Obstfeld, Maurice. 2009. "International Finance and Growth in Developing Countries: What Have We Learned?" *IMF Staff Papers* 56 (1): 63–111.

Ostry, Jonathan D., Atish R. Gosh, Karl Habermeier, Luc Laeven, Marcos Chamon, Mahvash Qureshi, and Annamaria Kokenyne. 2011. "Managing Capital Inflows: What Tools to Use?" IMF Staff Discussion Note 11/06, International Monetary Fund, Washington, DC, April 5. http://www.imf.org/external/pubs/ft/sdn/2011/sdn1106.pdf.

Prasad, Eswar S., Raghuram G. Rajan, and Arvind Subramanian. 2007. "Foreign Capital and Economic Growth." *Brookings Papers on Economic Activity* 38 (1): 153–230.

Prasad, Eswar S., Kenneth Rogoff, Shang-Jin Wei, and M. Ayhan Kose. 2003. "Effects of Financial Globalization on Developing Countries: Some Empirical Evidence." IMF Occasional Paper 220, International Monetary Fund, Washington, DC. http://www.imf.org/external/pubs/nft/op/220.

24

Managing Capital Inflows in Brazil

Márcio Holland

This chapter presents the recent Brazilian experience of dealing with capital inflows associated with domestic currency appreciation, and the use of macroprudential measures to cope with the capital surges. Restrictions on the financial account in Brazil are only some of the ingredients of the country's economic policy, which includes controlling inflation along with maintaining a conventional monetary policy, as well as macroprudential measures, a fiscal consolidation program, a solid financial system, a focus on investment and infrastructure, and a very comprehensive income inequality-reduction policy.

The consequences of the 2008–2009 international financial turmoil have not yet come to an end, as the world is still waiting to see advanced economies addressing important financial and political problems. In the United States, the Federal Reserve has become the main source of economic stimulus, having implemented the third round of quantitative easing, with only partial and less than satisfactory results for the United States but with negative consequences for emerging economies.

In Europe, the crisis still persists, mainly in euro zone's periphery, with severe economic and social consequences. Therefore, it is important that euro area countries come up with rapid and durable solutions, especially in terms of banking supervision and fiscal consolidation, so that economic growth picks up in the region. Since the fourth quarter of 2011, quarter-over-quarter economic growth in the euro area has been zero or below. European leaders are still struggling to find a solution that will put the region back on track.

In this particular circumstance, after establishing the monetary policy rates, central bankers in advanced economies began proposing a zero lower bound monetary policy that included aggressive quantitative easing. By 2013, more than US $9 trillion had been injected into the world's liquidity, with part of this huge amount of money searching for very rare positive returns, mainly in emerging market (EM) economies. The unconventional monetary-easing policies consist of central bank purchases of domestic government bonds or even the provision of explicit guidance on the future path of interest rates, with medium-term inflation or nominal output and unemployment rates as targets.

As a rational response, Brazilian monetary authorities have put into practice macroprudential measures that include restrictions on the capital accounts. Roughly speaking, these measures consist of increases in IOF (a tax on financial transactions) rates on short-term financial operations, including external loans up to one year, with the main aim being to reduce gains in carry-trade strategies. Foreign direct investments and even long-term financial operations are left aside.

This chapter highlights the fact that managing capital inflows is only part of the policy mix. Such a strategy has been effective in dealing with the increasing international liquidity and in preventing inflows of very short-term foreign capital, as well as in changing the composition of capital inflows toward better-quality capital inflows. Therefore, the exchange rate staunched its appreciation movement and since then has been less volatile. It is also worth noting that the interest rate may have increasing power to affect the exchange rate under such a policy.

We know how controversial the role and the effectiveness of capital controls are during crises. However, there has been a distinct scenario since 2008 suggesting that countries such as Brazil should care about its exchange rate and quality of capital surges. A combination of a zero lower bound monetary policy with quantitative easing, provoking exchange rate realignments across the world, is treated as part of the solution to the fragilities in advanced economies, but at the same time, it represents sizable constraints on EM economies. We are definitely in a noncooperative, non-zero-sum game, and thus EM economies are being harmed rather than benefited. Capital account management measures are a technical rather than an ideological issue. They join the policy toolkit, with successful results.

In the next section I examine the economic literature on capital controls and then describe the recent Brazilian experience.

The Literature

Several recent studies have reviewed the role played by capital controls in the context of a world economy emerging from a financial crisis. Even the IMF (2012) in its "institutional view" on capital controls suggests some signs of progress on the matter. The analysis of Ostry and others (2010) can be considered one of the first in the new context. They discuss not only the benefit of the capital inflows into emerging markets but also the appropriate policy responses. Baba and Kokenyne (2011) estimate the effectiveness of capital control in response to inflow surges in EMs such as Brazil, Colombia, Korea, and Thailand in the 2000s.

It is fair to say that the globalization of capital markets has been beneficial when it allows capital flows to move toward their most attractive destination, but at the same time this process has been associated with episodes of dramatic financial crises. In this scenario, there is an incipient debate regarding the role of international capital flows in triggering such crises, and if that is the case, capital controls become an important policy tool to be used by EM countries, as happened quite often during the 1990s.

Recently, a number of studies have argued that free capital mobility has created a highly unstable international financial system and that developing countries need to manage capital flows. It is important to note that this idea is not a new one and dates back to James Tobin (1978), who argued that reducing macroeconomic instability would require the adoption of a global tax on foreign exchange transactions to reduce speculation in international financial markets.

The rationale for imposing restrictions (capital controls) on international capital flows is associated with the belief that capital markets are usually characterized by market failures and distortions (information asymmetry), and that such imperfections are magnified by difficulties in enforcing contracts across borders and by a kind of herd behavior, such as when investors overreact to external shocks.

One of the reasons most often voiced in the defense of using capital controls during periods of crises is that it allows the central bank to stem the drain on foreign exchange reserves and that monetary authorities could initially raise interest rates; once capital controls are in place, it gives room for a lower and more stable interest rate, which acts in a procyclical way. It is also important to note that capital controls introduce a wedge between domestic and foreign interest rates, and the domestic interest rate policy does not need to follow international interest rates when facing the consequences of international crises and the breakdown of uncovered interest parity.

The discussion of some policy issues regarding the effectiveness of imposing capital controls should be carried out with the understanding of the required steps (sequencing reform) toward the liberalization of the capital account. The main issue is not whether or not capital controls should be eliminated but under what conditions (when and how fast) they would be effective in achieving desirable economic outcomes. Most countries' experiences with capital controls have shown that the private sector found ways of getting around capital controls, usually adopting strategies based on overinvoicing (underinvoicing) imports (exports) and mislabeling the nature of capital movements (short-term portfolio flows labeled as trade credit).

The majority of the studies have argued that before liberalizing the capital accounts, it is necessary to reverse major fiscal imbalances and achieve macroeconomic stability. The past experience of many developing countries, including Brazil in the 1990s, has shown that although price stability was obtained, it was still necessary to implement fiscal reforms to improve the overall macroeconomic fundamentals of the economy. Other than this, establishing a sound banking system is also necessary before developing countries can lift restrictions on capital mobility, as banks will intermediate the inflows of capital, which should not happen in an inefficient way.

Previous works, such as those by Reinhart and Smith (2002) and Kaminsky and Schmukler (2001), examined the role of temporary controls on capital inflows, emphasizing that capital controls have two crucial features: they are asymmetric (the target is capital inflows rather than capital outflows) and temporary. The authors examined possible reasons for policymakers to adopt controls on capital inflows and two types of shocks that can result in excessive capital inflows (temporary changes in the foreign interest rate and in domestic monetary policy). The major empirical findings are that the tax rate on capital inflows should be very high to affect the capital account balance, that the economic benefit of taxing capital inflows is not significant, and that taking too long to remove capital controls can reverse welfare benefits.

Malaysia and Thailand are two EM countries making use of capital controls during episodes of financial crises in the recent past; the experiences of those countries were examined by Edison and Reinhart (2001). Their main empirical findings suggest that capital controls help reduce interest rate volatility but there is mixed evidence for avoiding exchange rate volatility. Another important finding refers to a wider and more variable bid-ask spread during control periods, and little evidence that capital controls were effective in reducing volatility spillovers.

Kaminsky and Schmukler (2001) dealt with the question of whether or not capital controls affect the link between domestic and foreign stock market prices and interest rates—in other words, whether they matter for international market integration. The authors found little evidence that capital controls can segment domestic and foreign markets, and even when they do, the effects do not last long. Finally, they found that it is difficult to distinguish the effects of controls on inflows and outflows.

The Chilean experience during the 1990s has been examined in detail by De Gregorio, Edwards, and Valdes (2000), who developed work that addressed the issue of whether or not controls on capital inflows are efficient through the use of unremunerated reserve requirement. They also examined the effects on interest rates, the volume and composition of capital inflows, and the real exchange rate. Their main empirical findings suggest that it is difficult to find long-run effects, and that capital controls generate an increase in the interest rate differential only in the short run, no effects on the real exchange rate, and a significant effect in the composition of capital inflows in favor of a longer maturity.

Another study linked to the Chilean experience with controls on inflows and outflows of capital during the 1990s was reported by Edwards (1999), and the empirical results suggest that controls on outflows are not effective, whereas controls on inflows have the advantage of affecting the maturity of foreign debt, which is a desirable outcome for the monetary authorities. The three main goals of Chile's capital controls were to slow down the inflow of capital and change its composition toward capital of longer maturities, to reduce and postpone real exchange rate appreciation, and to help the monetary authorities adopt an independent monetary policy (maintaining an interest rate differential). The author also found that controls on capital inflows are not sufficient to eliminate financial instability. The GARCH—generalized autoregressive conditional heteroskedasticity—estimation reveals that the restrictions on capital inflows were successful in reducing stock market instability, but not short-run interest rate volatility.

Generally, the discussion about the effects of restrictions on capital inflows has shown that controls are important to explaining changes in the composition of capital flows in the direction intended (reducing the share of short-term and portfolio flows, and increasing foreign direct investment). The literature addresses the issue of whether external factors (international interest rates and liquidity) or internal factors (domestic fundamentals) are more important to explaining the increase in the financial flows to emerging economies, and relate this to the question of how these countries respond to an increase in capital flows.

The empirical evidence has indicated that capital inflow is more volatile in Latin America than in Asia, and short-term capital is more volatile than all other types of capital flows. The adoption of sterilized intervention increases the volume of total capital flows through short-term capital, and capital controls have no significant effect on reducing the overall volume of flows, but they affect the composition of capital flows in favor of foreign direct investments. Finally, short-term flows are not sensitive to changes in international interest rates, although the composition of capital flows does respond to such changes.

After the 2008 financial crisis, as some important economies reestablished restrictions on their financial capital account as part of the policy toolkit, academics, policymakers, and international institutions alike have been trying to shed new light on such controversial issues. Thus, we next present Brazilian recent practices and policy responses in the context of the crisis.

The Brazilian Experience

First, it is important to distinguish the current global scenario from that faced by Latin American economies in the 1990s. At that time, it was observed that the liquidity curb was more related to weak domestic macroeconomic fundaments in such economies than to international pressures caused by central banks in advanced economies. Financial and currency crises associated with debt defaults used to be commonplace in the developing world. Those crises were usually explained either by wrong domestic economic policies (*crazy policymakers* in the developing economies) or by wrong economic agents (*crazy agents* under self-fulfilling features). Asian crises were explained by *wrong markets*, to the result of contagious and herd behaviors (see Frankel and Wei 2004).

On the other hand, according to the IMF (2012, 6), "Capital flow liberalization has been part of the development strategy in several countries, in recognition of the benefits that such flows can bring." Actually, it is a novel strategy associated with unconventional monetary policies developed by the central economies trying to resume growth. That denotes a very different nature of capital flow surges experienced nowadays in comparison with past practices. It is "liquidity injection" rather than "capital flows liberalization," usually parsed as "removal of restrictions."

This distinction makes quite a difference to policy recommendations, especially with respect to how EM economies should deal with it. It is also not a matter of "unrestricted convertibility of local currency in international financial transactions." (IMF 2012, 10) It seems that the recent capital surges are more associated with the less convertible currencies combating devaluation in international currencies.

The relationship between growth and the exchange rate (devaluations, misalignments, and volatilities) has been approached in the economic literature from different perspectives.[1] It is still a controversial topic, though it is fair to state that devaluations foster growth through different channels, mainly the trade one. Weak domestic markets in advanced economies result in an excessive inventory of manufactured goods searching for international markets; thus, devaluation would be very helpful.

Under such specific circumstance, the capital flow management measures put forward in EM economies are a rational response, and as beneficial as they are prudential.

The current context for implementing capital controls is quite different. Currently, problems are caused by *crazy policymakers* in advanced economies. Unconventional monetary policy—including rude quantitative easing programs under a zero lower bound monetary policy—has been urged by central banks in advanced economies. Figures 24.1 and 24.2

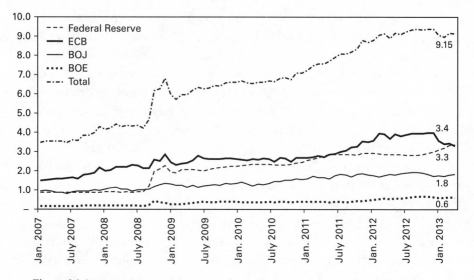

Figure 24.1
Expansion of International Liquidity (US $ trillion).
Notes: European Central Bank; Bank of Japan; Bank of England.
Source: Bloomberg, http://www.bloomberg.com.

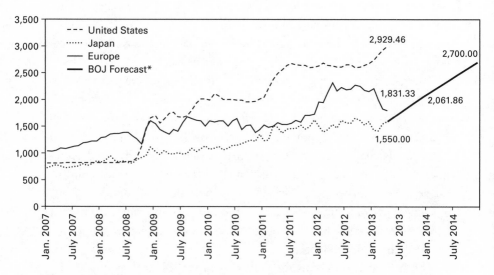

Figure 24.2
Expansion of the Monetary Base in Advanced Economies, 2007–2014 (US $ billion).
Note: * Bank of Japan estimated in April 2013.
Source: Bloomberg.

show how sizable the expansion of international liquidity is as a result of this practice.

As can be seen from these figures, central bankers in advanced economies, such as the United States, Europe, and Japan, have introduced very aggressive expansionary monetary policies. Notwithstanding the benefits of such monetary stances, EM countries are concerned that the surge in capital inflows could cause problems for their economies. Exchange rate appreciation, reserve accumulation with some fiscal costs, and incentives to excessively borrow abroad, risking a domestic credit boom, are only some consequences that have recently been observed. It should be added that the international interest rates are pretty low and have remained so for a long period of time, especially in comparison with normal interest rate levels in EM economies, which constitutes an incentive to make loans abroad in international currencies. It can also amplify currency mismatches, with the well-known propensity for instability in EMs during a sudden cessation of capital flows, sometimes leading to unexpected exchange rate devaluations.

In the Brazilian case, an increase in international liquidity created excessive pressure on the exchange rate. Consequently, the economic authorities created a transaction tax (IOF) on new capital flows. Table 24.1 shows the evolution of the IOF on portfolio investments and external loans, which can be summarized as follows (observations to June 2013):

1. Portfolio investments include fixed income and derivatives. They were all taxed at a 6 percent rate, with exception of capex and infrastructure bonds (there has never been an IOF on external flows to these bonds). Also, an IOF has not been applied to equities.

2. Short-term (up to one-year) inbound loans and offshore bond issues (overseas debt) are subject to an IOF at a rate of 6 percent.

3. There has not been a 1 percent IOF tax on foreign exchange short positions held by banks, funds, and companies.

It is worth noting that when it became necessary to do so, the Brazilian authority promptly withdrew such measures, indicating that they are additional tools to manage capital flows. That was the case observed in June 2013, when the IOF applied to portfolio investments, including fixed income instruments and derivatives, was reduced to zero.

Table 24.1
Brazil: Tax on Financial Transactions, 2008–2013 (%)

Portfolio:	December 3, 2008	October 19, 2009	October 4, 2010	October 18, 2010	July 26, 2011	December 1, 2011	February 29, 2012	March 9, 2012	June 13, 2012	December 4, 2012	June 4, 2013	June 12, 2013
Fixed income	1.50	2.00	4.00	6.00	6.00	6.00	6.00	6.00	6.00	6.00	0.00	0.00
Long-term corporate bonds	1.50	2.00	4.00	6.00	6.00	0.00	0.00	0.00	0.00	0.00	0.00	0.00
Equity	0.00	2.00	2.00	2.00	2.00	0.00	0.00	0.00	0.00	0.00	0.00	0.00
Derivative margin deposit	0.38	0.38	0.38	6.00	6.00	6.00	6.00	6.00	6.00	6.00	0.00	0.00
External loan up to:												
90 days	5.38	5.38	5.38	5.38	6.00	6.00	6.00	6.00	6.00	6.00	6.00	6.00
270 days	0.38	0.00	0.00	0.00	6.00	6.00	6.00	6.00	6.00	6.00	6.00	6.00
1 year	0.38	0.00	0.00	0.00	6.00	6.00	6.00	6.00	6.00	6.00	6.00	6.00
2 years	0.38	0.00	0.00	0.00	6.00	6.00	6.00	6.00	6.00	0.00	0.00	0.00
3 years	0.38	0.00	0.00	0.00	0.00	0.00	6.00	6.00	0.00	0.00	0.00	0.00
5 years	0.38	0.00	0.00	0.00	0.00	0.00	0.00	0.00	0.00	0.00	0.00	0.00
Excessive long positions on BRL	0.00	0.00	0.00	0.00	1.00	1.00	1.00	1.00	1.00	1.00	1.00	0.00

Source: Ministry of Finance, Brazil.

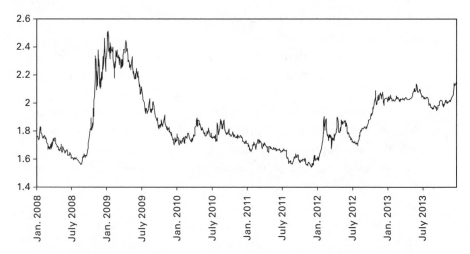

Figure 24.3
Nominal Exchange Rate (real per dollar), 2008–2013.
Source: Central Bank of Brazil.

The appreciation path of the Brazilian exchange rate was interrupted by the financial crisis of September 2008, which was reversed with the quantitative easing monetary policies adopted by developed economies. To reduce the vulnerability and procyclicality of capital flows, Brazil introduced measures to manage its capital account through prudential regulation. These measures are also illustrated over the time in figure 24.3. From this figure it is possible to infer that after controls on surges of capital inflows were initiated, the Brazilian real realized an appreciation and moved to a new stable equilibrium.

As can be seen in figure 24.3, the effectiveness of the restrictions on capital control has been longer than expected by the economic literature. Results include a more stable exchange rate and less vulnerable balance sheets, both in domestic companies and in the financial system. There are some plausible explanations for such successes.

First, the Brazilian economy is much less dollarized than it was a decade ago. The dollarization of an economy is strongly associated with both current inflation and inflation risk.[2] It is a rational response of agents to deal with inflation. As inflation and the risks of high inflation have decreased substantially in Brazil, along with sovereign risks, currency mismatches in balance sheets have shown a sizable reduction. As a result, capital account management measures do not change foreign investors' perceptions about the country.

Second, the composition of the capital inflows changed very clearly after restrictions were placed on short-term financial inflows. As described in the literature, restrictions on capital flows play an important role in capital allocation, changing the composition of capital inflows in favor of foreign direct investments. In Brazil, foreign direct investment has been as high as it was before the restrictions were placed on capital inflows. Meanwhile, as the returns on the carry-trade strategy turned out to be negative (see figures 24.4 and 24.5), short-term capital inflows have been reduced.

As shown in figure 24.6, long-term capital inflows remain stable at a very high level, while portfolio investment has decreased toward a level not seen since before the 2008–2009 financial crisis. Neither intercompany transactions nor equity have been affected by such measures.

Third, Brazil has put forward a set of macroprudential policies, including capital account management, along with conventional monetary policy. Consistent fiscal results have been accomplished; thus, the ratio of public debt to GDP has decreased very quickly. In addition, Brazil has left behind any probability of fiscal insolvency. The international investor's confidence in the Brazilian sovereign bonds has increased, as shown in figure 24.8. According to this figure, the difference between the yields on 10-year Brazilian and US bonds has narrowed consistently since 2011. A commitment to fiscal responsibility throughout the years, combined with economic growth, has contributed to a reduction in credit risk in Brazil.

Finally, the medium-term growth prospect also plays an important role, encouraging the foreign direct investments to search for opportunities, and Brazil today is one of the best countries in the world in which to invest. The Brazilian government has just launched a comprehensive program of concessions in the infrastructure sector, including airports, ports, railways, high-speed trains, oil, gas, and electricity, for a total amount of US $235 billion. It is just the first step toward addressing the entire spectrum of the country's infrastructure needs. Many investment projects in different sectors, such as in automobile, chemistry, health care, and others, are being set up. As a middle-class society, Brazil has a dynamic domestic market with a low unemployment rate and lower income inequalities.

(a)

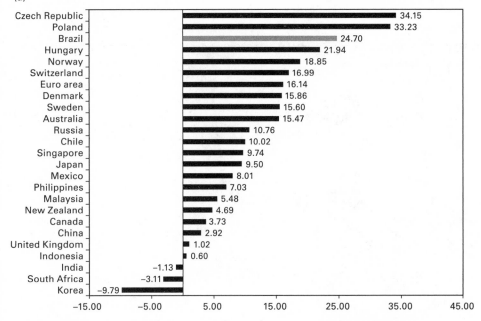

(b)

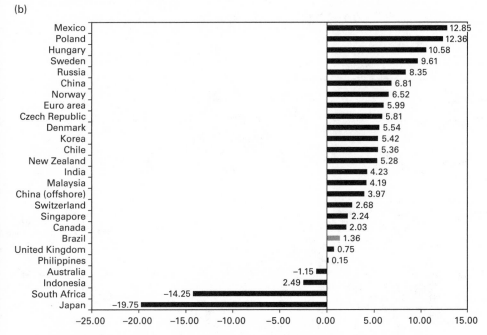

Figure 24.4
Returns on Carry-Trade Strategies in Selected Countries, 2008 and 2013 (%, 12-month accumulated). a. June 2008. b. June 2013.
Source: Bloomberg.

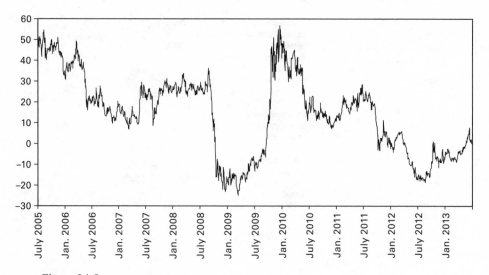

Figure 24.5
Brazil: Returns on Carry-Trade Strategy (2005–2013) (% per annum).
Source: Bloomberg.

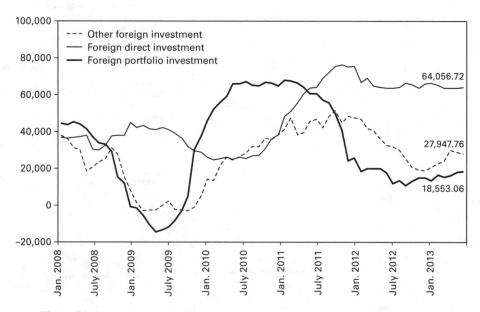

Figure 24.6
Brazil: Financial Accounts, 2008–2013 (US $ billion).
Source: Central Bank of Brazil.

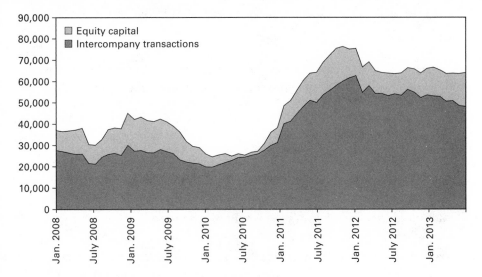

Figure 24.7
Brazil: Foreign Direct Investment, 2008–2013.
Source: Central Bank of Brazil.

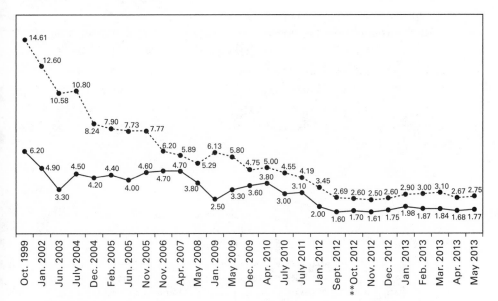

Figure 24.8
Yield* on 10-year Brazilian and US Bonds, 1999–2013 (%).
Notes: *Measured by the difference in yields on issue date on 10-year Brazilian bonds denominated in US dollars and yields on US Treasury bonds (same maturity) traded on the secondary market on the same date. ** From October 2012, yields on 10-year Brazilian and US Treasury bonds (same maturity) traded on the secondary market on the same date.
Source: Ministry of Finance, Brazil, and Bloomberg.

It seems that growth prospects and investment opportunities matter to foreign investors more than restrictions in short-term capital inflows do.

Summary

Excessive international liquidity has provoked side effects in EM economies, and Brazil is more a rule than an exception among them. To cope with the effect of unconventional monetary policies implemented by advanced economies' central banks, Brazil has introduced a set of macroprudential policies that includes capital account management, along with conventional monetary policy. Capital account management is much more a technical issue than an ideological one. Successful results have been obtained under the circumstances. The economic policy stance includes measures to foster investments in the context of inflation under control, a growth-friendly fiscal consolidation program, a solid financial system, and strong income-inequality reduction.

After restrictions on the country's financial account were implemented, the Brazilian real appreciated, moving upward until it stabilized at the parity of 2 reals per US dollar. It is fair to say that the effectiveness of the controls, begun in 2011, has lasted longer than expected. The benefits of the controls are generally greater than the eventual costs. As such measures are also prudential, borrowing abroad in other currency has been less leveraged.

Notes

1. See Holland and others (2013) for new empirical findings on the relationship between growth and exchange rate volatility. According to these authors, it seems that exchange rate volatility matters to growth more than misalignment does.

2. Financial dollarization is a topic associated with high inflation and inflation risk in Latin American economies, and Vieira, Holland, and Resende (2012) have associated such phenomena with sovereign risks as dollarization remains high, even after inflation and inflation risk decrease.

References

Baba, C., and A. Kokenyne. 2011. "Effectiveness of Capital Controls in Selected Emerging Markets in the 2000s." IMF Working Paper 11/281, International Monetary Fund, Washington, DC.

De Gregorio, J., S. Edwards, and R. O. Valdes. 2000. "Controls on Capital Inflows: Do They Work?" NBER Working Paper 7645, National Bureau of Economic Research, Cambridge, MA, April.

Edison, H., and C. M. Reinhart. 2001. "Stopping Hot Money." *Journal of Development Economics* 66 (2): 533–553.

Edwards, S. 1999. "How Effective Are Capital Controls?" *Journal of Economic Perspectives* 13 (4): 65–84.

Frankel, J., and Shang-Jin Wei. 2004. "Managing Macroeconomic Crises: Policy Lessons." Manuscript, Harvard University, Cambridge, MA.

Holland, M., F. V. Vieira, C. Gomes da Silva, and L. C. Bottecchia. 2013. "Growth and Exchange Rate Volatility: A Panel Data Analysis." *Applied Economics* 45 (26): 3733–3741.

International Monetary Fund (IMF). 2012. "The Liberalization and Management of Capital Flows: An Institutional View." International Monetary Fund, Washington, DC, November 14. http://www.imf.org/external/np/pp/eng/2012/111412 .pdf.

Kaminsky, G. L., and S. Schmukler. 2001. "Short- and Long-Run Integration: Do Capital Controls Matter?" Policy Research Working Paper 2660, World Bank, Washington, DC.

Ostry, Jonathan D., Atish R. Ghosh, Karl Habermeier, Marcos Chamon, Mahvash S. Qureshi, and Denis B. S. Reinhardt. 2010. "Capital Inflows: The Role of Controls." IMF Staff Position Note 10/04, International Monetary Fund, Washington, DC, February 19. http://www.imf.org/external/pubs/ft/spn/2010/spn1004 .pdf.

Reinhart, C. M., and R. T. Smith. 2002. "Temporary Controls on Capital Inflows." *Journal of International Economics* 57 (2): 327–351.

Tobin, J. 1978. A Proposal for International Monetary Reform. *Eastern Economic Journal* 4 (3/4): 153–159.

Vieira, F A. C., M. Holland, and M. F. Resende. 2012. Financial Dollarization and Systemic Risks: New Empirical Evidence. *Journal of International Money and Finance* 31 (6): 1695–1714.

25

Capital Account Management

Hélène Rey

Benefits of Financial Integration: Theory and Evidence

I will start by asking basic questions about international capital flows. Many policy discussions are based on the premise that international capital flows bring some important benefits to countries' economies. When asked more precisely, policymakers identify two main benefits of international capital flows: improvements in allocative efficiency and in risk sharing. Because of financial integration, capital can flow to places where it is put to its most productive use, that is, places where the marginal product of capital is highest. This view comes, of course, straight from the neoclassical growth model.

Policymakers would add that international capital flows are also beneficial because they enable better risk sharing, which is again a statement conveyed by many economic models.

Empirical Evidence

Numerous studies exist that actually try to look at the data for the effects of international capital flows on growth or on consumption volatility, trying to test for these two types of gains. Surprisingly, these effects are hard to find in macroeconomic data: the benefits of capital flows are remarkably elusive. As attested by the most recent surveys reviewing a long list of empirical papers, it is hard to find robust evidence of an impact of financial openness on growth or on improved risk sharing (e.g., Eichengreen 2002; Kose et al. 2006; Obstfeld 2009; Jeanne, Subramanian, and Williamson 2012).

To be fair, some papers point toward the existence of threshold effects: Capital flows would be beneficial only after a country has reached a certain amount of institutional or financial sector development. There are also some differences if one looks across different types of capital flows: Some capital flows seem better at delivering growth and risk-sharing benefits than others. But this evidence is not very conclusive because, often, the sample used seems to make a difference. Some papers using microeconomic data find a decrease in the cost of capital at the time of financial integration. So the question is, why don't we see more of an effect at the aggregate level?

There is also some recent research analyzing the role of global banks and looking at whether the large international capital flows that we see within the internal realm of global banks have had any effect on the real side of the economy. Cetorelli and Goldberg (2012) point toward a better allocation of liquidity within global banks. But one might wonder whether this comes together with a weakening of the monetary policy transmission, as global banks can reshuffle liquidity across borders to offset the effect of national monetary policies. If global banks can allocate liquidity among their various subsidiaries and branches, that may have benefits, but it might also be a way of circumventing the effects of monetary policy.

So, from the point of view of the empirical evidence, the jury is still out. So far, however, the evidence seems surprisingly less conclusive than what one might have thought, given both our strong theoretical priors and the sheer size of international capital flows in the world economy.

Calibrated Models

The neoclassical growth model is behind many of our economic intuitions regarding why the free flow of capital could be beneficial. Interestingly, even within that paradigm, realistic calibrations indicate that gains tend to be small. Gourinchas and Jeanne (2006) have shown, in the context of small open economies and in a deterministic setting, that gains were second order. All that international financial integration does in that context is to speed up transition toward the steady state of the economy. Coeurdacier, Rey, and Winant (2013) allow for uncertainty and estimate welfare gains from allocative efficiency and risk sharing together, within the context of a general equilibrium neoclassical growth model. They find that even in such a world, where the interaction between the precautionary savings motives and allocative efficiency effects is modeled explicitly, welfare gains are small. Such a model can, in particular, generate the realistic outcome that a volatile emerging market ends up exporting capital when it opens up its financial account (unless it is an extremely capital-scarce country, far away from its steady state at the outset). So both on the empirical side and on the theoretical side it is hard to find support, at this juncture, for large, quantifiable benefits of international financial integration.

I am not necessarily claiming that benefits to international financial integration do not exist, only that they have been elusive so far. In that light, it would be useful to identify more precisely the channels through which capital flows may be beneficial. We should look at more specific types of flows, and more closely at potential effects on total factor productivity.

Costs of Financial Flows

On the cost side, having gone through a number of crises in emerging markets and in advanced economies, we have some ideas about costs to international financial integration and capital flows. Reinhart and Reinhart (2008) wrote about capital flow bonanzas, that is, periods in which international liquidity is abundant and there are large capital flows into emerging markets, which may be subject to sharp reversal.

These large capital flows tend to be correlated with inflation in asset prices. There is a surprisingly large common component in risky asset prices (Miranda-Agrippino and Rey 2012). In other words, although we might think that risky asset prices around the world are largely determined by specific country macroeconomic conditions, local conditions, that would be wrong. There is an important global factor.

Associated with these capital flow bonanzas has been excessive appreciation of currencies, which strained the competitiveness of the tradables sector. Within the euro area the loss of competitiveness of the periphery has been to some extent caused by massive inflows of capital, which have bid up the price of real estate. The banking system has channeled massive capital flows into a number of countries, such as Spain and Ireland, fueling real estate investment booms that have increased nontradables' prices and unit labor costs.

Changes in the International Financial Landscape

The main change in the international financial landscape in the past 20 years has been the tremendous increase in cross-border *gross* asset flows and positions (see Lane and Milesi-Ferretti 2007; Gourinchas and Rey 2013). We need new frameworks, new ways of thinking through the benefits and costs of integration that take into account the importance of gross flows (in addition to net flows). That is to say, thinking about current account sustainability is not enough—we need to worry also about gross flows.

For financial stability purposes, gross flows matter, and they matter more as the external balance sheets of countries expand. In terms of the transmission of the 2008 financial crisis to Europe, for example, the position of the euro area vis-à-vis the United States was roughly balanced; there was no current account issue. But there were massive exposures through the gross positions of European countries. Their financial systems were exposed to US toxic assets, exchange rate movements, and funding risk. This illustrates that there are potentially massive valuation effects (capital gains and losses) when external balance sheets are large. This is really what has changed in the past two decades and what we need to take into account. It is no longer only about current account and net flows; it is also about gross flows and large gross positions at the financial sector and country level. Risk transmission can be heightened through various channels, including a currency mismatch between assets and liabilities or a maturity mismatch.

Procyclicality of Credit Flows

Credit flows are procyclical (Committee on International Economic Policy and Reform 2012; Bruno and Shin 2013). They grew at a fast rate in the 2003–2007 precrisis period. There is a positive feedback loop between greater credit supply, asset price inflation, and a compression of spreads. Smaller risk premiums amplify the credit boom; as measured, the risk is low and balance sheets look healthier as asset prices go up. By relaxing constraints, this creates additional space for lending and for credit, and so on.

This mechanism occurs when value-at-risk constraints operate in the banking sectors (Adrian and Shin 2012). This is a major positive feedback loop between credit supply and risk spreads, one that contributes to the procyclicality of credit flows and their importance in the run-up to the crisis.

Managing Balance Sheets

In the presence of positive feedback loops, we need circuit breakers. The traditional feedback loop that has confronted policymakers is the following. Large capital inflows into a growing economy tend to create inflation, exchange rate appreciation, and expectation of inflation. In such a situation, the central bank response is often to increase the interest rate to keep inflation under control, but because yields are now higher, capital keeps flowing in and the exchange rate keeps appreciating. This positive feedback loop justified the use of capital controls or, more broadly, capital flow management. Beside this traditional feedback loop is this new feedback loop described above, which has to do with credit flows and the procyclicality of leverage. High credit flows bid up asset prices, improve balance sheets, and lead to more flows and credit creation. The large balance sheets being built up have to be monitored carefully. This is all the more important because valuation effects can be of the same order of magnitude as current account movements (Gourinchas, Rey, and Truempler 2012).

When should one intervene? When should one activate circuit breakers to cut those positive feedback loops?

It is important, in my view, not to wait too long; not to wait, for example, for the quasi-certainty that there is a bubble in asset prices or real estate to intervene. Rather, one should continuously stress-test the balance sheet of the financial sector and of the country and judge whether large but realistic changes in asset prices could jeopardize financial stability. If so, macroprudential intervention or some type of capital flow management intervention should take place. I understand the difficulty of doing stress tests in general and estimating second-round effects in particular, but doing stress tests on a continuous basis, even if it is an imperfect process, is a necessary monitoring tool.

What are the tools available for intervention? The choice between macroprudential tools and capital management tools has to be somewhat pragmatic, depending on where the problems are and on the different institutional settings. Macroprudential tools tend to be more targeted. But capital controls may be appropriate if there is a lot of direct cross-border lending and the banking system is circumvented.

Conclusions

We should not forget in this whole discussion of circuit breakers that there are usually important domestic distortions that interact with capital flows. In practice, for political reasons, we see many subsidies to investment in real estate. These subsidies are instrumental in creating the initial bubble in real estate prices and investment. By all means, the first thing to do is to remove these distortions. It is also important to remember that excessive borrowing by a country means that someone else is lending excessively: Macroprudential policies apply to lenders just as well as they apply to borrowers.

I have discussed the use of capital flow management and macroprudential tools from an ex ante point of view (to prevent crises), but there may be also, in some cases, an important role for capital account management ex post (after a crisis). For example, capital controls can be used to avoid major capital losses for households and companies that borrowed in foreign currency and are heavily exposed to further exchange rate depreciation. This type of ex post policy intervention may have been useful in a country such as Iceland where there are large amounts of krona-denominated assets in portfolios of foreign investors and where massive capital flight and large, ensuing depreciation would have been likely in the absence of controls (see Baldursson and Portes 2013).

But we have to keep in mind that in this crisis, we have to deal with clearly subpar preventive policies, which have left us with a very difficult situation. Meanwhile, we must really think hard about better governance looking forward.

References

Adrian, T., and H. S. Shin. 2012. "Procyclical Leverage and Value at Risk." Federal Reserve Bank of New York Staff Report 338, Federal Reserve Bank of New York, New York. http://app.ny.frb.org/research/staff_reports/sr338.pdf.

Baldursson, F., and R. Portes. 2013. "Gambling for resurrection in Iceland: the rise and fall of the banks." CEPR DP 9664.

Bruno, V., and H. S. Shin. 2013. "Capital Flows, Cross-Border Banking and Global Liquidity." NBER Working Paper 19038, National Bureau of Economic Research, Cambridge, MA, May. http://www.nber.org/papers/w19038.

Cetorelli, N., and L. Goldberg. 2012. "Liquidity Management of US Global Banks: Internal Capital Markets in the Great Recession." *Journal of International Economics* 88 (2): 299–311.

Coeurdacier, N., H. Rey, and P. Winant. 2013. "Financial Integration and Growth in a Risky World." Manuscript, London Business School, London; NBER, Cambridge, MA; and Department of Economics, Sciences Po, Paris. http://www.helenerey.eu.

Committee on International Economic Policy and Reform. 2012. "Banks and Cross-Border Capital Flows: Policy Challenges and Regulatory Responses." Brookings Institution, Washington, DC. http://www.brookings.edu/research/reports/2012/09/ciepr-banks-capital-flows.

Eichengreen, B. 2002. "Capital Account Liberalization: What Do the Cross-Country Studies Tell Us?" *World Bank Economic Review* 15:341–366.

Gourinchas, P.-O., and O. Jeanne. 2006. "The Elusive Gains from International Financial Integration." *Review of Economic Studies* 73:715–741.

Gourinchas, P.-O., and H. Rey. 2013. "External Adjustment, Global Imbalances, and Valuation Effects." In *Handbook of International Economics,* ed. Gita Gopinath, Elhanan Helpman, and Ken Rogoff. Elsevier: North Holland.

Gourinchas, P.-O., H. Rey, and K. Truempler. 2012. "The Financial Crisis and the Geography of Wealth Transfers." *Journal of International Economics* 88 (2):266–283.

Jeanne, O., A. Subramanian, and J. Williamson. 2012. *Who Needs to Open the Capital Account?* Washington, DC: Peterson Institute.

Kose, M. A., E. Prasad, K. Rogoff, and S. J. Wei. 2009. "Financial Globalization: A Reappraisal." *IMF Staff Papers* 56:8–62.

Lane, P., and G. M. Milesi-Ferretti. 2007. "The External Wealth of Nations Mark II: Revised and Extended Estimates of Foreign Assets and Liabilities, 1970–2004." *Journal of International Economics* 73 (2): 223–250.

Miranda-Agrippino, S., and H. Rey. 2012. "World Asset Markets and Global Liquidity." Manuscript, London Business School, London. http://www.helenerey.eu.

Obstfeld, M. 2009. "International Finance and Growth in Developing Countries: What Have We Learned?" *IMF Staff Papers* 56 (1).

Reinhart, C., and V. Reinhart. 2008. "Capital Flow Bonanzas: An Encompassing View of the Past and Present." In *NBER International Seminar in Macroeconomics,* ed. Jeffrey Frankel and Francesco Giavazzi. Chicago: University of Chicago Press.

VII
Conclusions

26

The Cat in the Tree and Further Observations: Rethinking Macroeconomic Policy II

George A. Akerlof

I learned a lot from the conference, and I'm very thankful to all the speakers. I have been asked to give my overall view of the conference. Do I have an image of the whole thing? I don't know whether my image will help anybody at all, but my view is that it's as if a cat has climbed a huge tree. It's up there and, oh, my God, we have this cat up there. The cat, of course, is this huge economic crisis that has been upon us since 2008.

Everyone at the conference had some ideas about what we should do to get the poor cat out of the tree. What I found so wonderful about the conference was that the speakers all had their own respective images of the cat, with no two discussants of the same opinion. But occasionally those opinions meshed, in unexpected and productive ways. That's my view of what was accomplished. I will provide my own thoughts on the crisis and how well we've been doing relative to the cat. My thoughts are a slightly different angle from what everybody else has been saying, from their pervasively different vantage points. I will concentrate on the postcrisis United States, but the analysis also pertains internationally.

There is an excellent paper, by Oscar Jorda, Morris Schularick, and Alan Taylor (2011), which divided up downturns from 1870 to 2008 for 14 advanced countries into financial recessions and normal recessions. They looked at how GDP recovery varied in severity according to credit outstanding relative to GDP in the preceding boom. And their conjecture was strongly confirmed: not only are financial recessions deeper and slower in recovery than normal recessions, they also have slower recovery the greater the credit-to-GDP ratio is.

That is the history.

How do their findings reflect on the current crisis? Curiously, it depends on the measurement of credit outstanding. With bank loans to the private sector as the measure of credit, the United States' recovery is about 1 percent of GDP better than the mean recovery for financial recessions. When in addition the measure of credit also includes credit granted by the shadow banking system, the United States' recovery is about 4 percent better than the median recovery for financial recessions. The graphs in the paper by Jorda and others illustrate this point.

But with the onset of financial derivatives, we have no way of knowing how to measure "credit." If derivatives are used to hedge risk, then we would expect derivatives to soften the crash.

For example, if the buyer—rather than the seller—of a credit default swap goes bankrupt in the event of a default we would expect the credit default swap to soften the crash. On the other hand, if we think that derivatives escalate gambling, then we would expect them to exacerbate the crash. The conventional interpretation of the 2007–2008 crash in the United States holds that derivatives enhanced gambling in a different way. In parable, derivatives allowed a daisy chain of escalating valuation of mortgages—they were made, for example, in the Central Valley on the shadiest of bases, then passed through into derivative packages, which were rated A and higher. This was an environment in which junk did not affect ratings. So mortgage originators had no incentive to require down payments or borrower credibility. To a great extent, they didn't. In their creation and ratings of derivatives, the investment houses and the ratings agencies were mining their reputations as fiduciaries. This additional role of the derivatives suggests that a measure of credit based on loans out-standing, even taking into account the role of the shadow banks, yields a conservative measure of the benchmark for where the United States should now be.

That view also conforms with the common perceptions from the fall of 2008. At that time, the Great Depression was the benchmark for what would happen without government intervention. From that vantage point, macro policy has been not just good, but truly excellent. Alan Blinder's fantastic book, *After the Music Stopped* (2013), says the exact same thing.

Almost every program has been close to what the doctor called for. Those measures include the following:

Economic Stimulus Act of 2008

Bailout of AIG

Rescue of Washington Mutual, Wachovia, and CountryWide by adoption

Troubled Asset Relief Program (TARP)

Stress tests run by the US Treasury and the Fed

Declines in interest rates to close to zero

American Recovery and Reinvestment Act of 2009

Bailout of the auto industry

International cooperation in the spirit of the G20 meeting in Pittsburgh, at which the IMF played a leading role

There is only one major criticism of the policies put in place. We should have led the public to understand that we should measure success not by the level of the current unemployment rate but by a benchmark that takes into account the financial vulnerability that had been set in the previous boom. We economists have not done a good job of explaining that our macrostability policies have been effective. There is, of course, a good reason why the public has a hard time listening. They have other things to do besides becoming macroeconomists and macroeconomic historians.

But just a bit of common sense indicates why the policies have been so successful. If Lehman Brothers had been $1 in the red and it needed to be only $1 in the black to stay out of bankruptcy court, the expenditure of only $2 at just the right crisis moment could have saved us from a Great Depression. That $2 finger in the dike would have been all that was needed.

The expenditures for the bailout were, of course, more than $2; they will probably be positive and run to a few billion dollars. But they did literally stop the financial meltdown that was in progress. Relative to the tens of trillions of GDP that would have been lost with a repeat of the Great Depression, the savings from TARP are of the order of magnitude of 1,000 to 1. Figuratively, it is fair to call this a finger in the dike.

The expenditures by both the Bush and the Obama administrations on fiscal stimulus have achieved less bang for the buck, but almost surely they have been effective. Current estimates of government expenditure multipliers are something like 2. That number also makes intuitive sense. Liquidity-trap estimates of a balanced budget multiplier are approximately 1, both in theory and in estimation, and the tax multiplier is robustly measured as approximately 1. The government expenditure multipliers will be the sum of the two, so the stimulus bills have almost surely also had significant payoff.

In sum, we economists did a bad job of predicting the crisis, but the postcrisis economic policies have been close to what a sensible economist-doctor would have ordered. Those policies have come directly from the Bush and Obama administrations, and from their appointees. They have also been supported by Congress.

The lesson for the future is that good economics and common sense have worked well—we have had trial and success. We must keep this in mind with policy going forward.

References

Blinder, Alan S. 2013. *After the Music Stopped*. New York: Penguin Press.

Jorda, Oscar, Moritz H. P. Schularick, and Alan Taylor. 2011. "When Credit Bites Back: Leverage, Business Cycles and Crises." NBER Working Paper 17621, National Bureau of Economic Research, Cambridge, MA, November.

27

Rethinking Macroeconomic Policy

Olivier Blanchard

The IMF's second conference on rethinking macroeconomic policy in the wake of the 2008–2009 economic crisis has underscored the many challenges that lie ahead for policymakers. Rethinking and reforms are both taking place. But we still do not know the final destination, be it for the redefinition of monetary policy, or the contours of financial regulation, or the role of macroprudential tools. We have a general sense of direction, but we are largely navigating by sight.

In this chapter I review six examples raised at the conference to underscore our lack of knowledge concerning the "correct" trajectory to take in the coming years, and the possible outcomes of various regulatory moves. (More developed, though preconference, thoughts are given in the introductory chapter, written with Giovanni Dell'Ariccia and Paolo Mauro.)

Financial Regulation

There is no agreed-upon vision of what the future financial architecture should look like and, by implication, no agreed-upon vision of what the appropriate financial regulation should be. Here I am reminded of Paul Volcker's famous observation that the only useful financial innovation of the last 40 years has been the ATM. This is surely an exaggeration. But we are still unsure about the right role of securitization, the right scope for derivatives, the role of markets versus banks, and the role of shadow banking versus banking.

Still, it seems clear that some things should change, and indeed, policymakers are putting in place measures in the context of international or national initiatives. One example is the increase in required capital ratios.

It may not be a panacea, but it surely can make the financial system more robust. Even so, however, I am struck by the level of uncertainty and disagreement about the effects of capital ratios on funding costs and thus on lending. Reasonable people, as among them Martin Hellwig and Anat Admati, argue that we are not so far from the Modigliani-Miller world, and banks can afford substantially higher capital ratios. Others (and not only bankers) argue that such ratios would instead destroy the banking industry.

Another example is capital flows and, by implication, the role of capital controls. I was struck by Hélène Rey's discussion in chapter 25, in which she shows how surprisingly meager the hard econometric evidence is for the benefits of portfolio flows. I was also struck by Stanley Fischer's rhetorical question, what is the usefulness of short-term capital inflows? Clearly, how we think about the scope of capital controls depends very much on the answer to these basic questions.

The Role of the Financial Sector

It has become a cliché to say that macroeconomic thinking understated the role of financial factors in economic fluctuations. Much analytical work has taken place over the past five years to reintroduce the financial system into our models. But we are not there yet. For example, is there a credit and financial cycle separate from the business cycle, as Claudio Borio suggests? Or should we think of financial shocks as another source of disturbance and the financial system as just another source of amplification?

Was Stephan Gerlach right when he asked whether we should really reconsider all of macroeconomics for an event that may happen once every hundred years? Or, instead, are financial shocks and the financial system so central to macroeconomic fluctuations that the IS-LM model—which does not include an explicit financial system—is not an acceptable port of entry into macroeconomics?

By implication, there is no agreement on how or even whether to integrate financial stability and macrostability into the mandate of central banks. Does it require a tweak to inflation targeting or much more radical rethinking? The intellectually pleasant position is to argue that macroprudential tools will take care of financial stability, so monetary policy can still focus on its usual business: inflation targeting. I read, perhaps unfairly, Michael Woodford's discussion in chapter 4 as suggesting that the crisis should lead us to shift from inflation targeting to nominal income targeting, without a major emphasis on financial stability. I am skeptical that this is the right answer. I think we have to be realistic about the role that macroprudential tools can play and about the fact that monetary policy cannot ignore financial stability. This brings me to my third point.

Macroprudential Tools

At our first conference on rethinking macroeconomic policy, in 2011, macroprudential tools were, to use Andrew Haldane's phrase, very much the new kid on the block. It was clear that the two standard tools, fiscal policy and monetary policy, were not the right ones to deal with financial imbalances and risks. The question then was whether macroprudential policy was going to be the third leg of macroeconomic policy or just a crutch to help the first two.

We do not have the answer yet. But as more and more countries are using those tools, we are learning. I draw two lessons from the evidence and from the work presented in this volume.

First, these tools work, but their effects are still hard to calibrate, and when used, they seem to have moderated rather than stopped unhealthy booms. This is also my reading of Bank of Korea's Governor Kim's presentation in chapter 8.

Second, by their nature, they affect specific sectors and specific groups, and this raises political economy issues. This is clear from Stanley Fischer's discussion in chapter 7 of the use of loan-to-value (LTV) ratios in Israel.

Governance and Allocation of Tasks among Microprudential, Macroprudential, and Monetary Policy (or, as Avinash Dixit called them, MIP, MAP, and MOP)

How should microprudential and macroprudential regulation be coordinated? It is sometimes said that they are likely to conflict. Conceptually, I do not see why they should: I see macroprudential regulation as simply taking into account systemic effects and the state of the economy in thinking about bank regulation and the situation of each financial institution.

For example, I see macroprudential regulation requiring higher capital ratios from more systemically important banks or when aggregate credit growth appears too high. The question is how to work out the division of labor and the interactions between the two so that this is indeed what happens.

If not done right, it might mean that as a bust starts, the microprudential supervisor ignores systemic aspects and other events and asks for higher capital ratios, while the macroprudential supervisor rightly believes the opposite is needed. The United Kingdom's approach—the creation of a Financial Policy Committee that can impose capital ratios that vary over time and across sectors to maintain financial stability—seems like a good way to proceed. Andrew Haldane discusses the issues in chapter 5.

How macroprudential regulation and monetary policy should be combined raises more complex issues. There is little question that each affects the other: monetary policy affects risk taking, and macroprudential tools affect aggregate demand. So policymakers need to coordinate.

Given that monetary policy surely must stay with the central bank, this suggests putting both of them under one roof at the central bank. But this in turn raises the issue of central bank independence. It is one thing to give the bank independence with respect to the policy rate; it is another to let it set maximum LTV ratios and debt-to-income ratios. At some point, the issue of democratic deficit arises.

Maybe the solution is not so hard, namely, to give various degrees of independence to the central bank. Stanley Fischer gave us a marvelous analogy and pointed us toward the solution when he said that anybody who is married easily understands the notion of various degrees of independence. Again, the UK's approach, with its two parallel committees within the central bank, one focusing on monetary policy, the other on financial policy with a limited set of macroprudential tools (not including, for example, LTV ratios), seems like a reasonable approach.

The Sustainable Level of Debt

The rate of fiscal consolidation depends on, among other things, what we think a sustainable level of debt is. Many countries will be managing levels of debt close to 100 percent of GDP for many years to come. There is a standard list of textbook answers as to why high debt is costly, from lower capital accumulation to the need for higher and distortionary taxes. I suspect the costs are elsewhere. I see two main costs.

The first is debt overhang. The higher the debt, the higher the probability of default, the higher the spread on government bonds, and the harder it is for the government to achieve debt sustainability. But the adverse effects do not stop there. Higher sovereign spreads affect private lending spreads, which in turn affect investment and consumption. Higher uncertainty about debt sustainability—and thus about future inflation and future taxation—affects all decisions. I am struck by how limited our understanding is of these channels. Reduced form regressions of growth on debt can take us only so far.

The second related cost is the risk of multiple equilibria. At high levels of debt there may well be two equilibria: a "good equilibrium," at which rates are low and debt is sustainable, and a "bad equilibrium," at which rates are high and, as a result, the interest burden and the probability of default are higher. When debt is very high, it may not take much of a change of heart by investors to move from a good to a bad equilibrium.

I suspect that this phenomenon is partly behind the Italian and Spanish bond spreads. In this context, Martin Wolf in chapter 20 asks a provocative question: why are the spreads so much higher for Spain than for the UK? Debt and deficits are actually slightly lower in Spain than in the UK. No doubt, the overall economic situation of Spain is worse than that of the UK, but does this explain fully the difference in spreads? Could the answer lie in the difference in monetary policy? In the UK, investors expect the Bank of England to intervene if needed to maintain the good equilibrium, whereas they believe the European Central Bank (ECB) does not have the mandate to do so. These are central questions that we need to study more.

Multiple Equilibria and Communication

In a world of multiple equilibria, announcements can matter a lot. Take, for example, the case of the Outright Monetary Transactions program announced by the ECB. The announcement of the program can be interpreted as having removed one of the sources of multiple equilibria in the sovereign bond markets, namely, redenomination risk, or the danger that investors, assuming that a country on the periphery would leave the euro, ask for a large premium, thereby forcing exit from the euro in the process. The announcement has succeeded without the program actually having to be used.

From this viewpoint, the recent announcement by the Bank of Japan that it intends to double the monetary base is even more interesting. What effect it will have on inflation depends very much on how Japanese households and firms change their inflation expectations. If they revise them up, this will affect their wage and price decisions, and lead to higher inflation—which is the desired outcome in the Japanese deflation context. But if they do not revise them, there is no reason to think that inflation will increase much.

The motivation for this dramatic monetary expansion is primarily to give a psychological shock and to shift perceptions and price dynamics. Will it work, together with the other measures taken by the Japanese authorities? Let's hope so. But we are very far from the mechanical effects of monetary policy described in the textbooks.

Although I have had to spare mention of many contributions and insights from the conference captured elsewhere in this volume, the conference has left us with a clear research agenda. We at the IMF fully intend to take up the challenge.

28

Preventing the Next Catastrophe: Where Do We Stand?

David Romer

As I listened to the presentations and discussions, I found myself thinking about the conference from two perspectives. One is intellectual: Did we ask provocative questions? Were interesting ideas proposed? Were we talking about important issues? By that standard, the conference was very successful: the contributions and discussions were extremely stimulating, and I learned a great deal.

The second perspective is practical: Where do we stand in terms of averting another financial and macroeconomic disaster? By that standard, I fear we are not doing nearly as well. As I will describe, my reading of the evidence is that the events of the past few years are not an aberration, but just an extreme manifestation of a broader pattern. And the relatively modest changes of the type discussed at the conference—and that policymakers are putting into place in some cases—are helpful but unlikely to be enough to prevent future financial shocks from inflicting large economic harms.

Thus, I believe we should be asking whether there are deeper reforms that might have a large effect on the size of the shocks emanating from the financial sector or on the ability of the economy to withstand those shocks. But there has been relatively little serious consideration of ideas for such reforms, not just at the conference but in the broader academic and policy communities.

The Financial Sector as a Continued Source of Shocks

My view that we should think of financial shocks as closer to commonplace than to exceptional is based on history. Consider the United States over the past 30 or so years. By my count, there have been six separate times over that period when financial developments posed important macroeconomic risks. In three of them, the risks were largely averted and the costs ended up being minor. In two, the costs were modest to moderate. And in one, the damage was enormous.

Concretely:

• In the throes of the Volcker disinflation in the early 1980s, the combination of the severe recession and banks' exposure to Latin American debt caused many major banks to be in serious trouble. It was only a last-minute turn in policy and the willingness of regulators to ignore the banks' extremely shaky financial condition for a few years that kept the financial system from falling apart. So that was a danger averted.

• The 1987 stock market crash was a significant financial shock, but rapid and highly visible responses by the Federal Reserve to keep markets functioning and reduce interest rates again prevented large damage to the economy.

• The savings and loan crisis of the late 1980s and early 1990s did some damage to the economy through misallocation of investment and impaired lending, and somewhat more damage to the government budget through direct bailout costs.

• The Russian debt crisis and the collapse of Long-Term Capital Management (LTCM) in 1998 caused central bankers some sleepless nights as they worried about the stability of the world financial system. Stability was preserved through the arranged rescue of LTCM, lower interest rates, and other actions. That is the third case in which the danger was averted.

• The dot-com bubble and bust of the late 1990s and early 2000s caused a considerable misallocation of investment and, more important, a recession.

• And, obviously, we had the housing-price collapse and financial meltdown of the past few years, which have had catastrophic effects.

In light of that record for just one country over a third of a century, the idea that large financial shocks are rare, and that we therefore should not worry greatly about them, seems fundamentally wrong.

What I find striking about this list is not just its length but its variety. And if you look outside the United States, it is easy to find examples of other kinds of financial shocks. You see Iceland and Cyprus, where the financial shock came from a vastly expanded banking sector with huge foreign deposits. You see Greece, where the problem was disguised fiscal profligacy. You see the classic sudden stops. And I am sure that with a little more work, you could add even more types of financial shocks to the list.

In short, the range of potential financial shocks is long and varied. There are only a few on my illustrative list of domestic and foreign financial shocks that took the form of big run-ups in asset prices followed by some kind of crash. Indeed, there are only two, the dot-com episode and the recent crisis, that one could reasonably call "bubbles." So I think the right conclusion to draw is that financial shocks are likely to be both frequent and hard to predict, not just in their timing but also in their form.

Small-Scale Solutions

The question, then, is what to do. Let me start with two small-scale policies, one of which I think is largely a nonstarter and one of which I think will be helpful but very far from a complete solution to the risks of future crises.

The nonstarter is using the short-term policy rate as a tool for dealing with financial imbalances and risks. Even if that were the only objective we were using the policy rate for, it is much too crude. Often the concern with the financial system involves a potential problem in one part of financial markets, or different types of problems in different markets. In such situations, a single tool that affects all markets is of limited value. Indeed, as Janet Yellen pointed out at the conference, often it is not even clear which direction you would want to move the policy rate to address a potential financial risk to the economy. And, of course, we want to use it for other very important purposes as well. So we can debate whether there is a little bit of benefit to taking financial developments more into account in the setting of interest rates, but at best it can improve outcomes only marginally.

The type of small-scale policy that I think is more promising is the one advanced in the discussions of macroprudential policies and capital account management. The positive way to put it is that it is the wise central banker model; the negative way to describe it is that it is the Whac-A-Mole strategy. Regardless of how one labels it, the idea is to use regulations and interventions creatively to address potential problems as they develop. For example, if you think a bubble is developing in the real estate market in Seoul, you adopt regulations directed specifically at mortgages in Seoul.

I was very impressed with the descriptions of policymakers' actions in such countries as Israel, Korea, and Brazil in dealing with a wide range of financial developments, and something I learned from the conference is that such targeted actions are a useful addition to the policy toolkit. But in light of the enormous range of potential financial shocks, the idea that we can stabilize the financial system by counting on very smart policy-makers to perceive each problem as it is developing and design a specific intervention to target it quickly is surely wishful thinking.

What I take from this is that we need to be thinking more broadly and creatively, looking for more fundamental solutions rather than particular interventions. At a general level, these can take two forms.

Deeper Solutions on the Financial Side

The first approach is to reform the financial system so that the shocks it sends to the real economy are much smaller. The discussion of micro-regulation showed that there are promising ideas in that area. Here I am thinking of stronger capital and liquidity requirements, special rules for institutions that create more systemic risk, and restrictions on the form or capabilities of what financial institutions can do, such as ring-fencing in the United Kingdom and the Volcker rule in the United States. Those approaches are broader than responding to individual problems as they arise, and they appear promising.

But at the end of the day, it is hard to believe that the relatively modest changes along these dimensions that were discussed at the conference are really big enough to give us a financial system that is so robust that it is not going to periodically cause severe problems. Shadow financial insti-tutions may escape the rules altogether; rules can be gamed; and shocks can be so large that they overwhelm the moderate changes that were considered.

Thus, I was disappointed to see little consideration of much larger financial reforms. Let me give four examples of possible types of larger reforms:

• There were occasional mentions of very large capital requirements. For example, Allan Meltzer noted that at one time 25 percent capital was common for banks. Should we be moving to such a system?

• Amir Sufi and Adair Turner discussed the features of debt contracts that make them inherently prone to instability. Should we be working aggressively to promote more indexation of debt contracts, more equity-like contracts, and so on?

• We can see the costs that the modern financial system has imposed on the real economy. It is not immediately clear that the benefits of the financial innovations of recent decades have been on a scale that warrants those costs. Might a much simpler, 1960s- or 1970s-style financial system be better than what we have now?

• The fact that shocks emanating from the financial system sometimes impose large costs on the rest of the economy implies that there are negative externalities to some types of financial activities or financial structures. This suggests the possibility of Pigovian taxes. So, should there be substantial taxes on certain aspects of the financial system? If so, what should be taxed—debt, leverage, size, other indicators of systemic risk, a combination, or something else altogether?

I do not know the answers to these questions, but it seems to me that they deserve serious analysis. Yet radical redesign of the financial system was largely missing from the conference.

Larger-Scale Solutions on the Macroeconomic Side

The other way to make large changes is to try to make the macroeconomy more resilient to financial shocks. I thought the lack of discussion of possible changes in this dimension was the largest gap in the conference. Let me discuss this issue in three areas of macroeconomic policy: measures to deal with shocks to a common currency area, monetary policy, and fiscal policy.

With regard to a common currency area, imagine that at some point in the not too distant future, the euro area is hit with another large financial shock that has asymmetric effects across different countries. Are things going to play out very differently than they have over the past few years?

There would surely be fewer late-night meetings, because policymakers have learned more about how to do short-term crisis management. But I see little progress toward measures that would cause fundamental changes in the effects the shock would have. Policymakers have taken, at most, baby steps toward addressing the instabilities created by the fact that the responsibility for cleaning up insolvent banks is at the level of individual countries rather than of the euro area as a whole. And even less has been done in terms of a fiscal union and mechanisms to deal with large differences in competitiveness.

Concerning monetary policy, inflation targeting appeared to be an almost ideal framework for its first 15 or 20 years. But we have now had an extended period during which it has shown itself incapable of providing aggregate demand at the level that is widely recognized to have been needed. So it seems important to think about whether we should have a different approach to monetary policy. But again, we have not gotten very far. The idea of targeting a nominal GDP path has been mentioned on and off for a few years, but the debate has not proceeded to serious quantitative analysis of its costs and benefits and of whether it could make the economy substantially more resilient. Other ideas for significant changes in the monetary policy framework have been discussed even less.

With regard to fiscal policy, the biggest idea that has achieved substantial support is that it would be desirable to have more fiscal space. But how to get from here to there, given the challenges of just getting back to the amount of fiscal space we had before the crisis, is a hard issue, and one on which progress has been minimal. And in light of the terrible problems that have afflicted some countries that entered the crisis with very responsible fiscal policies, fiscal space is clearly not a magic bullet.

I heard virtually no discussion of larger changes to the fiscal framework. The possibility of measures to make automatic stabilizers stronger (for example, through macroeconomic triggers for changes in fiscal policy) was not mentioned. And the status of this idea in the broader policy community resembles the status of targeting a nominal GDP path: the idea is mentioned from time to time, but the discussion has not proceeded to the point of concrete proposals and quantitative evaluation.

Another fiscal idea that has received little attention, either at the conference or in the broader policy debate, is the idea of fiscal rules or constraints. For example, one can imagine some type of constitutional rule or independent agency (or a combination, with a constitutional rule enforced by an independent agency) that requires highly responsible fiscal policy in good times and provides a mechanism for fiscal stimulus in a downturn that is credibly temporary. Roberto Perotti and Avinash Dixit raised the idea of fiscal rules or councils very briefly, but it got no further than that.

The fact that we are making so little progress in terms of larger changes to our approaches to macroeconomic policy appears to further strengthen the case for thinking about deeper financial reforms. But I also think we need broader thinking about the macroeconomic side.

Conclusion

After five years of catastrophic macroeconomic performance, "first steps and early lessons" (to quote the conference's subtitle) is not what we should be aiming for. Rather, we should be looking for solutions to the ongoing current crisis and strong measures to minimize the chances of anything similar happening again. I worry that the reforms we are focusing on are too small to do that, and that what is needed is a more fundamental rethinking of the design of our financial system and of our frameworks for macroeconomic policy.

29

The Lessons of the North Atlantic Crisis for Economic Theory and Policy

Joseph E. Stiglitz

In analyzing the financial crisis that began in 2007 and led to the Great Recession, we should try to benefit from the misfortune of recent decades: The approximately 100 crises that have occurred during the last 30 years—as liberalization policies became dominant—have given us a wealth of experience and mountains of data. If we look over a 150-year period, we have an even richer data set.

With a century and a half of clear, detailed information on crisis after crisis, the burning question is not *How did this happen?* but *How did we ignore that long history, and think that we had solved the problems with the business cycle?* Believing that we had made big economic fluctuations a thing of the past took remarkable hubris.

Markets Are Not Stable, Efficient, or Self-Correcting

The big lesson that this crisis forcibly brought home—one we should have long known—is that market economies, on their own, are not necessarily efficient, stable, or self-correcting. One of the reasons there were not only failures in preventing and forecasting the downturn but also in responding to it, was that many of the predominant models employed special assumptions, leading to views that markets were efficient, stable, and self-correcting. Because our models didn't adequately analyze the causes of the crisis, we could neither respond to the crisis in ways that would ensure a quick and strong recovery nor take appropriate actions to significantly reduce the likelihood of a recurrence. The result is that we continue to face a significant risk of another crisis in the future.[1]

That unfettered markets are not, in general, efficient whenever there are information imperfections and asymmetries, and/or when there is an incomplete set of risk markets, and/or when capital markets are imperfect or incomplete has been well established for more than three decades. These "market imperfections" are important in *every* economy, even the most advanced; and yet many of our regulators and the advocates of deregulation ignored not only the lessons of history but also these advances in our understandings of the limitations of markets.

Moreover, predominant macroeconomic models *before the crisis* underestimated market instability. They had focused on *exogenous* shocks as the source of the perturbations giving rise to fluctuations, and yet it's very clear that a very large fraction of the perturbations to our economy—including those giving rise to the worse downturns—are *endogenous*. The housing bubble and its bursting, like so many bubbles that preceded it, was a creation of the market itself. The models that focused on exogenous shocks simply misled us—the majority of the really big shocks come from within the economy. Moreover, some of the most important shocks are persistent and associated with long-run structural transformations—closely linked with the economy's (endogenous) innovative activities.

Finally, economies are not self-correcting. Whether or not they are could not, of course, be addressed within models that assumed that the economy was in equilibrium. It is not just that the economy does not return to full employment quickly after a strong, adverse shock. There are economic forces that may, on their own, exacerbate the downturn. Unemployment leads to lower real wages; lower real wages lead to lower aggregate demand; and lower aggregate demand can lead to still more unemployment. The implication of this is that a quick recovery may require *strong* government intervention. It's clear that we have yet to fully take on board this crucial lesson: it is obvious that the attempts to "fix" the economies of the United States and Europe in the aftermath of the crisis have failed to restore the economy to full employment. The loss in GDP between our potential and our actual output is in the trillions of dollars. Of course, some will say that it could have been done worse, and that's true, even if it's cold comfort.

The reason for this failure—in spite of the unprecedented loose monetary policy—is that fiscal policy was too tepid; the Keynesian policies were too small and not of long enough duration; and they were followed by contractionary policies, with far more austere policies in Europe than in the United States, and far worse economic performance in Europe than in the United States. Of course, the fiscal policies could have been better designed. But poor design was not the main source of failure. Even with the imperfect design, the stimulative effects (the multipliers) were strong.

More Than Deleveraging, More Than a Balance Sheet Crisis: The Need for Structural Transformation

We have roughly the same levels today of human resources, capital stock, and natural resources as we did before the crisis. But many countries have not regained their pre-crisis GDP levels, to say nothing of returning to the precrisis growth paths. It is clear that we are not using our resources well. In a very fundamental sense, the crisis is still not fully resolved—and there's no good economic theory that explains why that should be the case.

Real business cycle theory and modern-day descendants of those models suggest there was a negative productivity shock, a collective bout of amnesia that resulted in a reduced capacity to produce outputs from inputs. Putting aside the absurdity of such a position, the irony is that in this downturn, individual firms continued to increase productivity at a rapid rate. At the microeconomic level, there is no evidence of such amnesia.[2]

Some focus on the high level of debt (especially at the household level) as an impediment to recovery. But it is worth noting that in the standard models (on which policymakers relied so heavily in the years before the crisis, and which continue to be relied on in some circles) debt plays little role: it just changes claims on resources, transferring income from one individual to another. And in those models, such redistributions have no consequences. But even if such transfers lead to a lower level of aggregate demand (because creditors have a lower marginal propensity to consume than debtors), standard theory suggests that there is a change in prices that would restore the economy back to full employment. (Standard theory doesn't have much to say about the dynamics of these price adjustments. Indeed, one strand simply assumes that wages and prices are rigid, when of course in the Great Depression they were changing at a very rapid rate. The problem, as I hinted above, is that the adjustments may themselves have been counterproductive.)

Much of the popular discussion sees no prospects of wage and price adjustments restoring the economy quickly to full employment. It has effectively abandoned the "standard" model. It is argued that if we could only deleverage—get rid of the excessive debt—we could return to some version of normality. In this view, the prolonged downturn is a result of the slow pace of deleveraging.

But even as the economy deleverages, there is every reason to believe that it will not return to full employment, even if it does lead to some increase in aggregate demand. We are not likely to return to the precrisis household savings rate of zero—nor would it be a good thing if we did.[3] Moreover, even if manufacturing has a slight recovery, most of the jobs that have been lost in that sector will not be regained. Nor will large numbers of construction workers in the United States that were employed at the peak of the housing bubble quickly regain their jobs.

Some, looking at past data, have suggested that we should resign ourselves to this unfortunate state of affairs. Economies that have had severe financial crises[4] typically recover slowly. But the fact that things have *often* gone badly in the aftermath of a financial crisis doesn't mean they *must* go badly. To make matters go well, though, one has to understand why recoveries are often so slow.

In earlier work, Greenwald and I explained why recoveries from balance sheet recessions (where there were adverse shocks to firms' equity) were so sluggish, and why this was especially so when banks' balance sheets were badly hit.[5]

But this is more than just a balance sheet crisis. There is a deeper cause: the United States and Europe are going through a structural transformation. There is a structural transformation associated with the move from manufacturing to a service sector economy (just as earlier in the twentieth century there was a structural transformation from agriculture to manufacturing). Additionally, changing comparative advantages requires massive adjustments in the structure of the North Atlantic countries. Such transformations occur slowly. This is partly because the human and physical capital stock has to be restructured (workers have to be retrained, and often relocated).

Further, markets do not make such adjustments easily on their own, partly because those who have to shift do not themselves have the resources to finance the requisite investments, having lost much of their human and other capital as a result of the underlying forces giving rise to the structural transformation; and there are natural imperfections in capital markets arising out of imperfect and asymmetric information.

Keynesian policies to stimulate the economy are not only able to increase GDP but can also facilitate restructuring. This is especially so if public expenditure is appropriately directed. Conversely, austerity measures, such as those that many countries are undertaking today, impede the restructuring that is now required. With austerity, some of the sectors that would naturally expand (as manufacturing contracts, along with its share of employment) are service sectors in which public financial support has traditionally played a key role, for understandable reasons.[6]

Reforms That Are, at Best, Halfway Measures

As I have observed, markets by themselves do not in general lead to efficient, stable, and socially acceptable outcomes. This means we have to think a little bit more deeply about what kind of economic architectures will lead to growth, real stability, and a good distribution of income.

There is an ongoing debate about whether we simply need to tweak the existing economic architecture or whether we need to make more fundamental changes. I have two concerns. One I hinted at earlier: the reforms undertaken so far have only tinkered at the edges. The second is that some of the changes in our economic structure (both before and after the crisis) that were *supposed* to make the economy perform better may not have done so.

There are some reforms, for instance, that may enable the economy to better withstand small shocks but at the same time make it less able to absorb big shocks. This is true of many financial sector developments, which may have allowed the economy to absorb some of the smaller shocks but clearly made the economy less resilient to fatter-tail shocks. Many of the "improvements" in markets before the crisis actually increased countries' exposure to risk. Whatever the benefits that might be derived from capital and financial market liberalization (and they are questionable), there have been severe costs in terms of increased exposure to risk. We ought to be rethinking attitudes toward these reforms—and the IMF should be commended for its rethinking in recent years. One of the objectives of capital account management, in all of its forms, can be to reduce domestic volatility arising from a country's international engagements.

More generally, the crisis has brought home the importance of financial regulation for macroeconomic stability. But as I assess what has happened since the crisis, I feel disappointed. With the mergers in the financial sector that have occurred in the aftermath of the crisis, the problem of too-big-to-fail banks has become even worse. But the problem is not just with too-big-to-fail banks. There are banks that are too intertwined to fail and banks that are too correlated to fail. We have done little about any of these issues.[7] There has, of course, been a huge amount of discussion about too big to fail. But being too correlated is a distinct issue. There is a strong need for a more diversified ecology of financial institutions that would reduce incentives to be excessively correlated and lead to greater stability.

Also, we haven't done enough to increase bank capital requirements. Missing in much of the discussion is an assessment of the costs versus benefits of higher capital requirements. We know the benefits: a lower risk of a government bailout and a recurrence of the kinds of events that marked 2007 and 2008. But on the cost side, we've paid too little attention to the fundamental insights of the Modigliani-Miller theorem, which explains the fallacies of arguments that increasing capital requirements will increase the cost of capital.[8]

Deficiencies in Reforms and in Modeling

If we had begun our reform efforts with a focus on how to make our economy more efficient and more stable, there are other questions we would have naturally asked. Interestingly, there is some correspondence between these deficiencies in our reform efforts and the deficiencies in the models that we as economists often use in macroeconomics.

The Importance of Credit
We would, for instance, have asked what the fundamental roles of the financial sector are, and how we can get it to perform those roles better. Clearly, one of the key roles is the allocation of capital and the provision of credit, especially to small and medium-sized enterprises, a function it did not perform well before the crisis and arguably is still not fulfilling well.

This might seem obvious. But a focus on the provision of credit has not been at the center of policy discourse or of the standard macro models.

I believe we have to shift our focus from money to credit. In looking at a bank's balance sheet, the two sides are *usually* going to be highly correlated. But that is not always the case, particularly in the context of large economic perturbations. Especially in deep recessions, we ought to be focusing on the impediments to credit creation. I find remarkable the extent to which there has been an inadequate examination in standard macro models of the nature of the credit mechanism.[9]

But failing to analyze credit markets--and to manage credit creation-- is not the only lacuna in "monetary" theory and policy. There is also a lack of understanding of different kinds of finance. A major area in the analysis of risk in financial markets is the difference between debt and equity. But in standard macroeconomics, this has barely been given any attention.

Stability

As I have already noted, in the conventional models (and in the conventional wisdom) market economies were stable. So it was perhaps not a surprise that fundamental questions about how to design *more* stable economic systems were seldom asked. We have already touched on several aspects of this: how to design economic systems that are less exposed to risk or that generate less volatility on their own.

One of the necessary reforms, though it is not emphasized enough, is the need for more automatic stabilizers and fewer automatic destabilizers, not only in the financial sector but also throughout the economy. For instance, the movement from defined benefit to defined contribution systems may have led to a less stable economy.

Elsewhere I have explained how risk-sharing arrangements (especially if poorly designed) can actually lead to more systemic risk: the precrisis conventional wisdom that diversification essentially eliminates risk is simply wrong.[10]

Distribution

Distribution matters as well—distribution among individuals, between households and firms, among households, and among firms. Traditionally, macroeconomics focused on certain aggregates, such as the average ratio of leverage to GDP. But that and other average numbers often don't give a picture of the vulnerability of the economy. It was the fact that a large number of people at the bottom were at risk of being unable to make their debt payments that should have tipped us off that something was wrong.

Across the board, our models need to incorporate a greater understanding of heterogeneity and its implications for economic stability.

Policy Frameworks

Flawed models lead not only to flawed policies but also to flawed policy frameworks.

Should Monetary Policy Focus Just on Short-Term Interest Rates?

In monetary policy, there is a tendency to think that the central bank should only intervene in setting the short-term interest rate. Adherents to this view believe "one intervention" is better than many. Since at least 80 years ago with the work of Ramsey,[11] we have known that focusing on a single instrument is not generally the best approach.

The advocates of the "single intervention" approach argue that it is best because it least distorts the economy. Of course, the reason we have monetary policy in the first place—the reason why government acts to intervene in the economy—is that we don't believe that markets on their own will set the right short-term interest rate. If we did, we would just let free markets determine that interest rate. The odd thing is that while just about every central banker would agree we should intervene in the determination of that price, not everyone is so convinced that we should strategically intervene in others, even though we know from the general theory of taxation and the general theory of market intervention that intervening in just one price is not optimal.

Once we shift the focus of our analysis to credit, and explicitly introduce risk into the analysis, we become aware that we need to use multiple instruments. Indeed, in general, we want to use all the instruments at our disposal. Monetary economists often draw a division between macroprudential, microprudential, and conventional monetary policy instruments. In our book, *Toward a New Paradigm in Monetary Economics*, Bruce Greenwald and I argue that this distinction is artificial. The government needs to draw on all of these instruments, *in a coordinated way.* (I'll return to this point shortly.)

Of course, we cannot "correct" every market failure. The very large ones, however—the macroeconomic failures—will always require our intervention. Bruce Greenwald and I have pointed out that markets are never Pareto efficient if information is imperfect, if there are asymmetries of information, or if risk markets are imperfect. And since these conditions are *always* satisfied, markets are never Pareto efficient.[12] Recent research has highlighted the importance of these and other related constraints for macroeconomics—though again, the insights of this important work have yet to be adequately integrated into either mainstream macroeconomic models or policy discussions. For instance, privately profitable contracts (e.g., credit default swaps) may, as we noted earlier, enhance systemic risk. The reason we have financial and banking regulation is precisely because profit maximization on the part of private agents does not, in general, lead to socially optimal outcomes. There are large externalities, for instance, associated with the actions taken by certain agents which they naturally don't take into account: the bankers did not take into account the costs that their excessive risk taking would impose on the rest of society.

Price versus Quantitative Interventions
These theoretical insights also help us to understand the erroneousness of the old presumption among some economists that price interventions are preferable to quantity interventions. There are many circumstances in which quantity interventions lead to better economic performance.[13]

Rethinking Tinbergen's Analysis of Targets and Instruments
A policy framework that has become popular in some circles argues that so long as there are as many instruments as there are objectives, the economic system is controllable, and the best way of managing the economy in such circumstances is to have an institution responsible for one target and one instrument. (In this view, central banks have one instrument, the interest rate, and one objective, inflation.[14] We have already explained why limiting monetary policy to one instrument is wrong.)

Drawing such a division may have advantages from an agency or bureaucratic perspective, but from the point of view of managing macroeconomic policy—focusing on employment, growth, stability and distribution, in a world of uncertainty—it makes no sense. There has to be coordination among all the instruments at our disposal, taking into account the impacts on all societal objectives.[15] The equilibrium that arises when different people control different instruments and focus on different objectives is, in general, not optimal in achieving overall societal objectives. In particular, there needs to be close coordination between monetary and fiscal policy. Better coordination—and the use of more instruments—can, for instance, enhance economic stability.

Take This Chance to Revolutionize Flawed Models

It should be clear that we could have done much more to prevent the crisis that began in 2007 and to mitigate its effects. It should be clear too that we can do much more to prevent the next one. Still, we are at least beginning to identify the really big market failures, the big macroeconomic externalities, and the best policy interventions for achieving high growth, greater stability, and a better distribution of income.

To succeed, we must constantly remind ourselves that markets on their own are not going to solve these problems, and neither will a single intervention such as changing short-term interest rates. That this is so has been proved time and again over the last century and a half. We should not let ourselves be deceived again by overly simplistic models that suggest otherwise.

And as daunting as the economic problems we now face are, acknowledging this will allow us to take advantage of the one big opportunity that this period of economic trauma has afforded: the chance to revolutionize our flawed models, and perhaps even exit from an interminable cycle of crises.

Notes

This chapter, an extended version of a discussion presented April 17, 2013, at the IMF Conference "Rethinking Macro Policy II: First Steps and Early Lessons," is based on joint work with a number of my colleagues, cited below. I especially want to thank my long term coauthor Bruce Greenwald. Research assistance from Laurence Wilse-Samson and Eamon Kircher-Allen is also gratefully acknowledged. I also wish to acknowledge financial assistance from the Institute for New Economic Thinking, and to acknowledge its agenda to reexamine the foundations of macroeconomics in the light of the crisis.

1. I have elaborated at greater length on some of the lessons to be drawn from the crisis for macroeconomics in "The Financial Crisis of 2007–2008 and Its Macroeconomic Consequences," in *Time for a Visible Hand: Lessons from the 2008 World Financial Crisis*, ed. S. Griffith-Jones, J. A. Ocampo, and J. E. Stiglitz, Initiative for Policy Dialogue Series (Oxford: Oxford University Press, 2010), 19–49; "Rethinking Macroeconomics: What Failed and How to Repair It," *Journal of the European Economic Association* 9, no. 4 (2011): 591–645; "Rethinking Macroeconomics: What Went Wrong and How to Fix It," *Journal of Global Policy* 2, no. 2 (2011): 165–175; "Stable Growth in an Era of Crises: Learning from Economic Theory and History," *Economi-tek* 2, no. 1 (2013):1-39; and "Macroeconomics, Monetary Policy, and the Crisis," in *In the Wake of the Crisis*, ed. O. Blanchard, D. Romer, M. Spence, and J. Stiglitz (Cambridge, MA: MIT Press, 2012).

2. Economic downturns can lead to the destruction of organization and informational capital, as Bruce Greenwald and I have emphasized. See our *Towards a New Paradigm in Monetary Economics* (Cambridge: Cambridge University Press, 2003).

3. It is important to distinguish between arguments concerning the restoration of growth and those focusing on the restoration of the economy to full employment. It is conceivable that the economy could return to normal growth—creating new jobs in tandem with new entrants to the labor force—but that the level of unemployment remains elevated. Hence, it is possible that once the economy has deleveraged, growth might be restored. Here we are asking, would aggregate demand be sufficient to return the economy to full employment?

4. We note too that the fact that downturns that are associated with deep financial crises are longlasting tells us very little: if there are deeper fundamental causes to crises (as suggested in the next paragraph), then these deep and longlasting crises will result in financial crises; the financial crises are the consequence, not the (underlying) cause. If that is the case, then the statement that "deep financial crises are longlasting" says nothing more than "deep crises are longlasting," a statement that, while true, is not very informative.

5. B. Greenwald and J. E. Stiglitz, "Financial Market Imperfections and Business Cycles," *Quarterly Journal of Economics* 108, no. 1 (1993): 77–114; and Greenwald and Stiglitz, *Towards a New Paradigm in Monetary Economics*.

6. The ideas in this paragraph are elaborated in D. Delli Gatti, M. Gallegati, B. Greenwald, A. Russo, and J. E. Stiglitz, "Mobility Constraints, Productivity Trends, and Extended Crises," *Journal of Economic Behavior & Organization* 83, no. 3 (2012): 375–393; and idem, "Sectoral Imbalances and Long Run Crises," in *The Global Macro Economy and Finance*, ed. F. Allen, M. Aoki, J.-P. Fitoussi, N. Kiyotaki, R. Gordon, and J. E. Stiglitz, IEA Conference Volume 150-III (Houndmills, UK, and New York: Palgrave, 2012), 61–97.

7. See Joseph E. Stiglitz, "Witness Testimony of Joseph E. Stiglitz, Congressional Oversight Panel," Hearing on Impact of the TARP on Financial Stability, March 4, 2011, http://cybercemetery.unt.edu/archive/cop/20110401230935/http://cop.senate.gov/documents/testimony-030411-stiglitz.pdftranscript (accessed September 30, 2013) and "Too Big to Fail or Too Big to Save? Examining the Systemic Threats

of Large Financial Institutions," testimony at a hearing of the United States Congress's Joint Economic Committee, April 21, 2009, http://www.jec.senate .gov/public/?a=Files.Serve&File_id=6b50b609-89fa-4ddf-a799-2963b31d6f86 (accessed September 30, 2013).

8. See J. E. Stiglitz, "On the Need for Increased Capital Requirements for Banks and Further Actions to Improve the Safety and Soundness of America's Banking System," testimony before the Senate Banking Committee, August 3, 2011, http://www.banking.senate.gov/public/index.cfm?FuseAction=Files.View& FileStore_id=97cec3e1-2d1d-44fa-acd9-a0a1bc640bc4 (accessed September 30, 2013); A. Admati, P. M. De Marzo, M. F. Hellwig, and P. Pfleiderer, "Debt Overhang and Capital Regulation," Stanford Working Paper, 2012, http://www.gsb .stanford.edu/news/packages/PDF/AdmatiDebt032612.pdf (accessed July 16, 2013); and Anat Admati and Martin Hellwig, *The Bankers' New Clothes: What's Wrong with Banking and What to Do about It* (Princeton, NJ: Princeton University Press, 2013), and the references cited there. There are numerous other regulatory issues (e.g., dealing with the transparency of derivatives and having them trade over well-capitalized exchanges). Even a brief exploration of these would take me well beyond the confines of this short note. I simply observe that in virtually each of these arenas, the regulatory reforms have fallen short of what is desired or needed.

9. Doing so was the objective of my book with Bruce Greenwald, *Towards a New Paradigm in Monetary Economics*. There is, of course, a large microeconomic literature on banking and credit, but for the most part, the insights of this literature have not been taken on board in standard macro models.

10. See J. E. Stiglitz, "Contagion, Liberalization, and the Optimal Structure of Globalization," *Journal of Globalization and Development* 1, no. 2 (2010), art. 2; idem, "Risk and Global Economic Architecture: Why Full Financial Integration May be Undesirable," *American Economic Review* 100, no. 2 (2010): 388–392; and S. Battiston, D. Delli Gatti, M. Gallegati, B. Greenwald, and J. E. Stiglitz, "Liaisons Dangereuses: Increasing Connectivity, Risk Sharing, and Systemic Risk," *Journal of Economic Dynamics and Control* 36 (2012): 1121–1141.

The intuition behind these results is simple: when we identify a group of individuals with a contagious disease, we don't "diversify"—sending them to all quarters of the earth. We quarantine them. Economists have intuitively recognized that economic crises can spread like a contagious disease, but that happens because of one form of interdependence or another. High levels of interdependence enable a disturbance in one part of the system to be transmitted elsewhere. Well-designed "architectures" balance the advantages of interdependence with the disadvantages, and attempt to introduce design features ("circuit breakers," capital controls) that mitigate the risks of adverse contagion. In the standard models, the risks of contagion were ignored (at least before crises occurred, which they did with increasing frequency), and thus no attention was paid to policies that might reduce these risks—and indeed, capital controls were adamantly opposed.

11. F. P. Ramsey, "A Contribution to the Theory of Taxation," *Economic Journal*, 1927, 47–61.

12. See J. E. Stiglitz and B. Greenwald, "Externalities in Economies with Imperfect Information and Incomplete Markets," *Quarterly Journal of Economics* 101, no. 2 (1986): 229–264.

13. The classic reference is Weitzman (M. L. Weitzman, "Prices vs. Quantities," *Review of Economic Studies* 41, no. 4 [1974]: 477–491). Since then, there has been a wealth of literature in different contexts showing that quantity interventions may be preferable; for example, quotas may be preferable to tariffs (P. Dasgupta and J. E. Stiglitz, "Tariffs Versus Quotas As Revenue Raising Devices Under Uncertainty," *American Economic Review* 67, no. 5 [1977]: 975–981), or quantity interventions in capital account management may be preferable to price interventions (J. E. Stiglitz, José Antonio Ocampo, Shari Spiegel, Ricardo French-Davis, and Deepak Nayyar, *Stability with Growth: Macroeconomics, Liberalization, and Development*, The Initiative for Policy Dialogue Series [Oxford: Oxford University Press, 2006]).

14. A fortiori, simple rules, like inflation targeting, that call for an increase in the interest rate when the inflation rate exceeds the targeted level are even more misguided. Such rules do not take into account the source of the disturbance to the economy or the most efficient way of restoring the economy to the desired "equilibrium" after a perturbation. The obvious illustration was provided by inflation in developing countries arising out of the global food and oil price rises of 2007. The increase in the interest rate in a small country obviously would have a negligible effect on these global prices; if the average rate of inflation were to be brought down to the desired level, it would require such large constrictions in the nontraded sectors that the cure would be worse than the disease. Fortunately, most governments have recognized this, and even those that have retained an inflation-targeting framework have adopted "flexible" frameworks.

15. Jan Tinbergen's analysis was, of course, based on a very simple model, with very stringent assumptions. Evidently, those relying on his insights did not appreciate just how critical these assumptions were, and that the results were not even approximately correct in more general contexts.

Contributors

George A. Akerlof, a 2001 Nobel Laureate, is Guest Scholar at the International Monetary Fund and Daniel E. Koshland Sr. Distinguished Professor Emeritus at Berkeley.

Sheila Bair served as Chairman of the Federal Deposit Insurance Corporation from June 2006 through June 2011.

Lorenzo Bini Smaghi is currently a Visiting Scholar at Harvard's Weatherhead Center for International Affairs. He was formerly a Member of the Executive Board of the European Central Bank.

Olivier Blanchard is the Economic Counselor and Director of the Research Department at the IMF. He is also the Robert M. Solow Professor Emeritus at MIT.

Anders Borg is a Swedish economist who serves as Minister for Finance in the Swedish government.

Claudio Borio is Head of the Monetary and Economic Department at the Bank for International Settlements (BIS).

Agustín Carstens is Governor of the Banco de Mexico. He is also a member of the Steering Committee of the G-20 Financial Stability Board, and the Chairman of the BIS Economic Consultative Council and the Global Economy Meeting.

José De Gregorio is Professor at the University of Chile. He was the Governor of the Central Bank of Chile from 2007 to 2011.

Giovanni Dell'Ariccia is Assistant Director in the Research Department of the IMF.

Janice Eberly is the James R. and Helen D. Russell Distinguished Professor of Finance at the Kellogg School of Management at Northwestern University. She was Assistant Secretary for Economic Policy and Chief Economist at the US Treasury from 2011 to 2013.

Stanley Fischer is currently at the Council on Foreign Relations. He was Governor of the Bank of Israel from 2005 to 2013 and First Deputy Managing Director of the IMF from 1994 to 2001.

Andrew Haldane is Executive Director for Financial Stability at the Bank of England.

Márcio Holland is Secretary of Economic Policy for the Brazilian Ministry of Finance since 2011 and also Professor at the São Paulo School of Economics/FGV.

Choongsoo Kim is the Governor of the Bank of Korea and the Chairman of its Monetary Policy Committee.

Mervyn A. King was Governor of the Bank of England from 2003 to 2013.

Paolo Mauro is an Assistant Director in the African Department of the IMF.

Roberto Perotti is Professor of Economics at Università Bocconi in Milan.

Hélène Rey is Professor of Economics at London Business School.

David Romer is the Herman Royer Professor of Political Economy at the University of California, Berkeley.

Nouriel Roubini is Professor of Economics at New York University's Stern School of Business and Chairman and Cofounder, Roubini Global Economics.

Jay C. Shambaugh is Professor of Economics and International Affairs at the George Washington University.

Jeremy C. Stein is a member of the Board of Governors of the US Federal Reserve System and has served as Professor of Economics at Harvard University.

Joseph E. Stiglitz is University Professor at Columbia University. He was awarded the Nobel Prize in Economic Sciences in 2001.

Duvvuri Subbarao was Governor of the Reserve Bank of India from 2008 to 2013.

Jean Tirole is Chairman of the Foundation J. J. Laffont–Toulouse School of Economics (TSE), Chairman of the Executive Committee of the Institute for Advanced Study in Toulouse (IAST), and Scientific Director of the Institute for Industrial Economics (IDEI).

Adair Turner is Senior Fellow at the Institute for New Economic Thinking. From 2008 to 2013 he was the Chairman of the UK Financial Services Authority (FSA).

John Vickers is Warden of All Souls College, Oxford, and was Chairman of the UK Independent Commission on Banking 2010–2011.

Martin Wolf is Associate Editor and Chief Economics Commentator at the *Financial Times*, London.

Michael Woodford is the John Bates Clark Professor of Political Economy at Columbia University.

Janet L. Yellen is the Vice Chair of the Board of Governors of the Federal Reserve System.

Gang Yi is Deputy Governor of the People's Bank of China and the administrator of the State Administration of Foreign Exchange (SAFE).

Index